The Digital Condition

The Digital Condition

Class and Culture in the Information Network

Rob Wilkie

FORDHAM UNIVERSITY PRESS

NEW YORK 2011

Fordham University Press has no responsibility for the persistence or accuracy of URLs for external or third-party Internet websites referred to in this publication and does not guarantee that any content on such websites is, or will remain, accurate or appropriate.

Fordham University Press also publishes its books in a variety of electronic formats. Some content that appears in print may not be available in electronic books.

Library of Congress Cataloging-in-Publication Data

Wilkie, Robert.
  The digital condition : class and culture in the information network / Robert Wilkie.—1st ed.
    p. cm.
  Includes bibliographical references (p.   ) and index.
  ISBN 978-0-8232-3422-6 (cloth : alk. paper)
  ISBN 978-0-8232-3423-3 (pbk. : alk. paper)
    1. Information technology—Social aspects. 2. Digital divide. 3. Computers—Social aspects. 4. Information superhighway—Social aspects. I. Title.
  HM851.W553 2011
  303.48′33—dc23

                                    2011016177

Printed in the United States of America
13 12 11   5 4 3 2 1
First edition

for Lily and Nicholas

CONTENTS

ACKNOWLEDGMENTS

A book is never the project of an isolated individual but depends profoundly on the help and assistance of many others. I am thankful for the support of my family—Robert, Christine, Terry, Vikki, Dennis, Christopher, Jim, Leslie, Allan, Debbie, and above all Kim—without which this project would not be possible. In addition, I thank everyone at Fordham University Press, including Michael Koch, Eric Newman, Mary-Lou Peña, and especially Fredric Nachbaur, for their interest in and support for this project. I would also like to recognize the many scholars who, at different times during the completion of this book, have offered advice and discussed the issues raised in the book with me.

In this book I have drawn material from an essay published in the e-book of the conference proceedings of the "Transforming Culture in the Digital Age" conference. Several texts on which I have drawn in different chatpers of this book were originally published in different versions in *The Red Critique*. I would like to acknowledge the editors of both publications for their intellectual support.

The Digital Condition

Introduction

One of the foremost issues facing cultural theory today concerns the meaning of the *digital condition*. Most people who talk about the emerging digital society often associate it with technological developments such as the Internet and MP3 players, DVRs and smart phones, videogames and digital cameras—in other words, with consumer products that provide people with new ways of accessing an endless stream of information and that are said to be ushering in a new age of personal empowerment. Similarly, much of cultural theory is inundated with proclamations that the emerging digital reality is leading us beyond all of the structures of the past, requiring in turn a fundamentally new mode of analysis that gives up totality for fragmentation, class for the multitude, and the global for the local and the contingent.

However, as I argue in the following chapters, in the context of a growing set of violent global contradictions—from the wars in Afghanistan and Iraq to the crises in finance, housing, food, water, and the environment that have, at one point or another, dominated the news over the past decade—it is perhaps time to undertake a different approach to the contemporary moment. It is time for a critique of the digital times. This is because, I suggest, how people think about our "digital times" has increasingly important consequences. The acceleration in developments in science, technology, communication, and production that began in the second half of the twentieth century and that has condensed into the concept of the digital has resulted in what might be the most contradictory moment in human history. On the one hand, the advances in the productive forces of society have made it more possible than ever not only to imagine but to realize a world in which the tyranny of social inequality is brought to an end. On the other hand, despite the potential productivity of human labor, the reduction of these developments to an unprecedented level of accumulation of private profits means that rather than the end of social inequality we are witness to its global expansion. The digital world, in other words, is the site of class conflict. What is represented as our so-called new digital reality is in actuality the technological and cultural manifestation of underlying class relations that are concealed through the dominant discourses of the digital today— discourses that, having declared the death of depth in the analysis of social life, focus on the intricate surfaces of culture. As new technological advances that could end "the wretched servitude of having to struggle for daily bread"[1] are used instead to expand the wealth of a few by exploiting the labor of the many, it is no longer the case that technology can take on the appearance of a simple or neutral aspect of human society. What this means is that what the digital represents is not yet fixed but is ultimately to be determined by the class struggle between capital and labor—the "two great hostile camps . . . directly facing each other" over the future of humanity.[2] *The Digital Condition* is a contribution to the debate over the meaning of the *digital* that aims to open a space within cultural studies to talk about the *digital condition* from the position of what Marx and Engels call "the property question"[3]—the economic, political, and social organization of society around the ownership of private property and the way in which this division of ownership determines all aspects of social life, including culture. As I argue throughout this book, it is the contradictory relation of property in capitalism—between those who own the means of production and those who own nothing but their labor power—that will ultimately determine the direction that the digital takes.

In many ways, Jean-François Lyotard's influential analysis of the emerging technological age in *The Postmodern Condition* remains one of the predominant theoretical guidebooks for thinking about the digital condition. Arguing that at the end of the twentieth century "knowledge has become the principle force of production over the last few decades,"[4] Lyotard famously proposes that this transition brings with it a fundamentally new cultural and economic condition defined by a crisis of legitimacy and an "incredulity towards meta-narratives."[5] In response he argues that the praxis of critique has to be replaced with the playful pragmatics of "paralogy," or the concern with "undecideables, the limits of precise control, conflicts characterized by incomplete information, *'fracta,'* catastrophes, and pragmatic paradoxes."[6]

In fact, in the wake of Lyotard's separation of knowing the particular from understanding the totality, it has become almost standard protocol for contemporary cultural analysis to begin by defining culture as a fluid site of competing, but never fully determining, discourses. From this framework, it is argued that to read culture as shaped by economics or politics is too totalizing and reductive and therefore unable to recognize the multiple ways in which culture operates at local levels as a space of resistance to the status quo. For instance, Lawrence Grossberg argues that while cultural theorists "need to be involved with notions and analysis of labor . . . in the classroom, in the university, in the media and consumer culture, in the nation and in the world,"[7] they should nonetheless "reject the assumption that production is determinacy in the last instance"[8] and refuse "to see everything locked in place by, guaranteed by, economic relations."[9] In other words, the explanation of culture in terms of its *outside* (its political economy) is no longer possible because the outside is beyond understanding. Instead, cultural studies should be about "describing how people's everyday lives are articulated by and with culture, how they are empowered and disempowered by the particular structures and forces that organize their lives, always in contradictory ways, and how their everyday lives are themselves articulated to and by the trajectories of economic and political power."[10] The assumption here is that only the *immanent* is knowable and that the praxis of critique, which seeks to connect the immanent with the outside to produce understanding of the existing, no longer has any explanatory value as we enter the digital age.

It is this same postcritique logic that we find written throughout contemporary theories of digital culture. For example, it is said that in place of the "hard-edged certainties of industrialization, Enlightenment empiricism, and modernity" the digital is defined by "malleable concepts of postindustrialism, technoscience, and postmodernity."[11] Similarly, cultural theorist and one of the leading writers on cyborg theory, Chris Hables Gray writes, "We do not live in the seemingly stable modern world our grandparents did. Their belief in inevitable, comfortable progress has been supplanted by our realization that scientific and technological innovation are relentless and quite ambiguous"[12]; in their self-described "Manifesto" entitled "On Cultural Studies, Technology and Science," Stanley Aronowitz and Michael Menser argue, "although technology and science may be everywhere, there is no determinism anywhere, if by determinism we signify a one-to-one correspondence between the causal agent and its effects."[13] In other words, the digital common sense is that we are entering a new stage of society more fuzzy than economically structured, more fluid than fixed by class division, and, despite tremendous technological development, more unfinished than at any other time in history.

In fact, one finds this same theory of a break between culture and the economic, between knowing and understanding, even among theorists who are calling for a more "critical" approach to Internet culture. Geert Lovink, for instance, argues in *Zero Comments: Blogging and Critical Internet Culture* that "nothing is as fluid, fragile—and unsustainable—as today's network landscape"[14] and that "the very notion of a network is in conflict with the desire to gain an overview."[15] In this context, Lovink writes that despite the fact that "the contemporary worker faces more job uncertainty than her proletariat precursor,"[16] it is time to shift away from "soft constructivism and *Ideologiekritik* toward a nonjudgmental approach"[17] called "distributed aesthetics." Like Lyotard's theory of paralogy, "distributed aesthetics" is a postbinary, postdialectical logic. In claiming that it is time to go "beyond poles such as real–virtual, old–new, offline–online, and global–local"[18] and instead to "dig into the dirty everyday doings of the network society,"[19] Lovink's theory of "distributed aesthetics" is ultimately a proposal for a pragmatic theory of the existing digital culture. That is to say, despite suggesting that we move beyond such binaries as the "local" and the "global," to focus only on the "everyday doings" means remaining stranded at the level of the immanent, without recourse to a way of understanding the outside forces that shape it. We are, in other words, always stuck at the level of the local.

It is on these terms that the dominant reading of technology in cultural theory has responded to the contradictions of digital society by reading the digital as an engine of difference—suggesting that the expansion of mass production around the world has meant the explosion of opportunities "for greater and greater numbers of people (men *and* women)—with however little money—[to] play the game of using things to signify who they are."[20] If class exists today, it is said to be simply one of a range of possible differences that shift, reverse, come together, and fall apart, depending upon the contingent and contextual needs of individuals who wish to define themselves as members of a group. Class, on these terms, has been replaced by "networked multitudes" that "create temporary and voluntary forms of collaboration" that exceed any and all attempts at homogenization.[21] In fact, what has made this reading of the digital condition so popular in cultural studies today is that it does not ignore class (which would place one completely outside of the realm of "seriousness") but rather rewrites it so as to be less disruptive, less explosive, and therefore more palatable to the dominant class interests. It is not uncommon for so-called progressive and radical cultural theorists at the center of the discipline—such as Mark Poster, Donna Haraway, N. Katherine Hayles, Slavoj Žižek, Michael Hardt, and Antonio Negri—to describe the details of a world that is divided by "the ecological crisis, the consequences of the biogenetic revolution, imbalances within the system itself (problems with intellectual property; forthcoming struggles over raw materials, food and water), and the explosive growth of social divisions and exclusions."[22] It is not that cultural theory simply fails to describe the economic inequalities of digital society; it is that in the context of contemporary theories of digital culture—which focus on consumption over production, desire over need, and lifestyle differences rather than class—cultural studies turns class into a safe concept that can be discussed in polite company. This is another way of saying that *class* is used descriptively and is hollowed out of any explanatory power. Using class descriptively thus allows cultural theorists to demonstrate an awareness of growing economic contradictions (and even their interconnections with matters of race, gender, the environment, disability, and health care)—but not in a way that these theorists are likely to be confused with "vulgar" thinkers who understand class as shaping all other aspects of social life. Class becomes an affective category based more on the perceptions of class collectivity and the effects of inequality than objective position in the relations of production.

On the contrary, I argue that what is necessary today if we are not only to *know* the expanding and complex relations of the digital condition but to *understand* them is the praxis of critique that connects the inside of the new cultural forms and theories with their economic outside. Drawing upon Marx's argument that the "ideal is nothing else than the material world reflected by the human mind, and translated into forms of thought,"[23] I argue that capitalism's global networks of production that have created the conditions of the digital cannot be understood through the *spontaneous, discontinuous, networked,* and *fragmentary* because what appear to us as such are, in actuality, reflections of social and historical forces that shape our lives. On these terms, I propose that in order to understand the contradictions of digital culture it is necessary to begin from a conceptual framework in which social contradictions do not become the basis for rejecting critique but rather serve as an opportunity to deepen our understanding of the world in which we live and labor. In other words, rather than the paratheory of Lyotard's postmodern condition that begins with disconnections and discontinuities, what is most needed today is the *meta* theory of Marx that works to connect the *nonmimetic* reflections of the economic as they shape and define the digital condition.

It is through the praxis of critique that Marx addressed the "meta-theoretical" question of theory and its relationship to modes of social organization. For example, both the 1857 introduction to the *Grundrisse* and the 1859 preface to *A Contribution to the Critique of Political Economy* are essentially inquiries into the relationship between theory and reality. Always a historical materialist and a dialectician, Marx in both texts argues that the emergence of contestations within theory is neither a formal process shaped by its own internal immanent force nor a natural given, such that, for example, each generation will simply view the world differently from the way its predecessors did. Rather, Marx argues, developments and contestations in theory are the effect of history or, to be more precise, the outcome of the formation and re-formation of modes of production. "Mankind," he writes in the preface, "always sets itself only such tasks as it can solve; since, looking at the matter more closely, it will always be found that the task itself arises only when the material conditions for its solution already exist or are at least in the process of formation."[24] Sigmund Freud's unconscious, Werner Heisenberg's theory of quantum mechanics, Franklin Roosevelt's New Deal, Pierre Bourdieu's New Internationalism—these are not instances of the workings of an autogenetic and self-delighting (that is, ahistorical) reason but acts of social engagements. For example, Freud's theory of the unconscious is a way of explaining the growing contradiction between what Marx identifies as "use-value" and "exchange-value." Whereas the humanist theory of the self as a rational, and therefore free, individual corresponds to the moment when private property comes to dominate social life and explains this development as the movement toward a more ideal reality, Freud's theory of the self is a pathologizing theory of the social in which the rational is understood to be driven by the irrational and the unknowable. It is a theory, at a moment of advanced industrialization and heightened global conflict between imperialist nations, that explains the irrationality of production for profit as an inevitable consequence of the forces of desire that operate beyond rational understanding and critique. My point is that social theories are historical and an effect of the mode of production. A concept becomes the site of debate when what it represents—in this case, the ends to which human labor will be directed—can no longer remain neutral.

In this sense, *The Digital Condition* takes up the challenge posed by Terry Eagleton in "Lenin in the Postmodern Age":

> You can attain anti-capitalist consciousness simply by looking around the world with a modicum of intelligence and moral decency, but you cannot attain a knowledge of the global trade mechanisms or the institutions of workers' power in this way. The distinction between spontaneous and acquired political consciousness, whatever historical disasters it may have contributed to, is itself a valid and necessary one.[25]

Through an analysis that looks at both high theory as well as the concrete cultural practices of digital culture, I argue for a counter mode of reading the digital—namely, the historical materialist theory of nonmimetic reflection—that reconnects questions of culture to the objective relations of class, labor, and production. I believe that there is an urgent need for cultural analysis to help serve as a guide for social agency and that the basis of such a project lies in understanding the complex ways in which "the property question" determines all aspects of social life. By analyzing the culture and theory of the digital condition, I demonstrate why what matters is that even as the sites of production expand across the globe, what defines the logic of the digital network remains the basis of capitalism in the exploitation of labor. In other words, in contrast to the argument that we are entering a *network capitalism* beyond the contradictions of class, what is necessary is a theory of *capital networks*—the way in which all aspects of life today are determined by the unequal property relations between those who own and control the means of production and those who own nothing but their labor power. *The Digital Condition* is a contribution to the struggle of working people to bring about a society in which technology is placed not in the service of profit but in the interests of the meeting and expansion of the needs of all.

The Spirit Technological

Many of today's theories of digital culture treat digital technologies like a *deus ex machina*—these technologies seem to appear out of nowhere and yet become the primary means for resolving all social contradictions. According to this model, we are undergoing a fundamental change in how we live and work and we consequently require fundamentally new ways of understanding the world that break with all past models and theories, especially theories that focus on class. Through a close examination that connects some of the core texts and assumptions of digital culture to commodities such as the iPod, I challenge the dominant representations of digital technologies. I argue that most representations disconnect the new technologies and the culture which surrounds them from the economic relations of class and explain why a class theory of digital culture and technology is necessary if we are to understand contemporary society.

Reading Digitally and the Un-Reading of Labor

Reading *digitally* is the form ideology takes in what might be referred to as the era of the *digital condition*: a regime of accumulation that emerges in the post–World War II period in which developments in production, communication, and transportation have enabled capitalism to encircle the globe. It is the means by which the exploitation of labor is obscured behind a "spiritual aroma" that suggests that humanity is entering a postcapitalist, postnational, postlabor, posthierarchy, postwork society in which consumption rather than production drives the economy and developments in science and technology have replaced labor as the source of surplus value. What the *digital* refers to, however, is not simply imaginary or fictional but material developments in the means of production that have heightened the contradictions between capital and labor, putting the question of the future of society at the forefront of cultural theory. In one sense, it corresponds to technological advances in computing, communication, and transportation that have resulted in the tremendous growth in the productivity of labor such that the possibility of meeting the needs of all has perhaps more than ever been materially possible. Yet, insofar as all technological growth under capitalism is subjected to the logic of profit, these developments are restricted in their use to the expansion of the conditions of exploitation and the universalizing of capitalism across the globe. It is for this reason that the digital has become a site of class struggle. That is to say, it is not simply that the digital is plural nor is it that all readings of the digital are equal. In the hands of capital, the concept of the digital has become an example of the way in which this contradiction turns into what Marx calls "an inverted world-consciousness" that is the product of an "inverted world."[1] The *digital* thus refers both to the process by which capital appropriates the products of labor and turns them into the tools of private accumulation that are then wielded against the working class as a means of extending the capitalist system globally, as well as the way in which this process is naturalized as an inevitable consequence of technological development.

To read the world digitally is another way of saying that the dominant theories of the digital today define the developments of technology in the interests of capital by excluding any understanding of the real possibilities that could be achieved if the private ownership of the means of production were eliminated. Instead, much of what passes for serious thinking about digital technologies is an increasingly celebratory theory that is declared sophisticated because it abandons the "reductive" and "crude" theory of class in favor of a social theory of multiplicity and difference. In this image, digital society is made to appear as the other of class inequality because it is said to be a fundamentally new version of capitalism—a capitalism of digital networks—that suspends all prior economic and social relations by replacing the "hard" world of production with the "soft" world of consumption and exchange. What supposedly differentiates the so-called network capitalism from earlier incarnations of the capitalist mode of production is that "Information, in the form of ideas, concepts, innovation and run-of-the-mill data on every imaginable subject—and replicated as digital bits and bytes through computerization—has replaced labour and the relatively static logic of fixed plant and machinery as the central organizing force of society."[2] In this context, the digital condition is said to refer to a society in which the vertical hierarchies of the industrial system have been replaced with horizontal digital networks of exchange that defy the exploitative logic of earlier modes of capitalism by dematerializing the means of production and thereby erasing the class antagonism of private ownership. As the German sociologist Helmut Willke puts it, "it is not important where you are as long as you are with or within the network."[3] Instead of a system in which the value created by workers flows upward to the owners, network capitalism is defined as a system in which value flows outward to anyone (and everyone) who can access and participate in the circulation of information—a process that occurs after the commodity has been produced, in the realm of consumption.

The problem is that knowledge cannot replace labor as the engine of the economy because it is not the other of labor but the product of labor. Regardless of whether it is the development of a microscope that enables scientists to examine the properties of a virus so as to be able to cure disease or advances in computing that have created the capability of storing and transmitting an entire library for a fraction of what doing so would have cost previously, the ability to expand our understanding of the world around us requires that labor be applied to the development of new technological means for advancing abilities of labor power in the future. But these developments do not occur within a social vacuum. Technology does not have an independent existence from society. As Frederick Engels writes, it is too often the case that the history of technology is presented as if the new technologies had simply "fallen from the sky." Instead, as he proposes, what drives the development of society is not technology but industry and the needs of labor:

> If society has a technical need, that helps science forward more than ten universities. The whole of hydrostatics (Torticelli, etc.) was called forth by the necessity for regulating the mountain streams of Italy in the sixteenth and seventeenth centuries. We have known anything reasonable about electricity only since its technical applicability was discovered.[4]

Furthermore, insofar as labor does not take place in a social vacuum either, the ends to which labor makes use of technology and knowledge are determined by the relations of production. What is posited as a contradiction between knowledge and labor in digital theory is the effect of the social division of labor that creates the appearance of a conflict between manual and intellectual labor. The real division of the digital condition is not between ideas and things but between the interests of capital and the interests of labor.

In so-called digital theories of the social, however, the transition to a digital economy results in not only a contradiction between *ideas* and *things* but a crisis at the level of ideas itself. Whether it is the articulations of a networked economy in high theory or the cultural representations of a cut-and-paste consumer society in the pages of popular magazines and iPod advertisements, the dominant argument is that it has become impossible to understand the world with any certainty because the digital condition represents the fragmentation of society into a thousand different markets with a thousand different desires. *Reading digitally* therefore means accepting that in an increasingly fragmented world *to think* means to be aware of the impossibility of understanding beyond the local and the contingent. For example, in defining the role of theory in the digital age, Timothy Druckery writes, "Perception, memory, history, politics, identity, and experience are now mediated through technology in ways that outdistance simple economic or historic analysis."[5] Similarly, Douglas Kellner and Steven Best argue that "contemporary developments exhibit so many twists and turns, and are so highly complex that they elude simply historical sketches, reductive theoretical explanations and facile generalizations" and, as such, "the social maps called classical social theories are to some extent torn, tattered, and fragmented, and in many cases outdated and obsolete."[6]

The target of the argument that classical social theories are "outdated and obsolete" and that technological developments undo simple (that is, reductive) "economic or historic analysis" is any theory that attempts to connect the form that capital accumulation takes with the underlying economic logic of capitalism in the exploitation of labor. Instead, the social is read as irreducible to the economic, even as capitalism has reduced the history of class antagonisms from several to two.[7] In other words, the digital economy of network capitalism has come to represent the moment when the economic conflicts between capital and labor will be replaced with what Bill Gates calls the "friction-free economy"[8] or what Thomas L. Friedman refers to as the "flat world"[9]—a time when class differences no longer matter because capital will be able to extract tremendous profits from virtually every aspect of daily life without having to exploit labor, and consumers will escape the limits of the working day and shape and reshape their identities at will through access to an ever-expanding global market. As digital enthusiast Nicholas Negroponte exclaims, "Some people worry about the social divide between the information-rich and the information-poor, the haves and the have-nots, the First and Third Worlds. But the real cultural divide is going to be generational."[10] The generational is what replaces class in a progressive theory of history with the perfection of capitalism as its end. In other words, according to the logic of the generational it is only a matter of time before capital finally "gets it right" and succeeds in eliminating all social inequality. In this vision of the world, to raise the question of why inequality exists in the first place and to put forward even the slight possibility that capitalism results in social inequality is not because of a lack of technology but because of the division of ownership that determines to what ends new technological developments are put is to speak in "old" discourses that have no place in the digital celebration.

In reality, the difference between so-called old and new theories is determined not generationally but ideologically. Capital has to regularly reproduce the ideological distinction between the old and the new because as the forces of production develop, they come into conflict with the relations of production. In turn, those concepts that at one moment provide a seamless explanation of the existing at another moment come apart at the seams. At such moments, it becomes necessary to redefine the boundaries of intelligibility so that, in inverted fashion, what *is* always appears on the side of the new while what *could be* is always relegated to the side of the old. Fredric

Jameson's theory of the "postmodern turn" is a prime example of the reshuffling of boundaries between the old and the new to accommodate developments in production. Jameson argues that we are entering a new economic regime which necessitates new economic theories that can account for the expanded role of consumption in the determination of value. This is because "aesthetic production today has become integrated into commodity production more generally: the frantic economic urgency of producing fresh waves of ever more novel-seeming goods (from clothing to airplanes), at ever greater rates of turnover, now assigns an increasing essential structural function and position to aesthetic innovation and experimentation."[11] According to Jameson, the incorporation of culture into production means "a prodigious expansion of culture throughout the social realm, to the point at which everything in our social life—from economic value and state power to practices and to the very structure of the psyche itself—can be said to have become 'cultural' in some original and yet untheorized sense."[12] In other words, the new is so new that it operates beyond the realm of any prior theories of the relation between the cultural and the economic levels of society. Having displaced any theoretical understanding of culture that seeks out the deep connections between the cultural and economic in favor of a contingent and reversible knowledge that presupposes contemporary culture is somehow so different that it exceeds such theories, Jameson argues that "if the idea of a ruling class were once the dominant (or hegemonic) ideology of bourgeois society, the advanced capitalist countries today are now a field of stylistic and discursive heterogeneity without a norm."[13] What Jameson proposes here is that to read capitalism in terms of class is to impose an old norm onto a new situation that cannot be adequately theorized. Or, rather, it can be theorized only if we accept the argument that capitalism has so fundamentally changed as to have become essentially unrecognizable.

It is in this theorization that we can begin to see why reading digitally has become so useful for capitalism. Reading digitally creates the conditions by which the workforce learns *how* to think about the complex interactions that a networked economy depends upon, while also learning not to worry about *why* the networked economy works the way that it does. What passes for theorization is, in other words, the ideological register of capitalist know-how. Even when Jameson argues, "postmodern culture is the internal and superstructural expression of a whole new wave of American military and economic domination throughout the world,"[14] following his own logic there is no way of making sense of such a statement. To read the world through a cultural lens, as Jameson proposes, is to read the question of global imperialism as simply one in a multitude of possible discursive formations that, insofar as there is no longer a capitalist norm, can just as easily exist alongside a range of alternative discourses. Without a theory of private property to explain the causes of "military and economic domination," we are left with only vague impressions as to the meaning of such domination for and impact on working people around the world. We might be outraged at what happens, but we will never be able to understand why it happens and how to transform it. A cultural theory of capitalism thus turns history into a reflection of the marketplace, where the heterogeneity of commodities is a poor substitute for freedom from exploitation.

Property, Class, and Digital Identities

As ideology, popular theories of the digital economy function as a means of displacing any discussion of property relations and the impact that property relations have on every aspect of society. It is, of course, precisely in the interests of capital to prevent such investigations because they bring to the surface the increasing contradiction between the developments in the forces of production that constitute the possibilities of the new technologies and the relations of production that undermine these possibilities by restricting the use of labor to the interests of the private accumulation of capital. Instead, one of the primary arguments is that material property does not have the same meaning in a digital society and that the only real property that matters is the idea. Or, as Robert Hassan suggests, what makes "Microsoft, or Apple, or Google what they are" is not "fixed assets" or labor, but "ideas."[15]

This line of thinking is extensively developed in *The Age of Access*, in which postwork and postproperty theorist Jeremy Rifkin argues that "a new kind of capitalism is journeying to the center stage of world history."[16] What we are witness to, he argues, is that

> the birth of a network economy, the steady dematerialization of goods, the declining relevance of physical capital, the ascendance of intangible assets, the metamorphosis of goods into pure services, the shift in first-tier commerce from

a production to a marketing perspective, and the commodification of relationships and experiences are all elements in the radical restructuring going on in the
high-tech global economy as part of humanity begins to leave markets and property exchange behind on its journey into the Age of Access.[17]

What defines the "Age of Access," in other words, is the end of traditional
property relations in which the ownership of material resources, and the
ability to use this ownership to command the labor of others, served as the
basis of wealth. "Wealth," he argues, "is no longer vested in physical capital
but rather in human imagination and creativity."[18] According to Rifkin, in
the contemporary moment "what is really being bought and sold are ideas
and images" and that if industrial capital was characterized "by the exchange of things" the network economy is characterized "by access to concepts, carried inside physical forms."[19] In this postproperty economy,
corporations no longer own property but lease it and instead of exclusion
and control look to create "partnerships" and "reciprocal relationships."[20]
What Rifkin is proposing is a capitalism that is beyond the market: a postproperty society "measured by the idea of what is mine is yours and what is
yours is mine" rather than "mine and thine."[21] While such pronouncements
might appear progressive, and perhaps even socialist to some, a closer look
at Rifkin's proposal will make clear that it is less about a fundamental transformation of capitalist property relations and more about a slight revision
of the terms of capital accumulation.

The problem is that while Rifkin eliminates property at the level of the
idea, he cannot do so in the realm of the material world. That this is the
case is marked by his having to acknowledge that even in the digital economy, social divisions still exist. According to Rifkin, "the gap between the
possessed and the dispossessed is wide" and in addition there is a growing
gap between "the connected and the disconnected."[22] In other words, Rifkin's world is one that is still divided economically. Yet, by turning the division of property into an issue of *access*, which is really another way of saying
being able to enter the marketplace, he erases the possibility of understanding why this division exists in the first place. In rewriting property as "access," the only possibility for eliminating the gap between the "connected
and the disconnected" becomes the *expansion* of capitalism. To gain access
is to be able to participate as a seller of one's labor power, which is precisely
the kind of "free access" that is the hallmark of capitalist property relations—namely, that those who own and control the means of production

provide "access" to these resources in exchange for labor power and all of the surplus value that the laborer produces.

Capitalism cannot eliminate private property because the existence of the owners who control the political economy of society is dependent upon their ability to buy the labor of a renewable class of workers who have nothing to sell but their labor power. The defense of this relation—what Rifkin is calling "free access"—was established early in the history of capitalist ideology as the basis of the "freedom" of the individual. Immanuel Kant, for example, in challenging the remaining vestiges of feudalism sought to establish the ownership of private property as the requirement for the development of civilization. In contrast to the "complex and hierarchical system of land tenure under feudal lords," in which there was no protection from the seizure of land by the aristocracy who controlled all land in the country because of their "divine right" as rulers, what Kant proposes is a more "simple" and "legal" system of ownership in which "everyone may acquire and own property" and that this right to own property is protected by the establishments of property rights against the seizure of property without cause or right.[23] Kant argues it is a principle of reason that society has the "authorization . . . to put all others under an obligation, which they would not otherwise have, to refrain from using certain objects of our choice because we have been the first to take them into our possession."[24] Although it is possible to conceive of property ownership prior to the establishment of the civil constitution, it is just *"provisionally rightful* possession." According to Kant, it is possible to achieve *"conclusive* possession" only with the establishment of an *"actual* civil condition."[25] In other words, property can exist *only* in community with other property owners, each of whom respects the property rights of the other members:

> For only in accordance with this principle of the will is it possible for the free choice of each to accord with the freedom of all, and therefore possible for there to be any right, and so too possible for any external object to be mine or yours.[26]

In this, Kant rewrites the aristocratic right to property in which property ownership is determined primarily through inheritance and military takeover as the bourgeois property right that is determined by a "legal" relation between owners—namely, property should "freely" go to whoever can "possess" it through purchase. If you cannot purchase it, then you cannot possess it. At the same time, by locating individual property ownership in the "spirit" of reason, it becomes natural and therefore equally unchallengeable by those who were denied this freedom because they lacked the means to acquire the now "freely accessible" property and thus were at the mercy of the new, legal property owners.

At the core of capitalism is a fundamental and unequal relation to property. By property, I do not mean the houses, cars, HDTVs, iPods, Blu-ray players, computers, and other consumer goods that people own and that fulfill certain historical needs that they may have. The problem of inequality, in other words, does not rest in personal acts of consumption. Rather, I am referring to the ownership of the means of producing these items. The division upon which the possibility of private accumulation of capital is based is a division between those who own and control the means of production and those who own nothing but their labor power. Marx writes, "Property [is] the right, on the part of the capitalist, to appropriate the unpaid labour of others or its product, and to the impossibility, on the part of the labourer, of appropriating his own product."[27] The "freedom" of the worker to sell her labor power on the market for a wage is based upon a precondition that she has no other means by which to meet her needs. As Marx explains, the capitalist system is built upon the necessary condition that in the market

> two very different kinds of commodity possessors must come face to face and into contact; on the one hand, the owners of money, means of production, means of subsistence, who are eager to increase the sum of values they possess, by buying other people's labour power; on the other hand, free labourers, the sellers of their own labour power, and therefore the sellers of labour.[28]

What is the basis of "freedom" for the worker is, in other words, that they have no other commodity to sell except their labor power. It is on these terms that Marx explains the economic process underlying the only guaranteed freedom in capitalism—namely, the "free" exchange of labor on the market:

> The immediate producer, the labourer, could only dispose of his own person after he had ceased to be attached to the soil and ceased to be the slave, serf, or bondman of another. To become a free seller of labour power, who carries his commodity wherever he finds a market, he must further have escaped from the regime of the guilds. . . . Hence, the historical movement which changes the producers into wage workers appears, on the one hand, as their emancipation

from serfdom and from the fetters of the guilds, and this side alone exists for our bourgeois historians. But, on the other hand, these new freedmen became sellers of themselves only after they had been robbed of all their own means of production, and of all the guarantees of existence afforded by the old feudal arrangements. And the history of this, their expropriation, is written in the annals of mankind in letters of blood and fire.[29]

It is on these terms that Marx writes that the existence of free labor is dependent upon the condition that workers are free in a double sense: "that neither they themselves form part and parcel of the means of production as in the case of slaves, bondsmen & c., nor do the means of production belong to them, as in the case of peasant proprietors; they are, therefore, free from, unencumbered by, any means of production of their own."[30] It is this fundamental division of property that determines one's class position in which those who do not own or control the means of production of society are not free but rather *compelled* through economic coercion either to sell their labor power to the capitalist or to give up all possibility of meeting their needs. Class, in short, is an objective relation to the means of production.

It is in this sense that even Rifkin's proposal that the logic of *leasing* represents a new form of property relations—the renting of an item for only so long as it is useful to a particular moment of production—does not challenge the logic of capitalist ownership but extends it. This is for two reasons. First, the development of leasing is similar historically to the development of the retail, banking, and service industries. The emergence of a retail industry, to take only one of the circulation industries under capitalism, enabled the manufacturing industry to lower costs by taking over the storage and sale of the final commodity for which the manufacturer would otherwise be responsible. While the manufacturer has to turn over part of the accumulated surplus value to the retailer in exchange for this service, this process still results in a smaller reduction in profit for the manufacturer than would result if the manufacturer had to address the storage and sale of the commodity internally. Similarly, if corporations are starting to lease rather than purchase equipment it is because they are willing to turn over a portion of the surplus value to a business that can take care of the maintenance and care of the machines for less than the previous cost. What Rifkin promotes as a postproperty theory of digital capitalism is in actuality a plan for capitalists to reduce costs of production and circulation. In no sense are the means of production turned over to the worker whose labor actually produces the surplus value that the capitalists divide among themselves. Private property does not go away because the means of production have been updated. The idea that advances in production in themselves change social relations is to substitute a change in forms for a change in logic. If increases in the productivity of labor have meant that more capital can be put toward the development of science and technology, or that new businesses have emerged which take up certain aspects of circulation that corporations used to do for themselves, we still remain within the structure of private ownership. Even in a digital economy, everything from the resources necessary for the production of knowledge (books, classrooms, electricity, buildings, oil, computers, and so on) to the means for disseminating that information (paper, computers, phone lines, fiber optic cables, television and radio networks, and so on) remains under the ownership of capital.

It is this reading of property that is central to seeing why a theory of class exploitation remains critical to understanding contemporary social relations. According to the predominant reading of the digital condition, in contrast to the rigid social hierarchies of the Industrial Age that created clear and recognizable divisions between owners and workers, class is said to have become too difficult to read in the digital age of production because the development of the economy is now based upon vertical relations and an increasing plurality of available commodities rather than on a division of ownership. Instead of a "whole, centered, stable and completed ego or autonomous, rational 'self,'" the subject today is defined as "more fragmented and incomplete, composed of multiple 'selves' or identities in relation to the different social worlds we inhabit."[31] Class, on these terms, shifts from an economic relation to a cultural one shaped as much as, if not more than, by how class is "perceived" as it is constituted in reality. The digital society is said to "confound any spectral politics based upon self-confident class identities of previous periods"[32] and to transform the social into a space of difference without consequence in which "there is no single underlying principle fixing—and hence constituting—the whole field of differences."[33] It is in these terms, for example, that the emergence of online forums such as Facebook and YouTube are read as potential sites of "cosmopolitan cultural citizenship . . . in which individuals can represent their identities and perspectives, engage with the self-representation of others, and encounter cultural difference."[34] But "cultural difference" is not in itself disruptive to capitalism. In fact, capitalism is an engine of cultural difference. It requires the production of an endless stream of lifestyles in order to market otherwise similar commodities. The problem is not, in other words, that capitalism abhors difference. It is that capitalism will ultimately tolerate any differences that do not challenge the one difference that it cannot eliminate—the difference between capital and labor. It is this difference that is obscured when class is read digitally.

For example, Zillah Eisenstein begins her critique of the digital economy by marking the fact that "some 800 million people are starving across the globe" and that "of the world's largest one hundred economies, fifty-one are corporations, not countries."[35] "Class exploitation," she writes, "seems to be back with a vengeance."[36] But, for Eisenstein, class is not an economic relation but a cultural one that defies a clear understanding. That is to say, she argues that a traditional class analysis in which class is defined as a division of property cannot account for the ways in which "consumer culture and consumerism," which for her as for most theorists today characterize the networked landscape of digital life, "are woven through a notion of individualism that seduces everyone, the haves and the have-nots alike."[37] An economic theory of class has lost explanatory power in defining the boundaries of contemporary culture, according to Eisenstein, because it no longer can explain the seemingly universal introduction of technology and the ways in which it has reshaped the lives of both the rich and the poor. In this context, she argues instead, power relations have become "multiple and complex"[38] because digital technologies have the ability to allow the user to deconstruct the very class structures to which he or she was previously bound. "The emergence of 'digital technology,'" she concludes, "has the potential to undermine existing relations of power. The flow of information cannot be contained. The Internet creates new lines of communication and challenges old constrictions of private/public dialogue."[39] But, class is not simply a matter of power. Power *is an effect of* class relations, not its cause. What determines power in capitalism are the relations of property between owners and workers. By representing class as power, Eisenstein places class on the level of the political and the cultural rather than on the level of the economic. As a result, cultural critique moves toward the surfaces and effects of capital while leaving its logic intact.

The problem is that while such arguments displace class in the aroma of a digital spiritualism, on Earth the class division has not lessened but has in fact grown. As such, even as digital theorists claim that class has ceased to be a material reality, it seeps back into their discourse but in other terms. In other words, the economic realities of contemporary capitalism mean that to be *serious* one cannot simply ignore class, and yet to speak in a discourse that will be recognized by other cultural studies scholars requires that class be "revised" in terms that excuse exploitation. So, for example, in place of class as an economic binary, one finds class as a "cultural" or "political" binary, such as in the "digital divide,"[40] the gap between the "interacted" and the "interacting,"[41] or the conflict between "empire" and the "multitude."[42] In other words, in a world divided by a class binary, reality cannot but shape the image of a world divided into two. These arguments begin with the effects of property relations—they turn class into a matter of access to commodities, not the production of commodities. Class, however, is not a matter of lifestyle, consumer choice, market access, or representation. It is an objective relation between those who own and control the means of production and those who do not and, therefore, are forced to sell their labor power to those who do. This is the reality of capitalism, not the digital spiritualism of postclass market harmony.

Mark Poster's *What's the Matter with the Internet?* is a clear example of the way in which the economic divisions of the digital condition are rewritten as conflicts other than those shaped by the relations of production. What makes Poster's book particularly effective in this respect is that it is a reflection of the contradiction between the proclamations that class has become a plural identity without structure and the material reality that continues to simplify class relations. That is to say, it combines the more celebratory rhetoric of the past claims of the ability of technological development to supersede the economic conflict between capital and labor— found, for instance, in the work of Alvin Toffler (*The Third Wave*) and Daniel Bell (*The Coming of Post-Industrial Society*)—with the more tempered theorizations of technology by Geert Lovink (*My First Recession: Critical Internet Culture in Transition*) and Kevin Robins and Frank Webster (*From Information Society to the Virtual Life*) that have emerged following the crash of the dot-com bubble in the United States into a more subtle third way approach that is neither too celebratory nor too critical. It is precisely in writing of capitalism as an in-between subtlety that Poster's work has been recognized as a serious take on digital society, even as declining real wages, rising unemployment, and an expanding gap in wealth between the rich and the poor show that far from becoming more equal, digital society is synonymous with inequality.

Beginning with the assumption that as a result of recent technological advances we are entering an entirely new moment beyond the social divisions and inequalities of the past, Poster writes that in the digital society, "Nothing stands outside of the cultivatable, and so culture itself must be regarded as constructed rather than as given, historically contingent rather than timeless and certain,"[43] and, as such, "the magic of the Internet is that it is a technology that puts cultural acts, symbolizations in all forms, in the hands of all participants."[44] Poster sees digital technologies as creating the conditions for suspending class conflict because they give everyone access to the tools of representation that previously were available only to a select few. Of course, Poster cannot simply dismiss class. He writes that a digital society "is surely no total departure from all previous history" and that technological developments thus far tend to "favor the wealthy and the educated everywhere."[45] Yet according to this analysis what is different about contemporary culture is that it has become more flexible and can accept a wider array of difference within the existing, such that class is just one aspect of a broader social picture that no longer is centered on any norm. Echoing Baudrillard's theory of the contemporary as a culture of simulation,[46] as well as the corporate interest in fostering "market diversity," Poster argues that culture has become a "problem" on the basis of the disconnection between the original and the reproduction that emerges in the potentially endless copying of digital culture. For this reason, he proposes that culture has "lost its boundary"[47] and "fits badly"[48] with previous modes of understanding it. Prior analyses of culture, he suggests, assumed as a starting point a clear and definable relation between those who produced culture and those who consumed it. In contrast, Poster writes, "cyberspace means producing culture as you consume it."[49] In the tradition of the work of cultural theorists, such as Marshall McLuhan's *The Medium Is the Massage* and Manuel Castells's *The Internet Galaxy*, Poster declares the emergence of a global network of production and communication to be symbolic of a more decisive transformation that shakes the primary economic foundations of capitalist society, shifting it from a system based upon production and exploitation to one based on consumption and access.

That the digital reading of new forms of consumption having suspended the terms of class conflict that Poster offers here has become the primary way of making sense of the development of the networked economy can be seen in the fact that it is the reading most popular not only with savvy theorists of digital culture but also with those whose work is firmly within the established boundaries of corporate culture. For example, management theorist Peter Drucker calls the emergence of a global cyber economy a "Post-Capitalist Age" in which "[t]he basic economic resource—'the means of production' to use the economist's term—is no longer capital, nor natural resources . . . nor 'labor.' *It is and will be knowledge.*"[50] He goes on to argue that "the leading social groups of the knowledge society will be 'knowledge' workers. . . . [U]nlike the employees under Capitalism, they will own both the 'means of production' and the 'tools of production.'"[51] What is central to this argument is the idea that the substitution of knowledge for labor means the end of social inequalities precisely because of the inability of capital to control the production of ideas. The shift to knowledge work is thus understood as suspending the class divisions between owner and worker because of the way in which it takes the control over the means of production out of the hands of the owners and places it under the control of all workers. Rather than a class division between capital and labor, society is instead redefined by the relationship of the "info-rich" and the "info-poor." Insofar as all own the means of production—that is, everyone owns his or her "creativity," which is said to be the driving engine of the new economy, as Richard Florida proposes in *The Rise of the Creative Class*[52]— even this division is presumed to be short-lived, as it follows from this argument that such a division of information exists only until the fully networked economy is finally implemented. In this context, the argument is that technological developments alone will bring about the end of all social antagonisms as production is automated and exploited labor is replaced with the labor of machines.

It is within this framework that Poster defines the digital as signaling a "linguistic turn"[53] within capitalism in which "the initiative of questioning no longer gravitates towards production"[54] but instead focuses specifically on expanding access to the consumption of culture. By dematerializing the means of production and thus allowing "every receiver of a message to [also] produce a message," he argues, the same technological developments "confound the principles of capitalism."[55] He writes,

> In industrial technology, reproduction of commodities was the exclusive privilege and capability of the producer. Producer and consumer stood apart and were

differentiated precisely by this distinction. . . . But now all of this has changed. Information technologies place into the hands of the consumer the capacity to become a producer of cultural objects. The line dividing the two functions increasingly is blurred.[56]

What is "blurred" is said to be the status of private ownership. In fact, Poster argues that the production and circulation of knowledge commodities such as shareware and freeware mark the emergence of a postcapitalist age premised upon "an economy of sharing"[57] that "flies in the face of traditional free market enterprise economics."[58] What we are witnessing, his argument goes, is a deconstructive mode of accumulation in which the production of knowledge commodities disrupts the profit motives of capitalism by placing the means of representation into the hands of consumers, allowing them to create their own commodities independent from the interests of capital.

It is by severing the relationship between culture and class society that Poster's analysis of digital technologies re-articulates the status of representation and reflection as beyond the boundaries of economic determinacy, thereby shielding digital culture from class critique. Specifically, Poster argues that if capitalism has changed in the ways he suggests, the role of cultural studies must also shift to move away from questions of production and class—which are based on a mode of cultural critique that relies on an unreliable connection between economic and cultural developments— toward an analytics of consumption and the production of difference. That is to say, Poster extends this assumption of the "blurring" of property relations in capitalism's "linguistic turn" to cultural studies to argue that digital culture can no longer be read as a class society.

What Poster is proposing in the idea of social divisions as shaped not by property but in terms of the question of access to the means of communication is the theory of class-as-lifestyle that has come to serve as the most popular reading of class in cultural studies today. This is a theory of class in which class is no longer understood *relationally*—that is, as the relation between owners and workers at the point of production—but rather *differentially*, as part of a vast, fluid network of identities that are created by affinity (spirit) rather than economically (materially). Class-as- lifestyle is a broad categorization that depends less on objective relations than on subjective conceptions of social status. Such theories of class draw heavily from the work of Max Weber. What makes Weber's theory of class so appealing to the interests of capital is the way in which it ideologically opens class to a more complex reading by broadening the definition of class to include not only the relations of production but also income and political differences. Weber writes that while the "factor that creates 'class' is unambiguously economic interest, and indeed only those interests involved in the market," what must also be accounted for is the fact that "the concept of 'class-interest' is an ambiguous one: even as an empirical concept it is ambiguous as soon as one understands by it something other than the factual direction of interests following with a certain probability from the class situation."[59] That is, although the property relation can account in some instances for the ways in which people act in certain situations, it is not the prime factor. Weber writes that "class does not in itself constitute a community" and, in turn, that status groups—in which the rich and the poor might join side by side—play as big a part in organizing social life as any economic relations that might exist. People who think of themselves as, for example, *American* or *middle class* have the potential, according to Weber's analysis, to share the same class position.[60] In short, class, according to Weber, is most effectively understood as a plural and fluid designation of one's lifestyle.

One of the most famous examples of the theory of class-as-lifestyle is Stuart Hall's account of the ways in which oppressed peoples have taken over and remade the signs of the oppressive culture. Based upon his reading of "New Times" in which he argues that "the fact is that greater and greater numbers of people (men *and* women)—with however little money—play the game of using things to signify who they are,"[61] Hall reads the Rastafarian culture as an example of people constructing a space of resistance to hegemony from the inside through cultural reappropriation. He writes:

> In the case of the Rastafarians in Jamaica: Rasta was a funny language, borrowed from a text—the Bible—that did not belong to them; they had to turn the text upside-down, to get a meaning which fit their experience. But in turning the text upside-down they remade themselves; they positioned themselves differently as new political subjects; they reconstructed themselves as blacks in the new world: they *became* what they are.[62]

According to Hall's analysis, what makes an individual a member of a group is whether that individual *perceives* him- or herself as a member of the group. The Rastafarians are said to refigure their identities through a kind of resistance consumption, an argument that we see repeated endlessly today in relation to emerging cultural forms of remixing, blogging, and uploading videos to YouTube. However, just as with Jameson's theory of capitalism without a norm, we are once again left with no way of making sense of the reasons why the hegemony that the Rastafarians were resisting existed in the first place except a vague sense of power relations without determination. In other words, without understanding the economic history of slavery and colonialism, we are left with a reality that has no history.

What links all of these arguments is the idea that it is not property but the ways in which people *think* about property relations that determine their class. Class is, in other words, now shaped by perception (virtual), not property (material). But, as Lindsey German points out in response to similar arguments, "none of these subjective approaches really help in defining class, because they start with distribution and consumption, with the outcome of an unequal class society, rather than what creates class society in the first place."[63] That is to say, what writers like Eisenstein, Hall, and Poster assume as their starting point is a society that is *already* divided at the point of production and, instead, seek to mitigate those circumstances through the ways in which commodities are consumed. However, as German goes on to argue, "the actual class position of individuals [depends] not on what they feel about which class they are in, but whether they are forced to sell their labor power in order to survive."[64] In other words, "Going to the cinema, or on a trip to a theme park, or playing computer games, seems to appeal across the class divide,"[65] but in reality "even if a worker cuts across class stereotypes by, for example, listening to opera, there is something more fundamental which defines him or her than one particular leisure pursuit"[66]—namely, that the worker's ability to survive depends entirely upon an ability to sell his or her labor on the market. Class, in short, is an *objective* relation. It is determined not by the consumption of materials—whether, for example, both the lord and the serf eat from the same harvest and thus think of themselves as part of the same community or whether the owner and the workers spend their free time gaming online and consider themselves members of a gaming clan—but rather by the relationship to property that exists between these social groups.

Technology and Determination

In the contestation between the theory of class-as-lifestyle and that of class-as-property-relations there is also a deeper question about the role of technology and whether advances in communications, production, and transportation have rendered labor superfluous to the production of value. That is to say, the idea that production has been replaced by consumption depends upon a reading of the development of production in the postwar period as essentially deconstructing itself. It is the idea that capitalism has undergone a fundamental transformation from a Fordist industrial economy of mass production and class inequalities to a post-Fordist informational, cyber-economy of signs and the pluralizing of differences beyond class. For example, John Frow writes that with the "increased integration of the aesthetic in economic production,"[67] "the structure of a linear hierarchy" such as class "no longer seems applicable."[68] Similarly, Yochai Benkler argues in *The Wealth of Networks* that "the change brought about by the networked information environment is . . . structural,"[69] representing a "new mode of production"[70] in which "individuals are free to take a more active role than was possible in the industrial economy of the twentieth century."[71]

What defines these arguments is the idea that the primary focus of capitalism has become the production of knowledge commodities and that as a consequence of the shift from a Fordist to a post-Fordist society the boundaries between owners and workers, producers and consumers, and economics and culture have all broken down because of the ways in which culture itself has been incorporated into the production process. As John Allen explains, "the concept of 'Fordism' captures all things modern about an economy: it is associated with scale, progress, science, control, technology, rationality, including the sea of disciplined workers that poured through the gates."[72] "Ford*ism*," he goes on to write, "is conceived of an era of mass, standardized goods produced for mass markets, created by an interventionist state which gave people the spending power to make mass consumption possible"[73] in which "it is *manufacturing* which acts as the 'engine' of growth within an economy" and "it was this connection, between mass production and mass consumption, that was taken to be one of the hallmarks of the modern era."[74] On the contrary, the shift to post-Fordism, which is understood roughly as emerging in the period after 1945 and is marked most often by the mass introduction of microchip technologies, is characterized by a growing importance of "information technologies and networked offices rather than by coal or steam power and sprawling workshops."[75] Allen states:

> Opening up before us, it is claimed, is an altogether different kind of economy; one which is organized around flexible forms of production, in both the technologies used and in the kinds of work expected. In contrast to mass production and mass markets, it is argued that flexible production techniques are becoming increasingly important as a means of responding to the greater diversity of consumer demand and fragmented market tastes.[76]

The growth of the productivity of labor throughout the twentieth century, the argument goes, reduced the necessity of labor required to maintain production to such low levels as to be inconsequential to the overall accumulation that was generated, while at the same time it freed up formerly productive workers for the expansion of avenues of consumption. Alvin Toffler, for example, defines this shift in terms of his theory of the "prosumer"[77] for whom the new productive market becomes a means for individualized consumption and "the consumer, not merely punching the button that sets this entire process in action, will become as much a part of the production process as the denim-clad assembly line worker was in the [industrial/second wave] world now dying."[78] Similarly enthusiastic futurist Nicholas Negroponte declares that in "the post-information age, we often have an audience the size of one. Everything is made to order and information is extremely personalized."[79] In such declarations we find the precedent for the contemporary arguments about the iPod and the Internet as opening new spaces for individual self-fulfillment and the notion that consumption has become central to the global economy.

The theory of technology as the solution to socioeconomic problems does not have to take the *hard* form of theorists such as Jacques Ellul, who, from a conservative Christian position, argues in response to the changes of the postindustrial economy that "it is useless to rail against capitalism. Capitalism did not create our world; the machine did."[80] Rather, much of cultural theory today takes the form of a *soft* technological determinism that nonetheless continues to read technology as a space independent of the current economic conditions of capitalism in which labor is exploited, and this is the reason why it simultaneously operates as a site of what Constance

Penley and Andrew Ross call "popular refunctioning" to resist cultural norms.[81] One of the central figures in the development of this logic is Daniel Bell, whose work on the "Post-Industrial Society" in the 1970s has become foundational in establishing this reading of the role of science and technology in the economy. What has made Bell's analysis so influential is the way in which it works to incorporate technological progress into the analysis of culture in such a way as to insulate the relationship between technology and labor from critique.

Taking as its starting point the argument that the failure of Marx's analysis of capitalism is the idea that "the mode of production (the sub-structure of a society) determines and encompasses *all* other dimensions of a society,"[82] Bell first moves to separate the development of technology from the analysis of economic conditions, which he describes as a "false confrontation between two *different* conceptual schema."[83] In its place, he shifts the development of history away from labor and onto a spiritual theory of traditions. He argues that "societies are not unified entities. The nature of the polity—whether a nation becomes democratic or not—rests not on the economic 'foundation' but on historic traditions"[84]; further, he writes:

> The most grievous mistake in the social sciences is to read the character of a society through a single overriding concept, whether it be *capitalism* or *totalitarianism*, and to mislead one as to the complex (overlapping and even contradictory) features of any modern society, or to assume that there are "laws of social development" in which one social system succeeds another by some inexorable necessity.[85]

To prove his point that *traditions* (that is, culture) and not *economics* determine the development of society and the uses of technology, Bell argues that "the same forces of production (i.e., technology) exist within a wide variety of different systems of social relations" such that "one cannot say that the technology (or chemistry or physics) of the Soviet Union is different from the technology (or chemistry or physics) of the capitalist world."[86] Bell is also quick to remark that the division of the world at the time he was writing—locating the United States and the Soviet Union on the developed side of an "axis of technology" with countries such as Indonesia and China on the undeveloped side—is simply one of a range of possibilities.[87] As long as "one does not claim that the particular schema is exhaustive, and subsumes all others," he writes, "we can also specify different schemata of social development: feudal, capitalist, and socialist;

or pre-industrial, industrial, and post-industrial; or within the Weberian framework of political authority, that of patriarchal, patrimonial, and legal-rational bureaucracy."[88]

Although in this formulation Bell appeals to social complexity and challenges "the claim that the mode of production always determines the 'superstructure' of society,"[89] it becomes clear that what is at stake in the kind of pluralistic approach to sociology he opens with is developing a means of reading technology that situates technological development as independent from and equal to all other forces in shaping social life. That is to say, regardless of Bell's claim that his emphasis on technology "does not mean that technology is the primary determinant of all other societal changes,"[90] by isolating technology from economic, political, and cultural factors while simultaneously revising the history of human society in terms of its relationship to technological development it becomes clear that it *is* technology, divorced from historical conflict, that becomes the foundation of change in Bell's analysis. This becomes even more clear as he begins outlining the history of society:

> A pre-industrial sector is primarily *extractive*, its economy based on agriculture, mining, fishing, timber and other resources such as natural gas or oil. An industrial sector is primarily *fabricating*, using energy and machine technology, for the manufacture of goods. A post-industrial sector is one of *processing*, in which telecommunications and computers are strategic for the exchange of information and knowledge.[91]

What is significant about this schema is not simply the way in which it articulates the divisions between societies in terms of their mode of production, an approach of which, as I have noted, Bell claims to be critical. Rather, what is more important is that the changes he outlines—from extraction, to fabrication, to processing—are differentiated in terms of the level at which technology in society acts as a substitute for labor. It is precisely the displacement of labor by technology that Bell indicates marks one of the "vastly different" elements that distinguishes "post-industrial" society from the two previous modes of production.[92] He argues, "if industrial society is based on machine technology, post-industrial society is shaped by an intellectual technology. And if capital and labor are the structural features of industrial society, information and knowledge are those of the post-industrial society."[93] In other words, it is not that Bell is opposed to a reductive analysis of history in terms of the mode of production, for which he criticizes Marx.[94] It is that he is opposed to any analysis that sees labor and not technology as the source of social development. This becomes evident when, having argued that "[n]o conceptual scheme ever exhausts a social reality,"[95] he nonetheless concludes that "every society has existed on the basis of knowledge."[96]

The centralization of information and knowledge as a substitute for labor is thus the key to Bell's analysis. It is, in fact, in describing the differences between an industrial and a postindustrial economy that his work has become most influential for the dominant theories of the digital condition, particularly as it relates to the role of culture in the economy. He argues that "industrial commodities are produced in discrete, identifiable units, exchanged and sold, consumed and used up, as are a loaf of bread or an automobile" and that "information and knowledge are not consumed or 'used up'" but rather, "even when it is sold," knowledge "remains with the producer."[97] In other words, what is fundamentally different for Bell about the postindustrial society is the way in which the producer (worker) no longer turns over his or her product to the owner or consumer but rather retains control and thus, one could argue, cannot be considered exploited in the "industrial" sense. This is the implication of his reading of the status of labor in the postindustrial age. He writes:

> In a pre-industrial world, life is a game against nature in which men wrest their living from the soil, the waters, or the forests, working usually in small groups, subject to the vicissitudes of nature. In an industrial society, work is a game against fabricated nature, in which men become dwarfed by machines as they turn out goods and things. But in a post-industrial world, work is primarily a "game between persons." . . . Thus in the experience of work and the daily routine, nature is excluded, artifacts are excluded, and persons have to learn how to live with one another. In the history of human society, this is a completely new and unparallel state of affairs.[98]

Although Bell's analysis of technology and work is generally understood as coming from a conservative political position, his reading in this passage of a knowledge economy in which class is replaced by individual initiative and exploitation is rendered obsolete because the nature of the commodity produced has become extremely influential in cultural studies, particularly among those working in the post-Marxist tradition such as Aronowitz, Baudrillard, Deleuze and Guattari, Laclau and Mouffe, Lyotard, and Negri, to name only a few. To take as one example, Jean Baudrillard's thesis in *Symbolic Exchange and Death* rests on a similar assumption that capital has moved from an economy based upon the production of goods to an economy based upon the exchange of signs. He writes, "A revolution has put an end to [the] 'classical' economy of value, a revolution which, beyond the commodity form, stretches value to its most radical form,"[99] bringing with it "the end of labor, the end of production, and the end of political economy."[100] While Bell and Baudrillard differ on their terms—for Bell it is knowledge that drives the economy; for Baudrillard it is the sign—what is significant is the way in which knowledge is situated as the other of labor. Baudrillard's theory posits labor as a sign whose value depends upon its ability to stand in for the reality of production that is displaced in the move toward "simulacrum"—the final stage in the history of modes of production in which "the question of signs and their rational destinations, their 'real' and their 'imaginary,' their repression, reversal, the illusions they form of what they silence or of their parallel significations, is completely effaced"[101] Bell's theory of a "knowledge theory of labor" similarly assumes "it is the codification of knowledge that becomes directive of innovation."[102] However, despite these differences in idiom, what both theorists share is the underlying assumption of a soft technological determinism.

Technological determinism today is based upon the idea that there is a force other than labor that is able to create surplus value and thus has become the primary focus of the economy. While it is most commonly articulated as knowledge or, as Henry Giroux argues, the idea that "information has now become capital,"[103] such arguments are based upon the presupposition that it is ideas (what technology embodies) rather than labor that shape the world. Of course, I am aware that in many instances this determinism is projected onto Marxism, often in terms of a selective reading of Marx's statement that "the hand-mill gives you society with the feudal lord; the steam-mill, society with the industrial capitalist,"[104] for example in Robert Heilbroner's influential article "Do Machines Make History?" What is at stake, however, in Marx's analysis of this relationship between technology and social change is precisely what differentiates a materialist analysis of technology from the technological determinism that has become dominant. In the passage in question, for example, Marx is arguing precisely *against* a kind of technological determinism that erases the fundamental role of human labor in social change. Marx writes, "the economist understands very well that men make cloth, linen, silk materials in definite relations of production. But what he has not understood is that these definite social relations are just as much produced by men as linen, flax, etc."[105] In other words, in contrast to the attempt merely to describe the conditions of production as if they had emerged on their own and thus are beyond the power of individuals to transform them, Marx argues that we must understand the conditions themselves as the product of labor. It is in this sense that Marx continues by arguing, "social relations are closely bound up with productive forces. In acquiring new productive forces men change their mode of production; and in changing their mode of production, in changing the way of earning their living, they change all their social relations" before concluding that "the hand-mill gives you society with the feudal lord; the steam-mill, society with the industrial capitalist."[106] What is central to this conclusion is the fact that, as Marx argues, the acquisition of new productive forces—whether it is the "hand-mill," the "steam-mill," or the computer chip—is the result of human labor. In other words, it is the human labor in the past which produces the conditions that exist in the present, and it is the human labor in the present which makes possible the conditions that may exist in the future. Without human labor, to put it crudely, the technological developments do not exist, regardless of the level of development such advances have achieved.

Instrumentality and Labor

At the same time that technological determinism has emerged to isolate technological developments from historical conditions, there has developed what appears, at first glance, to be a counter-reading of technology which advances a kind of spiritual resistance to what is described as the "instrumental reason" of technology that seeks to resurrect a lost spiritual wholeness that has been displaced by the crushing logic of the technological and the scientific. The foundational theorist of this essentially religious critique of technology is Martin Heidegger, whose essay "The Question Concerning Technology" remains extremely influential in contemporary cultural theory because of the way it lends the appearance of radicalism to the notion that the problems of capitalism reside not on earth but at the level of the idea.

Heidegger opens the essay by drawing a distinction between technology and its essence. He writes,

> Technology is not equivalent to the essence of technology. When we are seeking the essence of "tree," we have to become aware that what pervades every tree, as tree, is not itself a tree that can be encountered among all the other trees. Likewise, the essence of technology is by no means technological. We shall never experience our relationship to the essence of technology so long as we merely represent and pursue the technological, put up with it, or evade it.[107]

While this distinction is not limited to Heidegger—although on different terms, dialectical theorists such as Hegel and Marx, for example, argue for the distinction between an object's appearance and its essence—what is significant about Heidegger's approach is that the purpose of drawing this distinction is not to uncover the essence of technology as much as to displace the essence that exists without substituting an alternative cause. For Heidegger, the problem of technology is the dialectical logic of causality it instills, and it is this critique of causality that remains so influential within cultural theory.

When asking about the essence of technology, Heidegger argues, one generally receives two answers:

> One says: Technology is a means to an end. The other says: Technology is a human activity. The two definitions of technology belong together. For to posit ends and procure and utilize the means to them is a human activity. The manufacture and utilization of equipment, tools, and machines, the manufactured and used things themselves, and the needs and ends they serve all belong to what technology is. The whole complex of these contrivances is technology. Technology is itself a contrivance—in Latin, an *instrumentum*.[108]

For Heidegger, to read technology either as a product of human labor (Marx) or as a product of human reason (Hegel) is to assume an instrumental approach to technology which reduces all possible meanings of technology to causes that are justified after the fact by the effects that result. He argues that the use of technology as the "means to an end" means that

> the instrumental conception of technology conditions every attempt to bring man into the right relation to technology. Everything depends on our manipulating technology in the proper manner as means. We will, as we say, "get" technology "intelligently in hand." We will master it. The will to mastery

becomes all the more urgent the more technology threatens to slip from human control.[109]

In other words, technology is symptomatic of a will to mastery over nature that continually increases as what he proposes as the "real" essence of nature is replaced by the "instrumental" essence of technology.

The will to mastery that Heidegger outlines here is what he defines as the effect of the technological consciousness of instrumental reason. The problem of this kind of mastery, he argues, is that it imposes on nature and on humanity the very results it seeks to find. For example, he writes that one of the problems of technology is that it "puts to nature the unreasonable demand that it supply energy which can be extracted and stored as such."[110] As a result, "everywhere everything is ordered to stand by, to be immediately on hand, indeed to stand there just so that it may be on call for a further ordering."[111] The reduction of things to "standing-by" means, for Heidegger, the imposition of a false causality such that the thing in question loses its "real" essence and, instead, becomes an object whose *essence* reflects its instrumental purpose. He argues, on these terms, that the introduction of a hydropower plant on a river turns the river into a water power station, and, in turn, "what the river is now, namely, a water-power supplier, derives from the essence of the power station."[112] In short, the world comes to appear as instrumental because this is the (false) logic through which the world is being read.

Heidegger goes on to argue that the reduction of things to an instrumental essence concerns not only nature but human activity. He states, "The forester who measures the felled timber in the woods and who to all appearances walks the forest path in the same way his grandfather did is today ordered by the industry that produces commercial woods, whether he knows it or not."[113] Heidegger, here, locates the alienation of the individual in contemporary society not in capitalism but in the instrumental logic of technology. He argues:

> As soon as what is unconcealed no longer concerns man even as object, but exclusively as standing-reserve, and man in the midst of objectlessness is nothing but the orderer of the standing reserve, then he comes to the very brink of a precipitous fall; that is, he comes to the point where he himself will have to be taken as standing-reserve. Meanwhile, man, precisely as the one so threatened, exalts himself and postures as lord of the earth. In this way the illusion comes to

prevail that everything man encounters exists only insofar as it is his construct. This illusion gives rise in turn to one final delusion: it seems as though man everywhere and always encounters himself.[114]

The reduction of human activity to instrumental reason and, in turn, the reduction of nature to the same logic is, for Heidegger, the real risk of technological development: "the possibility that it could be denied to [humanity] to enter into a more original revealing and hence to experience the call of a more primal truth."[115]

What Heidegger proposes as the solution to the alienation of instrumentality is a destructive mode of thinking that refuses to begin with or to draw conclusions. He begins this project by outlining what he argues is the logic of causality, writing:

> Whatever has an effect as its consequence is called a cause. But not only that by means of which something else is effected is a cause. The end that determines the kind of means to be used may be considered a cause. Wherever ends are pursued and means are employed, wherever instrumentality reigns, there reigns causality.[116]

For Heidegger, causality and instrumentality are an approach to nature that imposes an alternative use, rather than its essential purpose, primarily through human activity (that is, through labor). He argues that in contrast to this kind of causality—which he defines as the *causa efficiens*—there are, in fact, three other kinds of causality: the *causa materialis* (or natural materials), the *causa formalis* (the form or shape into which the materials are crafted), and the *causa finalis* (the ritual or purpose that determines what materials and which shape are to be used). Giving the example of a chalice, Heidegger redefines causality in terms of indebtedness and responsibility. He writes:

> Silver is that out of which the chalice is made. As this matter (*hyle*), it is co-responsible for the chalice. The chalice is indebted to, i.e. owes thanks to, the silver for that which it consists. But the sacrificial vessel is indebted not only to the silver. As a chalice, that which is indebted to the silver appears in the aspect of a chalice, and not in that of a brooch or a ring. Thus the sacred vessel is at the same time indebted to the aspect (*eidos*) of chaliceness. Both the silver into which the aspect is admitted as chalice and the aspect in which the silver appears are in their respective ways co-responsible for the sacrificial vessel.[117]

What he is proposing in this reading of the chalice is a reading of production in which human labor is only one aspect in a process to which he ultimately gives determinacy to the ritualistic purpose to which that product is used. He writes, "there remains yet a third something that is above all responsible for the sacrificial vessel. It is that which in advance confines the chalice within the realm of consecration and bestowal. Through this the chalice is circumscribed as sacrificial vessel."[118] This is an attempt to address the contradictions of exchange-value by placing the meaning of the commodity in the idea to which the commodity aspires. In other words, it spiritualizes the meaning of the commodity in an attempt to solve a social conflict that emerges when use value is subsumed under the logic of exchange value.

Having turned production into the process by which the "spirit" is materialized on Earth, Heidegger challenges the technological logic of instrumentality by substituting the logic of *poiēsis*. Heidegger takes up Plato's statement in the *Symposium*—"Every occasion for whatever passes beyond the nonpresent and goes forward into presencing is *poiēsis*"—to argue for a new understanding of technology not as instrumental but as "revealing" (*alētheia*). He writes, "The concept word [technology] stems from the Greek. *Tecknikon* means that which belongs to *technē*."[119] What is significant about this relationship, he continues, is that "*technē* is the name not only for the activities and skills of the craftsman but also for the arts of the mind and the fine arts. *Technē* belongs to the bringing-forth, to *poiēsis*; it is something poetic."[120] In other words, in production one must recognize the creativity of the laborer over the commodity produced. For Heidegger the worker (in this case, the silversmith) becomes a *causa efficiens* not because he has been reduced to an exploited wage laborer. Rather, the alienation of the worker results from the logic of instrumentality, which imposes upon him the status of means to an end. Instead, Heidegger argues that the silversmith must be understood as part of the process of revealing the true essence of nature, without imposing upon that essence the logic of "means." It is only through recognition of his role as part of a broader *spiritual* purpose that the worker can overcome the alienation of capitalist society.

It is interesting to see the way in which Heidegger's critique of technological instrumentality has itself become part of the ideology of the digital economy. In spite of his existential critique of *technē*, as capital relies more and more on technology, Heidegger's existential resistance softens to the extent that Bernard Stiegler, one of Heidegger's most perceptive critics writes, "the meaning of modern technics is ambiguous in Heidegger."[121] For example, in *High Technē: Art and Technology from the Machine Aesthetic to the Posthuman*, R. L. Rutsky looks to Heidegger's reading of *technē* as creative labor as a way of explaining the freedom provided to the individual in the new virtual landscape of digital culture. He writes, "whatever changes or mutations have occurred in contemporary cultures—whether one calls these cultures postmodern or not—seem to be based less on changes in technology per se than in the very conception of technology, of what technology is."[122] What Rutsky believes is that in contrast to industrial technologies, digital technologies redefine labor as "a more general concept of making or producing, including artistic production"[123] as articulated by Heidegger. That is to say, in contrast to the industrial, which was "defined in terms of an instrumental conception of technology, an instrumental or technological rationality that allows modern 'humanity' to know and control the world,"[124] Rutsky argues that the digital economy, "with its emphasis on issues of representation, style, and design, seems to signal a reemergence of [a] repressed aesthetic aspect within technology."[125] He continues, "Unlike modern technology, high tech can no longer be defined *solely* in terms of its instrumentality or function—as simply a tool or a means to an end. In high tech, rather, technology becomes much more a matter of representation, of aesthetics, of style."[126] It is the digital, Rutsky argues, that finally allows the worker to be "free" from the instrumental logic of capitalism.

Similarly, in *Mass Mediauras: Form, Technics, Media*, Samuel Weber follows Heidegger's argument in suggesting that the "representational thinking" underlying modern conceptions of technology treats objects and people as "calculable data, as information to be taken into account or accounted for,"[127] and he concludes that for this reason the technical has ceased to be "a way of bringing-forth" but has become instead "a driving- or goading-forth" and the basis of "ex-ploiting, ex-tracting, ex-pelling, inciting."[128] In contrast, Weber writes that just as Heidegger frees the creative logic of *poiēsis* from "a dependency upon an object (the product) or subject (a producer),"[129] we should no longer approach new technologies as establishing an "emplacement" that is fixed and determined. Instead, he argues that just as "the more technics seeks *to place* the subject into safety the less safe its *places* become," that "places and placing can no longer be taken *for* granted. Rather, they must be taken *as* granted" as opening "a way that can never be entirely secured."[130] In other words, by characterizing the contemporary as "an age of increasing uncertainty, when the solutions and answers that were taken for granted until recently no longer seem viable" and that this new age allows us to "confront problems without demanding recipes of salvation,"[131] Weber is essentially proposing, like Rutsky, that it is the very nature of digital technologies and their creative abilities to transform the ground of "certainty" that challenge the instrumental logic of the Industrial Age.

Even a more radical political theorization of instrumentalism, as David Golumbia advances in *The Cultural Logic of Computation*, ultimately ends up reproducing the same idealist logic that it aims to criticize. Arguing against "messianic claims about sudden, radical, and almost salutary changes in the fundamental fabric of politics, economics, and social formations,"[132] he proposes that differences between manual and service workers "may be far less salient to politics . . . than the degree to which members of a given institution in fact participate in the management of the organization or are instead subject to strong, hierarchical rule"[133] and that "both represent a significant separation of capital and responsibility from the human being operating in the name of the corporation."[134] According to Golumbia, however, this economic division is symptomatic of an epistemological divide, rather than a division of property. He proposes that the main problem of digital society is that instrumentalism or "computation" is "not a neutral technology" but "a means of expanding top-down hierarchical power."[135] In other words, what emerges from his analysis is a reading of capitalism in which the contradictions are not between capitalist and worker but between the powerful and the powerless. Further, as with Weber and Rutsky, what is ultimately privileged as resisting the homogenizing instrumentality of computation is an "anti-realism" that embraces the "inexact, fuzzy, analog features of the world that, while difficult to control and even at times to name, are nevertheless among the most vital facets of human life,"[136] such as "our primitive need to play."[137] He concludes, "Our societies function best when they are balanced between what we call here rationalism and whatever lies outside of it."[138] In other words, while Golumbia is critical of the connections between global capital expansion and instrumentalism, by simply embracing the other of rationalism we are left with an epistemological conflict with little direct attachment to the conditions in which people live. Instead, reality becomes an effect of ideas, and transforming social inequality is reduced to embracing the uncertain rather than changing material relations.

What Heidegger, and following him Rutsky, Weber, and Golumbia, presents as a "spiritual" renewal—creativity—is simply a recognition that it is the labor power of workers that creates value. This does not so much challenge the logic of exploitation as it places it on a higher plane, where it can remain the natural logic of capitalism. The spiritualization of exploitation shows only the extent to which the appearance of capitalism as an eternal system has taken hold at the level of ideology. What is obscured in the turning of labor into a spiritual act that can combat the materiality of the technological is the fact that it is not technology that alienates the worker but the appropriation of the worker's labor by capital that makes technology appear "*as something alien, as a power independent* of the producer."[139] The appearance that it is technology and not capital which causes the alienation of the worker conceals the fact that "the *alien* being, to whom labour and the product of labour belongs, in whose service labour is done and for whose benefit the product of labour is provided, can only be *man* himself. If the product of labour confronts him as an alien power, then this can only be because it belongs to some *other man than the worker*."[140] Heidegger and other "anti-rationalists" thus provide a "solution" to the alienation of labor that extends, rather than curtails, the logic of capitalism. His rewriting of causality erases the economic relations between people and turns this human relation, as is the ideology of capitalism, into a relationship between ideas and things. The limit of capitalism does not reside in bad ideas, however; it resides in the fact that the productivity of labor is put towards the limited ends of profitability.

In contrast to Heidegger's analysis of the chalice, I want to turn to Lenin's reading of the drinking glass because it demonstrates what it means to approach culture from the position that it is labor which takes place under specific social and historical conditions that determines the status and meaning of our reality. He writes:

> A glass is undoubtedly a glass cylinder and a drinking vessel. But a glass not only has these two properties, qualities, or sides, but an infinite number of other properties, qualities, sides, interrelations and "mediations" with the rest of the world. A glass is a heavy object which may be used as a missile. A glass may serve as a paperweight, as a jar to keep a captive butterfly in, a glass may have value as an object with an artistic engraving or design, quite apart from the fact that it can

be used as a drinking vessel, that it is made of glass, that its form is cylindrical, or not quite so, and so on and so forth.[141]

What Lenin outlines in this passage is a dialectical analysis that approaches an object not in terms of its formal characteristics but in terms of "all its sides, all connections and 'mediations.'"[142] What is particularly important about Lenin's examination of the glass is his insistence that in such an analysis, "the whole of human experience should enter the full 'definition' of an object as a criterion of the truth and as a practical index of the object's connection with what man requires."[143] We cannot assume the meaning of an object outside of the material conditions of its production, which are social and historical. Thus, if we apply this analysis to Heidegger's chalice, we must ask not only whether its use corresponds to an instrumental or natural essence but what the conditions in which the instrumental or the natural are determined are. These are not simply abstract categories. Their meaning is a reflection of social conflicts, and whether a glass is a chalice or a paperweight is historically determined. In capitalist society, both the glass and the chalice are commodities, produced for the purposes of exchange. The object's value is completely independent from its use. This is the spiritualism to which Heidegger's theory of the chalice ultimately appeals—it is the logic of exchange value that capitalism imposes on the products of labor.

The iPod and the Fetishism of Consumer Resistance

The digital spirit of anti-instrumentalism reaches perhaps its highest point in "the cult of iPod."[144] The iPod has become synonymous with the cultural freedom of the digital age and the idea that the freedoms of consumption, which is really another way of saying the wage since it is the wage that enables most people to purchase these items, is a more than fair exchange for the sale of labor power. It is described as "a near-universal object of desire"[145] that is "the symbol of the media's future" in which "the gates of access are thrown open, the reach of artists goes deeper, and consumers don't just consume, they choose songs, videos, and even their news their way."[146] Thomas L. Friedman, for example, uses the iPod as a prime example of what he calls the "flat world," a moment when capitalism turns from a hierarchical to a vertical system in which value no longer simply flows from bottom to top, but outward in an expanding network of exchange. In an anecdotal style that is intended to signify the "obviousness" of the new digital landscape, Friedman describes the iPod as bringing about the transferring of the ownership and control of culture from large corporations to the individual user. According to Friedman the iPod is empowering because it enables someone to take control over what they want to listen to when they want to listen to it. He writes, "Think about it: For decades the broadcast industry was built around the idea that you shoot out ads on network television or radio and hope that someone is watching or listening. But thanks to the flattening technologies" such as the iPod "that world is quickly fading away."[147]

It is not that the economic logic that shapes the broadcast industry is fading away in the digital age. In fact, the monopoly consolidation of the entertainment industry means that four companies sell 90 percent of all music, six companies control over 90 percent of revenue in the film industry, the three largest publishers of textbooks control over 70 percent of the U.S. market, and the two largest radio firms control more of the market than the next twenty-three competitors combined.[148] It is that as the commodification of everyday life expands, the ability to *see* the labor in the commodity becomes more difficult. The spiritual aroma of the iPod which means that labor "disappears" at the level of ideas and is replaced with consumption, is what Marx calls "commodity fetishism"—the way "a definite social relation between men, that assumes, in their eyes, the fantastic form of a relation between things."[149] It is not accidental that before its announcement the iPhone was often referred to as the "Jesus phone" because of all it (supposedly) represented.[150] It is the effect of the transformation of all use values into exchange value, a process that makes commodities appear transcendent of the relations of labor because of the way in which the commercial value comes to dominate their social value.[151] That is, when their value as objects produced for the purposes of private accumulation takes over for their value as objects of use. What appears as transcendence is, in actuality, the reduction of all aspects of life to the process of commodification.

What commodity fetishism means is that the more commodification becomes the dominant logic of society the more that commodities appear to transcend commodification and the more that the role of labor is hidden behind the hieroglyphic of the commodity. A posting to a public technology newsgroup is a prime example of this logic of consumer "freedom":

> The iPod has become more than just an MP3 player; it is a fashion statement and symbol of being "cool." Certainly there are better MP3 players with more functionality at lower prices, but that is no longer the point of owning an iPod. The closest analogues are in clothing and cars. Sure, you could get "very functional" clothes and cars, but some of us choose to buy more expensive items because we have the money and the inclination to make a fashion statement.[152]

The description of the iPod as "more than just an MP3 player" but a "fashion statement"—that its meaning is not defined by use but by exchange—demonstrates how the logic of exchange value has become the logic of the everyday. It is this logic which explains the dominant readings of the iPod as not just a commodity but an object of "technotranscendence" that, according to Markus Giesler, allows consumers to "transcend the here and now through the use of technology."[153] The beauty of the iPod, according to Giesler, is that it "reduces the complexity of consumption" while at the same time shifting consumption from "materiality to information—the Internet; from ownership to access—file sharing; and from pattern to randomness—the iPod."[154] But this "simplicity" is an ideological effect of the complexity of the division of labor, in which workers only encounter the objects of production on the market, and thus the labor that has produced this commodity is nowhere to be found.

What is supposed to make the iPod so different as a commodity is the way in which it places the ability of the individual consumer to determine the reality they want to live in. Other commodities might allow the individual to control their identities by projecting meaning outward, but they still require the individual to inhabit a collectively determined public space. On the contrary, the iPod is described as allowing the individual to retreat inward, creating a private audioscape that enables them to take greater control over reality by allowing them to define on their own terms how they interact with the world. As Michael Bull argues, by allowing iPod users to "reinscribe mundane linear time with their own very personalized meanings, transforming the intolerable into the tolerable" the iPod empowers the user "to wrest back some control from the multiple and invasive rhythms of daily urban life."[155] In this sense, the iPod is said to "confound the traditional distinction between work and leisure time as users construct a seamless auditory experience from work to home."[156]

What this erases, however, is that work time and leisure time are not simply ahistorical givens, their development and their meaning is an effect of developments in the means of production and take on the shape of the mode of production. As Ernest Mandel writes, "The producer in a primitive society does not usually separate his productive activity, 'labour,' from his other human activities."[157] Far from being a peaceful integration of labor and leisure, this level of society is defined by the "tyranny" of nature over the productive development of human labor. In other words, "This high degree of integration of his whole life is more an expression of the poverty of society and the extreme narrowness of his needs than a conscious effort towards the all-around development of all human potentialities."[158] It is the productivity of labor that enables humanity to transform the natural into the social and "as the productive forces increase, mankind frees himself more and more completely from the tyranny of the forces of nature."[159] Yet, as society moves from "absolute poverty" to "relative scarcity," what emerges is the simultaneous movement from "a society harmoniously united to a society divided into classes."[160] In other words, "As man frees himself from the tyranny of natural forces he falls more and more under the tyranny of blind social forces, the tyranny of other men (slavery, serfdom), or the tyranny of his own products (petty commodity production and capitalist production)."[161] What this means is that the appearance of daily life as a struggle between leisure time and work or "alienated" time is, in reality, a struggle between those who have been freed from having to work by appropriating the work of others and those whose work has been appropriated. It is the consequence of a system of production in which workers lose all control over their labor because they must sell it piecemeal to the capitalist in order to acquire the means of survival. It is the reflection of a society in which "everything is bought and sold."[162]

The iPod is a mass-produced commodity. Its value resides in the fact that it is an object produced for exchange. Whatever appearances it takes on at the level of culture, it remains a commodity and thus the embodiment of labor power that has been appropriated by capital for the purposes of private accumulation. Although Apple has long asked its users to "Think Different," the iPod produces surface differences that cover the primary difference of class. The more iPods are sold the more the owners of Apple are able to realize the surplus value of the labor they have appropriated from their workers in the form of private profits. No matter how ubiquitous the iPod becomes, it cannot but expand the economic division between capital and labor.

However, in contrast to a society of alienation that requires individuals to retreat into their own private worlds as the only way of tolerating their lives, what is becoming possible as a result of the productivity of labor is the material conditions for bringing about the end of an alienated society in which only a few have been "freed from the burden of having to work for a living."[163] Instead of a world in which the majority must live as "prisoners of the same dull fate, shut up within the same restricted horizon by the same wages, dressed in the same mass-produced clothes, reading the same sensational newspapers, relaxing in the same sports stadiums or in front of the same television programs,"[164] the freeing of labor from the restrictions of commodity production would mean that everyone, and not just those who own and control the means of production, would eliminate the alienation that currently exists between work and leisure. Freedom from the confines of wage labor means that "human energy will be concentrated in art and science, in education and in physical and mental well-being."[165] No longer will social differences result in economic inequality. Rather, the end of the private ownership of the means of production will allow each individual to develop fully the differences of their talents and aspirations.

The contradictions of the digital condition are neither technological nor spiritual. The class contradictions that have resulted in increasing, rather than lessening, inequality have as their cause the development and use of technology in a system based upon private ownership of the means of production. Under capitalism a few own and control the means of production while the majority who are without the means to meet their needs must sell their labor for a wage. This is what Marx defines as the "working day"—the conditions under which the entire being of a person is reduced to that of a commodity, traded on the market like all other commodities without any security for the seller that their labor will be purchased and, having no other means by which to meet their needs, that they will be able to earn enough in wages to support themselves and their families. However, as Marx explains, what differentiates labor power, defined as "the aggregate of those mental and physical capabilities existing in a human being,"[166] from all other commodities, including technological developments in manufacturing, is that it "not only produces its own value, but produces value over and above it."[167] Unlike other commodities, because labor power is sold by time and not by what it can produce in that time, labor power produces value over and above its cost and thus is the basis for producing surplus value. In a system in which the primary drive is the accumulation of profit, it is the purchasing of labor power by the owners from the workers who have nothing else to sell that drives the system.

Capitalism differs from all prior modes of production because it is a dynamic system based on increasing the productivity of labor and thus increasing the rate at which the worker is able to produce surplus value to be accumulated by the capitalist. As Marx argues in the first volume of *Capital*, the drive to accumulate an increasing amount of surplus value from the purchased labor power of the worker results in the necessity of constantly driving down the costs of production: "The starting point of Modern Industry is . . . the revolution in the instruments of labor."[168] The role of technological advancement in capitalism is to create the conditions for increasing the production of surplus value by increasing the productivity of the worker, thereby reducing the time it takes to produce a commodity while simultaneously driving down the cost of labor power by lowering the cost of the commodities needed by workers reproduces their labor power for another day. It is the drive to further exploit the productivity of labor that requires from the beginning that capitalism become a "revolutionary" system:

> Modern Industry never looks upon and treats the existing form of a process as final. The technical basis of that industry is therefore revolutionary, while all previous modes of production were essentially conservative. By means of machinery, chemical processes and other methods, it is continually causing changes not only in the technical basis of production, but also in the functions of the laborer, and in the social combinations of the labor-process. At the same time, it thereby also revolutionizes the division of labor within the society, and incessantly launches masses of capital and of workpeople from one branch of production to another.[169]

What a materialist theory of technology enables is an approach to technological development that analyzes technology not only in terms of the changes in its concrete forms—from hand-mills to computer chips—and how these changes have impacted people's lives, but more importantly *why* such developments take the forms that they do. The image of a postclass, postproduction, postexploitative society in which technology alone will eliminate social divisions by eliminating labor, thus ignores that the very production of technology depends upon a division of labor between those who own and control the means of producing new technologies and those whose labor actually produces technology. Technology cannot replace labor because technology is a product of labor and as long as there exists a division between those who labor and those who live off of the labor of others, technology will only work to heighten this contradiction. As Marx argues, the more capitalism develops, and the more the productive forces are put to the restricted use of private accumulation, the more "the law that surplus-value does not arise from the labour-power that has been replaced by machinery but from the labour-power actually employed in working with the machinery asserts itself."[170] What we are witnessing in the development of the digital economy is not the superseding of production by consumption nor the discursive breakdown of older modes of thinking, but rather the restriction of the tremendous advances in production that are concentrated and centralized in the hands of a few and used for the purposes of private accumulation.

To posit technological development as in itself transforming the relations of production, as existing somehow beyond the class struggle over the means of production, is to invert the relationship between technology and labor in order to provide an ideological alibi for exploitation. As Marx argues, under capitalism,

> almost all the new inventions were the result of collisions between the worker and the employer who sought at all costs to depreciate the worker's specialized ability. . . . [I]n short, with the introduction of machinery the division of labor inside society has increased, the task of the worker inside the workshop has been simplified, capital has been concentrated, the human being has been further dismembered.[171]

Rather than representing a new theory for new times, the dominant theories of the digital society are instead keeping up with the new technological developments through which capital increases exploitation. In other words, they are taking what is really a very one-sided view of technological change—which does provide the benefits of increased cultural "freedom" for those who already have achieved economic freedom as a result of their class position—and presenting it as if it were a universal condition, available to all. While most theories of the digital condition claim, in other words, to be a theory of networks and connections—they are founded instead upon a primary disconnection—the disconnection between the exploitation of labor and commodity production. Only by reconnecting the study of culture and class will the field of cultural studies be able to grasp the contemporary and act as a material force for social change.

Global Networks and the Materiality of Immaterial Labor

This chapter focuses on one of the central issues in contemporary debates over the status of labor in the digital economy: the issue of immaterial labor. Writers such as Antonio Negri and Manuel Castells—who provide the basic framework of assumptions for all contemporary theories of immaterial labor—propose that digital technologies change the way in which value is produced and, as a result, that the economy is shifting away from the production of material commodities and toward immaterial commodities including information and affect, as well as the terms of life itself. In effect, they represent digital technologies as shifting the economic terrain of the global economy away from issues of class and exploitation and toward a new form of capitalism based upon immaterial labor. In contrast, I offer an extended analysis of the contemporary global economy and explain why we are actually witnessing the heightening of the economic contradictions between labor and capital rather than their resolution.

The Class Contradictions of Digital Globalization

Concepts are abstractions of the actual conditions of life and, for this reason, historical maps of the social conflicts that determine which theories are taken as accurate representations of reality and which are marginalized or excluded as "terrorist" threats to the existing order[1] In other words, although concepts reflect the material developments of labor and therefore must be understood in relation to what *is*, they are never simply neutral reports of the existing but instead represent a divided space in which competing classes "become conscious of the conflict" over the existing and "fight it out."[2] It is in this context that since its first emergence in the 1980s, *globalization* has become one of the primary—and at the same time highly contested—concepts in cultural and social theory for describing the emergence of a regime of capital accumulation that developed in the years following World War II, covering the period from what is known as the long boom, through the period of global economic recession described as the long downturn, and up to the contemporary moment.[3]

In mainstream and popular presses, globalization is championed as the period of capitalism's ultimate triumph over communism with the end of the Cold War and, furthermore, the transcendence of its own internal contradiction between capital and labor in the apparent centrality of cultural production and immaterial labor to the digital "revolution" of society. For example, according to Yochai Benkler in *The Wealth of Networks*, the emerging digital technologies are bringing with them a "new mode of production"[4] that "allows people to reach across space and political divisions."[5] Similarly, Clay Shirky proposes in *Here Comes Everybody* that "for the last hundred years the big organizational question has been whether any given task was taken on by the state, directing the effort in a planned way [socialism], or by businesses competing in a market [capitalism]."[6] However, with the advent of digital technologies, he writes, there is now a "third alternative"—namely, "action by loosely structured groups, operating without managerial direction and outside the profit motive."[7] While this representation of a world remade in the image of digital technologies has become, in the words of Chris Harman, a "new orthodoxy" that is "used to mean that the world economy has reached a new stage, which governments and workers alike are virtually powerless to withstand,"[8] the reality is that what is presented in contemporary theory as a seamless transition to a new digital and global world functions ideologically to banish any discussion of the exploitation of labor that is at the core of capitalist production by substituting changes in how something is produced or where production takes place for a transformation in the fundamental logic that governs production under capitalism.

In order to understand the centrality of exploitation to the global expansion of capitalism it is important to examine the way in which the digital reading of globalization is based upon the presupposition that "more or less everyone has learned to accept, if not necessarily love, capitalism—in much the same way as they have democracy" and "at this time, no one can see any effective alternatives to the combination of a market economy and a democratic political system."[9] This conclusion is generally dependent upon two interrelated arguments. First, it is argued that globalization corresponds to a "broad cultural shift . . . away from a dominance of production over our everyday lives to a dominance of consumption,"[10] in the sense that the primary source for the accumulation of new value is said to no longer be labor or manufacture (material commodity production), but knowledge and its embodiment in communications and other digital technologies. According to sociologist Helmut Willke, the shift to a digital economy means that "digital goods are weightless and they move along the fiber optic lines at the speed of light" and thus operate beyond the former political and economic controls of industrial, national capitalism.[11] It is on these terms that the so-called digital globalization is understood to constitute a new stage of capitalism based upon the seemingly inexhaustible resource of information, which, it is assumed, disrupts the economics of scarcity that is manifest in the class inequalities of capitalism and removes the divisions of ownership that constituted class identities in the predigital age by placing the means of production in the hands of every creative person. As Mark Poster argues, "there is no need for a capitalist market in the area of digital cultural objects, and these objects need not become commodities . . . indeed, digital cultural objects *resist* market mechanisms" and, in turn, transform "the nature of the producer and the consumer, blurring the boundary between them."[12] Accordingly, the global expansion of a new regime of capital accumulation based upon knowledge has the effect of creating spaces of cultural heterogeneity and exchange in which the "fixities of nation, community, ethnicity and class," as Jan Nederveen Pieterse states, "become fragments" dispersed in the flows of financial markets and cultural exchanges.[13] Or, as Ulrich Beck concisely puts it, "the notion of a class society remains useful only as an image of the past."[14] The elevation of digital over analogue production is therefore represented as ushering in a more "democratic" globalization because of the ways in which it supposedly re-maps cultural and political institutions as spaces defined in the terms of individual desire and personal lifestyles, rather than social need.[15] As management theorists Klaus Görtz and Nadine Bleher write, "technological innovations have enabled an increasing number of individuals to choose, create, and cultivate transnational communities according to their personal interests, values, habits, and attitudes."[16]

Second, it is argued that the development of postlabor means of production creates the conditions for the expansion of capital globally, in turn disrupting the traditional boundaries between nations, thereby creating a "flat" or "borderless" world of free cultural and financial exchange.[17] What *flat* or *borderless* signifies is an increased capitalization in the post–World War II period of formerly socialist and Third World nations and their incorporation into the global system of production, either through the shifting of manufacture from the global North (the United States, Canada, the European Union, Russia, Japan, Australia, as well as Singapore, South Korea and Taiwan) to the global South (Central and Southeast Asia, the Middle East, Africa, Mexico, and South America) through outsourcing or off-shoring or by becoming integral players in a postnational supply chain that has been enabled by advances in communication as well as the opening up of trade and financial barriers to free up the flow of formerly trapped or unproductive capital.[18] Proponents of the flat world thesis point to the expansion of international trade which, according to the IMF, "has grown five times in real terms since 1980, and its share of world GDP has risen from 36 percent to 55 percent over this period."[19] This "flattening" of the global economy, in which it is said that the expansion of production and trade relations between nations constitute the emergence of a level playing field between formerly unequal or hostile nations, is essentially premised upon a theory of a "universal evolution in the direction of capitalism" in which there is no longer any "outside" to capitalism.[20] In this reading, the developed economies of the North have moved beyond the traditional economic cycle, while transplanting the conditions of new growth and prosperity to the underdeveloped nations in the South. As Martin Wolf writes, "In the post-war era, the most successful route to development seems to have been via the export of labor-intensive manufactures, the route on which China has followed Hong Kong, Singapore, Taiwan and South Korea."[21]

The problem for the ideologists of capital and their image of globalization as leveling the world is that insofar as concepts are abstractions of reality the continuing existence of deep social and economic inequalities cannot be solved at the level of ideas and thus still have to be explained. That is to say, even though globalization has become synonymous in theory with the end of the economic challengers to capitalism's dominance, this does not change the fact that the expansion of capitalism globally has corresponded in actuality with a rising level of inequality and a sharpening of the class divide, both between the so-called developing and developed national blocs, as well as within the respective countries of each. This is because capitalism is a system that depends upon the exploitation of labor. Regardless of whether or not the primary location of production is the North or the South, or whether the workers work in factories that are highly mechanized or newly digitalized, it is the production of surplus value extracted from the surplus labor of workers by owners that drives capitalism forward. That exploitation remains even in the global factories of today is supported by a 2007 study from the World Bank which, despite touting the results of "free-market" globalization as having reduced the number of people living in poverty—defined as the ridiculously low, and ultimately arbitrary, sum of less than $1 per day—by 260 million from 1990 to 2004, nonetheless also showed that real inequality between the rich and poor has actually *increased* during this time in forty-six of the fifty-nine developing countries surveyed.[22] Over the same period, a study by the International Monetary Fund also found that "inequality has been rising in countries across all income levels, except those classified as low income" and that overall "the income share of the richest quintile has risen, whereas the shares of the remaining quintiles have declined."[23] That the two main representatives of capitalist finance found rising inequality and a sharpening of the class divide despite representing globalization as moving beyond class binaries is due to the fact that the economic contradiction between capital and labor does not reside at the level of the concept—that is, the conflict over globalization is not simply a political or intellectual struggle over how to best define the term—but rather in the property relations that enable the owners of the means of production to accumulate capital at the expense of those who own only their labor power. As Marx argued more than one hundred fifty years ago and which is proven once again by the increases in class inequality globally, "even the *most favorable situation* for the working class, namely, the most rapid growth of capital, however much it may improve the material life of the worker, does not abolish the antagonism between his interests and the interests of the capitalist."[24] Although developments of labor productivity result in new, higher standards of living for some workers, these developments are always restricted under capitalism to the accumulation of surplus value and thus it is always the directives of profit that will take precedence over the needs of the working class.

Insofar as these social contradictions cannot simply be ignored if one is to be taken seriously as a social critic, economic divisions have to be explained in terms that will be recognized institutionally as explanations of the existing while at the same time reassuring everyone that the problem is not with the economic status quo. This is the function of ideology: to make the exploitation that is inherent in the exchange of labor for wages appear as "fair" in the eyes of common sense. In this context, what one finds in the most popular cultural and economic discourses is an inverted and distorted representation of the existing social divisions which responds to actual developments in production but places the effects of exploitation in front of the causes and substitutes a range of pluralizing concepts for social binaries such as class. Instead of the rigid social structures of industrial/national/analogue capitalism, we are told across a range of so-called progressive texts that postindustrial/global/digital capitalism "transcends the 'us' versus 'them' dualism that prevails in cultural and political arenas,"[25] that "there has been a sharp move . . . away from bipolarity and the coming into being of a much more multipolar international circumstance,"[26] that "the notion of class retains a material value which is indispensable to make sense of the experience of concrete historical subjects" but "does not explain or make sense of the heterogeneity and yet commonalities of Internet users,"[27] that "inequalities by no means disappear" but are "redefined in terms of an *individualization of social risks*,"[28] that "class cannot be ignored" but that it "is not the single, ultimately determining instance" of globalization,[29] and if class stratification still exists "that stratification pattern is now focused on possibilities for consumption rather than production."[30] Any theory of globalization that situates the growing worldwide economic divisions as a result of property relations at the point of production is defined as too reductive to effectively address the plurality of contesting forces engendered by the process of globalization which "have arguably served to reinforce the sense of the significance of identity and difference."[31] Yet, class does not simply disappear. Instead, class becomes in these discourses an amorphous and fluid relation of power that has no recognizable ties in the mainstream readings to capitalist exploitation. This is what has made the ideology of the digital condition so effective for maintaining the status quo—it takes up actual developments in production, but frames the entire debate and its impact on global society as if there is no exploitation in the wage labor/capital relation, and thus ultimately nothing wrong with the capitalist system itself.

Globalization, particularly for many on the left, is situated instead as a struggle for cultural hegemony between the homogenizing tendencies of the global and the heterogeneous forces of the local.[32] According to this reading, the main problem with globalization is the dominance of the global marketplace by Western commodities such as McDonald's, the Gap, and Coca-Cola and the threat that this cultural homogeneity poses to local diversity and difference. Against this corporate homogenization of culture, the means for resistance are located in local acts of daily consumption that take place in "the streets, the houses, the churches, the workplaces, the bars, and the shops that lie beyond the business or tourist centers."[33] George Ritzer, for example, writes that "we live in an era in which, truly for the first time, capitalism is unchained and free to roam the world in search of both cheap production facilities and labor as well as new markets for its producers."[34] And yet, he concludes from this that "it is important not to reduce all of this to (capitalist) economics alone."[35] Instead, Ritzer argues that too much attention has been paid to what he calls "productivism" when the main battle today is between the homogenizing forces of "nothing," which he defines as "centrally conceived and controlled social forms that are comparatively devoid of distinctive substantive content,"[36] or "grobalization"[37] and the resistance of "something," defined as "a social form that is generally indigenously conceived, controlled, and comparatively rich in distinctive content"[38] or "glocalization."[39] Based upon the reading of globalization as the conflict between "grobalization" versus "glocalization," Ritzer declares that to "go beyond capitalism"[40] is to find and celebrate a series of "ethical" lifestyle choices of going to the "local farmers' market,"[41] "flea markets, craft fairs, and co-ops,"[42] and above all becoming "craft consumers . . . who single out parts, or a segment, of the available mountain of nothingness and alter them, sometimes so dramatically that they become virtually unrecognizable."[43] According to Ritzer, it is the use of commodities by regular people, regardless of their class status, which shapes the meaning of the commodity and thus provides the solution to corporate hegemony. It is, in short, a theory of spiritual values in the market place. What matters is not the broader logic of production, but the local intentions of the decidedly middle-class consumer. If those intentions are "ethical" or "creative"—in other words, if they are spiritually just—then the problems of inequality no longer carry material significance and class is simply one difference among many. Differences, in this sense, are always local and reside on the surfaces of capital, in the spaces of cultural consumption.

On the right, one also finds economic differences rewritten as cultural differences, and in many of the same terms, but the sides are reversed. Instead of the image of encroaching corporate homogenization led by the United States imposing its cultural will on the local communities in the South, it is precisely U.S. and European capital that is the guarantee of heterogeneity and difference. As David Pryce-Jones writes in "Why They Hate Us," "Democracy means Us *and* Them. Yet nothing in the history or the culture of Arabs and Muslims allows them to put this into any form of political practice. From long ago they have inherited a cast-iron absolute system, in which the ruler does as he pleases, and the rest have no redress, indeed going to the wall."[44] According to this logic, which has perhaps been most popularly advanced in Samuel Huntington's *The Class of Civilizations*, global conflict is driven today by a cultural divide between the values of "democracy" and "free enterprise" in the West and authoritarian, closed, anticapitalist regimes in the East. Huntington writes, "In the post–Cold War world, the most important distinctions among peoples are not ideological, political, or economic. They are cultural."[45] It is in these terms that Huntington rewrites social differences as cultural ones. He argues, "In this new world the most pervasive, important, and dangerous conflicts will not be between social classes, rich and poor, or other economically defined groups, but between peoples belonging to different cultural entities."[46] Again, sharpening global divisions are constructed as those between homogeneity and heterogeneity in which the West represents a heterogeneous civilization of "democracy, free markets, limited government, human rights, individualism, the rule of law" with the "Rest" who are said to represent homogenized societies opposed to such values.[47] These divisions are then naturalized as the source of capitalist development and expansion—an updated version of Weber's "protestant ethic" in which values and attitudes produce reality, rather than reality as the source of ideas. Although Huntington himself believes it to be "immoral" to impose Western cultural values on the East (for the "paternalistic" reason that the East is not "prepared" or "interested" in any form of "democracy" or "human rights") others on the right, such as "anglobalization" historian Niall Ferguson, take this thesis and argue that globalization is the means by which to spread through a new colonial project the culture of democracy, free markets, and individual liberty to what he describes as the "failed states" of the global South that lack the "cultural values" of the global North.[48]

In the substitution of the discourse of culture and values for class relations what is placed outside the boundaries of "real" discourse by both the left and the right is any theory of globalization as imperialism, in which the drive of capital expansion is explained as a necessary effect of the material conditions for the further accumulation of capital. This is what has made globalization such an effective concept for global capital—it substitutes for economic imperialism a world of spiritual conflicts and cultural bargains. In this context, while a number on the right are calling for reconsideration of imperialism as a way of spreading democracy, many on the left have simply abandoned the theory of imperialism and argue, as Pieterse does, that "the term imperialism may no longer be adequate to address the present situation . . . [which] is less coherent and less purposeful than imperialism."[49] Or, as Hardt and Negri put it more succinctly, "imperialism is over."[50] To draw connections between the global expansion of capitalism and rising inequality is to be too reductive and trapped in the metanarratives of the past. Instead, a digital world is described as "multidimensional,"[51] "without borders and spatial boundaries,"[52] and "a complex, overlapping, disjunctive order, which cannot be understood in terms of existing center-periphery models."[53] What is at stake for both the right and the left in deploying the rhetoric of cultural difference as a substitute for class divisions is obscuring the economic realities of imperialism in order to maintain the illusion of the possibility of capitalism without exploitation.

In contrast to these narratives, which are what might be called superficial readings in the sense of describing rather than analyzing recent economic developments and therefore remaining on the surfaces of society instead of addressing its fundamental logic, I argue that by going global capitalism has become *more* itself, not less, and that the most effective means for understanding the role of new digital technologies for global interests of capital remains the historical materialist theorization of imperialism. While the dominant approach to the issue of globalization obscures any discussion of the material conditions in which global society is currently being produced by inverting the relationship between culture and the economic, what is represented as the emergence of a fundamentally new moment in capitalism based in communication technologies, cultural and economic networks, and immaterial labor is best understood as the global mode of accumulation corresponding to the stage of monopoly capitalism as explained by Lenin in *Imperialism, The Highest Stage of Capitalism*: namely the increasing concentration and centralizing of production in monopolies, the subsequent development of *finance capital* and the export of capital to regions in the Third World required by the rising level of organic capital in the First World, and the division of the world's markets and resources between the economic monopolies. What makes such a view so controversial today is that while theories of globalization have increasingly had to attend to the growing contradictions of global capitalism—marked, for example, by the recent publication of four different books entitled *Globalization and its Discontents*, including books by Joseph Stieglitz, Saskia Sassen, Roger Burbach (with Orlando Nunez and Boris Kargarlitsky), and Stephen McBride and John Wiseman—it still remains almost universally accepted, even among more radical social theorists who argue that capitalism is a global system of exploitation, that the labor theory of value, which Marx and Lenin argue is essential to understanding why capital must expand globally and why it can be transformed into socialism, no longer has any explanatory value.[54] Instead, as Žižek claims, "the rise of 'intellectual labor' . . . to a hegemonic position" effectively "undermines the standard notion of exploitation, since it is no longer labor-time which serves as the source and ultimate measure of value."[55]

In contrast to the dominant cultural readings of globalization in which the culture, politics, and economics of globalization exist in "overdetermined" relation to one another, I argue that it is necessary to return to the work of Marx and Lenin to explain why globalization is a social theory whose meaning is determined by property relations, in the division between those who own and control the means of production and those who own only their labor power, and furthermore to show that this view is supported by the actual developments of the global economy in the post–World War II period. What one finds is that in contrast to the end-of-imperialism narrative, capitalism has in actuality become even more universal than ever before. In order to develop this thesis, I address two aspects of mainstream globalization theory in which digital technologies play a particularly central role. First, I address the digital theory of *networks*, and in particular the theories of Manuel Castells and Thomas L. Friedman, because of the way in which the image of the network increasingly operates as both the metaphor for, as well as the new managerial logic of, global capitalism. Following this, I take up the theory, advanced most prominently in the work of Michael Hardt and Antonio Negri, that global capitalism is increasingly dependent upon immaterial labor and that this new economic source of value brings about the blurring of the class divide. What I show is that the development of mass production and exchange on a global scale, which is central to the arguments that network capitalism has replaced imperialism as the logic of globalization, cannot in itself constitute a break from the fundamental structures of capitalist society such that production and labor are replaced by consumption and immaterial labor, nor is this break supported statistically. Through an analysis of the arguments that the culmination of the globalization lies in the production of a postclass, postcapitalist, postimperialist network economy, I argue that what is at stake in reading globalization is the question of the organization of production in society: whether society will continue to be divided in terms of owners and workers or, on the contrary, whether the inequality of class society will be transformed through the collectivity of the international working class.

The Ideology of New Economic Formations

The dominant ideology today is that the labor theory of value has lost its explanatory effectivity because globalization represents a fundamental transformation in the relations between capital and labor resulting from the shift from an industrial, to a postindustrial, and now to a digital economy in which value is created not through the exploitation of labor but the generation of knowledge and the consumption of commodities. More specifically, the emergence of globalization as "*the* concept, the key idea by which we understand the transition of human society into the third millennium"[56] is said to correspond to the development of a new economic dynamic defined by the evaporation of social boundaries of nationality, ethnicity, class, and region and the opening of cultural flows across all borders. This view is shared by cultural theorists and management theorists alike. In *The Global Market*, for example, management theorists John Quelch and Rohit Deshpande differentiate between globalization and previous forms of international and transnational production on the grounds that "globalization implies economic activity in the absence of national boundaries, whereas internationalization implies an increasing number of transactions across the borders of nation-states."[57] Similarly, Mike Featherstone describes globalization in the introduction to *Global Culture* as "cultural integration and cultural disintegration processes which take place not only on an inter-state level, but processes which transcend the state-society unit and can therefore be held to occur on a trans-national or trans-societal level."[58]

Perhaps the most influential of the early postnational theorists of globalization is management guru Kenichi Ohmae who in *The Borderless World* and *The End of the Nation State* argues that the expansion of capital globally effectively draws a close to the historical necessity of the nation-state. According to Ohmae, capitalism is increasingly organized around regions rather than states and, in turn, nation-states "need to cede meaningful operational authority to the wealth-generating region states that lie within or across their borders."[59] This is because, Ohmae argues, "in terms of real flows of economic activity, nation states have *already* lost their role as meaningful units of participation in the global economy of today's borderless world."[60] Instead, in his work as a management theorist and consultant to global corporations, Ohmae proposes that capital needs to move towards an "interlinked" economic model in which goods and companies "change hands across borders as easily as paintings, patents, and real estate."[61] This postnational economy is premised upon the ability to generate more value outside of the imperialist model of globalization in circuits of trade and exchange, if imperialism is understood solely in terms of direct colonialism. "Wealth," he writes, "is now created in the marketplace rather than in colonies and in soils that contain natural resources."[62] What the "borderless" theory of globalization is responding to is the reorganization of production globally in the post–World War II period, in which the global integration of production and markets that exists at the beginning of the twentieth century and which sharply declines with two intra-imperialist wars and the collapse of the colonial division of the world begins to re-emerge in the 1950s and which receives a sharp boost postcolonial, post–Cold War era of the twenty-first century. This theory ideologically disconnects the expansion of global capital from the logic of exploitation in order to represent as *new* what is necessary for capitalist production—the constant global search for cheaper sources of labor and raw materials.

The fact that capital is a global system is not new. As Marx and Engels wrote more than one hundred fifty years ago, "The need for a constantly expanding market chases the bourgeoisie over the whole surface of the globe. It must nestle everywhere, settle everywhere, establish connections everywhere."[63] What we are witnessing, then, is not a new social formation, but a heightening of the inherent tendencies of capitalist production. It is at the beginning of the twentieth century that, while the logic of capitalism does not change, one starts to see the global logic of capital as theorized by Marx and Engels become the dominant mode of organizing production. As Chris Harman describes,

> Until the 1880s most industries consisted of a multiplicity of small producing units. This began to change at the end of the century with the concentration of production within each major company into trusts and combines which set out to conquer world markets from rivals abroad.[64]

Similarly, Hirst and Thompson mark that from the emergence of manufacturing multinationals in the second half of the nineteenth century, "international business activity grew vigorously in the 1920s as the truly diversified and integrated MNC matured, but it slowed down during the depressed 1930s and war-torn 1940s."[65] Although global capital expansion slows in the middle of the twentieth century as a result of the capitalist World Wars, in the 1960s the levels of international integration of production and trade start to return to the pre–World War I levels.[66] What happens in the post–World War II period, emerging first in the United States and later in Europe and Japan, is a restructuring of the global economy enabled by investment in technology during the war, increasing productivity, and the availability of capital for investment abroad. The first evidence of this global restructuring emerges during what is known as the *long boom*, the period between between 1950 and 1973 when "the advanced capitalist world experienced record rates of growth"[67] and investment in developing new areas of production outside of the home market surged. For example, "between 1957 and 1968, manufacturing investment by majority-owned foreign affiliates of US companies in new plant and equipment overseas grew at an astonishing annual rate of 15.7 per cent."[68] As the long boom gave way to global economic downturn after 1973, due more to a falling rate of profit and subsequent crisis of overproduction than the oil crisis alone as Duménil and Lévy convincingly argue,[69] it is in the 1980s that capital once again begins to restructure and return to the development of global manufacture, aided in part by advances in computers and telecommunications that "made possible unprecedented levels of coordination between geographically separated productive units."[70] For example, in a sector of the economy not normally considered part of the digital revolution but nonetheless effected by it, "ocean freight costs per short ton, in 1990 U.S. dollars, have come down to less than $30 in 2000, having been $100 in 1930" because of "the development of new technologies in transport and telecommunications."[71]

The developments in digital technologies (computing and telecommunications) and a slow growth in both levels of productivity and the rate of profit during the 1970s results in the necessity for finding the most effective use of technology and capital reserves for expanding capitalist production. It is in this climate that one begins to find in the 1980s the emergence of "borderless" theories of organizing production on a global scale. As developments in technology enable corporations to advance the global division of labor, what becomes necessary is the development of economic and social theories that can theorize how to put labor, technology, and capital reserves to their most productive use. It is in this sense that contemporary cultural theory reflects the development of new forms of organization of labor. The concept of the *network* has emerged to explain the global expansion of capital, the importance of digital technologies to this growth, as well as the means by which this growth is separated at the level of ideas from the growing levels of inequality between capital and labor that have developed over the same period.

Networks, Supply Chains, and the Labor Theory of Value

The concept of a network structure is defined as "a collection of links between elements of a unit."[72] In simple modes of organization, such as those between the elements or parts of an atom, it is argued that a hierarchical or static set of relations is adequate to account for the connections between elements. "When matter becomes more complex," however, network theorists argue that it becomes necessary to develop more complex forms of organization that can "produce order out of chaos" by linking the elements in a more dynamic fashion.[73] That is to say, a network is a conceptual structure in which, rather than a hierarchical or vertical organization of agents or information, the system consists of semiautonomous but interconnected nodes, each with a productive, yet transitional, relation to the whole. The image of society as a network has become so popular, in fact, that one finds it not only within the discourses of digital culture and corporate management theory, but also as the basis of a new historiography (Mattelart's *Networking the World, 1794–2000*), a new biology (Johnson's *Emergence: The Connected Lives of Ants, Brains, Cities and Software*), and a new sociology (Barabási's *Linked: How Everything Is Connected to Everything Else*). What links these accounts of contemporary society is the idea that the history of human society is best conceptualized as increasingly driven by an overdetermined set of social interactions in which politics, culture, and economics exist in an interrelated and interconnected web without any determinacy. As Tiziana Terranova argues,

> To think of something like a "network culture" at all, to dare to give one name to the heterogeneous assemblage that is contemporary global culture, is to try to think *simultaneously* the singular and the multiple, the common and the unique. When seen close up in detail, contemporary culture (at all scales from the local to the global) appears as a kaleidoscope of differences and bewildering heterogeneity . . . each with its own identity and structure, they appear to us as a meshwork of overlapping cultural formations, of hybrid reinventions, cross-pollinations and singular variations.[74]

For Terranova, the network represents the emergence of a new social formation in which binaries such as the local and the global, the past and the future, the inside and the outside, and owner and worker have lost their material force and instead are replaced with a constantly changing series of relations without a singular organizational principle. The attractiveness of such a concept for organizing production is that it corresponds to the ability capital has acquired in the digital age to move resources more effectively to where they can be put to the most profitable use. As Chwo-Ming Joseph

Yu writes, "a network approach, focusing on patterns of relationships that surrounds a firm, has captured the attention of academics and business writers" because of the way in which "vertically disaggregated and spatially concentrated production networks are sometimes a more viable and often desirable alternative to the vertically integrated corporation."[75] With this new form of capital and market integration, it is argued that a *network* logic calls into question all hierarchical social relations as well as deeper class divisions and replaces them with a rhizomatic series of interconnections without any singular organizing logic such as exploitation.[76] In other words, the development of network capitalism is supposed to mean the end of a binary class relation between capital and labor and, in turn, the conditions of monopoly capital that result in imperialist conflict.

In his book *The Rise of the Network Society*, foundational network theorist Manuel Castells advances the idea that developments in information technology are transforming "the material basis of society"[77] from the industrial age of labor and production to an informational age of knowledge and cultural exchange. As a result of the application of new scientific developments in communication and management technologies to production, he writes, "a new economy has emerged in the last two decades on a worldwide scale. I call it informational and global to identify its fundamental distinctive features and to emphasize their intertwining."[78] Although Castells writes that "for the first time in history, the capitalist mode of production shapes social relationships over the entire planet"[79]—meaning that the social and political changes we are witnessing are, in essence, the effects of the economic motives of capitalism—he also argues that what differentiates the new "informational" stage of capitalism[80] from previous modes of production is the way in which information has become "the key ingredient of our social organization" and "flows of messages and images between networks constitute the basic thread of our social existence."[81] According to Castells, the social and cultural changes resulting from technological advances in production and communication represent not just a development within capitalist relations, but a more fundamental social restructuring in which "money has become almost entirely independent from production" and "the social relationships between capital and labor are profoundly transformed."[82] That is to say, the organization of production according to the logic of networks means not only new ways of managing business. It is ushering in a fundamental change to social relations in which capitalism itself becomes virtually unrecognizable. While, he argues, capitalism in the pre-Industrial and Industrial Age depended upon a strict property relation between owners and workers, he proposes that network capitalism blurs such class divisions by opening the production of capital to the flows of finance and thus to a more plural theory of ownership in which anyone with access to culture (and credit) can participate in the shaping of its meaning. "In the new informational mode of development," Castells writes, "the source of productivity lies in the technology of knowledge generation, information processing, and symbol communication"[83] and value is "mainly generated by innovation."[84] For Castells, then, what is significant about the emergence of global economic networks is the way in which they destabilize class relations by creating new sources of value in cultural exchange that, insofar as they are "enacted by informational networks in the timeless space of financial flows,"[85] no longer depend upon the extraction of surplus value from the labor of workers. Instead, the new universality of capitalism is founded on the interconnection of informational networks and the global flows of messages and images; in short, on expanding the avenues of consumption after production. On these terms, instead of a class conflict over the control of the means of production, Castells describes global capitalism as a cultural struggle over consumption between the "interacting," who, he argues, are able to "selec[t] their multidirectional circuits of communication,"[86] and the "interacted," who are limited to "a restricted number of prepackaged choices."[87] As a result, he concludes, "the new economy cannot be characterized as being centered any longer on multinational corporations, even if they continue to exercise jointly oligopolistic control over most markets . . . because corporations have transformed themselves into a web of multiple networks embedded into a multiplicity of institutional environments"[88] and that "who are the owners, who the producers, who the managers, and who the servants, becomes increasingly blurred in a production system of variable geometry, of teamwork, of networking, outsourcing, and subcontracting."[89] In a posthierarchical organization of production and exchange, Castells writes, "who are the winners and the losers changes by the year, the month, the day, the second . . . "[90] because,

> under the new technological, organizational, and economic conditions . . . the capitalists . . . are certainly not the legal owners of the means of production, who range from your/my pension fund to a passerby in a Singapore ATM deciding

to buy stock . . . yet neither are the corporate managers . . . for managers control specific corporations, and specific segments of the global economy, but do not control, and do not even know about, the actual, systematic movements of capital in networks of financial flows, of knowledge in the information networks, of strategies in the multifaceted set of network enterprises.[91]

It is this "blurring" of social relations, particularly within the social division of labor, which is said to be the defining characteristic of network capitalism. While, on the one hand, the network is theorized by Castells as the thousands of business and communities linked up in a vast global communications systems, he also situates it as something more: The primary feature of a network society is an increasingly decentralized set of relations without a determining locus or center. "A network architecture," he writes, "cannot be controlled from any center, and is made up of thousands of autonomous computer networks that have innumerable ways to link up, going around electronic barriers."[92] It is,

> a culture of the ephemeral, a culture of strategic decision, a patchwork of experiences and interests, rather than a charter of rights and obligations. It is a multifaceted, virtual culture, as in visual experiences created by computers in cyberspace by rearranging reality.[93]

The key to understanding the logic of this argument is the way in which the fluid, ephemeral nature of the network—in which any connection, regardless of how big or how small its initial capital, has the opportunity to generate new and innovative ideas without having to depend upon either the productivity of labor—is said to bring an end to the domination of the more hierarchical modes of organization and the rise of more flexible and adaptable modes of organization which can "survive and prosper in a fast changing environment."[94] In other words, the network society is understood to be a more flexible mode of economic and social organization because it creates a structure that can more quickly adapt to local changes. According to this logic, because the network expands horizontally rather than vertically anyone can enter and thus fundamentally transform the structure of the network because the structure of the network is never finally determined and is therefore not bound to any particular formal arrangement. In the new economic model of network capitalism, this argument goes, property relations are no longer determinant of who controls the economy—class is no longer an objective relation determined at the point of production, but rather a matter of access to knowledge and thus, in the most basic terms, all that matters is a good idea. Or, as Steve Lohr argues, the network society represents "a big step in the democratization of information technology" because:

> The old story of technology in business was a trickle-down affair. From telephones to computers, big companies came first. They could afford the latest innovations, and they reaped the benefits of greater efficiency, increased sales and expansion into distant markets. . . . Now that pattern is being challenged by a bottom-up revolution . . . a cost leveling that puts small companies on equal footing with big ones, making it easier for upstarts to innovate, disrupt industries and even get big fast.[95]

The most popular version of this narrative is advanced by Thomas L. Friedman, the foreign affairs columnist for the *New York Times* and winner of three Pulitzer prizes for his work on globalization. What has made Friedman's work so popular is the way in which it normalizes economic relations by presenting them in an anecdotal fashion, thereby making the unnatural relations of capitalism appear more natural because we are meant to read his stories as front-line reports unmediated by the abstractions of theory. Yet, the fact that he essentially vetted his book *The World Is Flat* with leading capitalists such as Bill Gates, Michael Dell, and the strategic planning committee of IBM before publishing it, demonstrates clearly that despite his rhetorical populism, his discourse is firmly on the side of capital.[96]

In *The World Is Flat*, Friedman puts forward his take on network capitalism as the "flattening of the world." He observes, "we are now connecting all the knowledge centers on the planet together into a single global network, which—if politics and terrorism do not get in the way—could usher in an amazing era of prosperity and innovation."[97] In particular, Friedman advertises the emerging network society as creating a capitalism that is more than ever working in the interests of the individual because more than ever the individual is in control of their labor. The network society, he states, is dependent upon "the new found power for individuals to collaborate and compete globally . . . Individuals must, and can, now ask where do *I* fit into the global competition and opportunities of the day, and how can *I*, on my own, collaborate with others globally."[98] And, reminiscent of Castells' argument, Friedman maintains that this new structure means the end of rigid and unequal social hierarchies: "Everywhere you turn, hierarchies are being challenged from below or transforming themselves from top-down structures into more horizontal and collaborative ones."[99]

At the center of Friedman's theory of the flat world is the *supply chain*, which he describes as "a method of collaborating horizontally—among suppliers, retailers, and customers—to create value."[100] The importance of the supply chain for Friedman is that it combines the technological developments of the digital age with the open borders of the post–Cold War period. The primary example he uses is Wal-Mart, "the biggest and most profitable retailer on the planet."[101] Over the past two decades, Friedman argues, Wal-Mart has been at the forefront of the network society:

> In 1983, Wal-Mart invested in point-of-sale terminals, which simultaneously rang up sales and tracked inventory deductions for rapid supply. Four years later, it installed a large-scale satellite system linking all of the stores to company head-quarters, giving Wal-Mart's central computer system real-time inventory data and paving the way for a supply chain greased by information and humming down to the last atom of efficiency . . . Now Wal-Mart, in its latest supply-chain innovation, has introduced RFID—radio frequency identification microchips, attached to each pallet and merchandise box that comes into Wal-Mart [. . . which . . .] allows Wal-Mart to track any pallet or box at each stage in its supply chain and know exactly what product from which manufacturer is inside.[102]

What the supply chain represents, according to Friedman, is a more open and democratic way of organizing capitalist production, one that benefits both workers and owners equally. On the business side, supply chains promote the universalization of the most effective productive practices for capital:

> Supply-chaining is both enabled by the flattening of the world and a hugely important flattener itself, because the more these supply chains grow and proliferate, the more they force the adoption of common standards between companies (so that every link of the supply chain can interface with the next), the more they eliminate points of friction at borders, the more the efficiencies of one company get adopted by the others, and the more they encourage global collaboration.[103]

On labor's side, even if Friedman finds that Wal-Mart is an example of extreme corporate "ruthlessness" in its treatment of workers,[104] he writes that supply chains are the great global equalizer "because they deliver us all sorts of goods—from tennis shoes to laptop computers—at lower and lower prices."[105]

Ultimately, the theory of a "flat world" is most dismissive of the theory of imperialism. In the example of Wal-Mart, Friedman describes how trade between Japan and the United States was first established at the end of a bayonet, but has since become a more "co-operative" exchange. He writes, "Commodore Matthew Calbraith Perry opened a largely closed Japanese society to the Western world on July 8, 1853 when he arrived in Edo (Tokyo) Bay with four big black steamships bristling with guns."[106] Of course, as might be expected given Friedman's defense of corporate global-ization generally and his importance as a popularizer of this reading for capital, this forced exchange was not really a problem because it "led to an explosion of trade between Japan and the United States, helped open Japan to the Western world generally, and is widely credited with triggering the modernization of the Japanese state, as the Japanese realized how far behind they were and rushed to catch up."[107] Leaving aside the irony that Fried-man's theory of the supply chain was, in fact, first developed in Japan and was initially seen as a threat by U.S. capitalists to their economic domi-nance,[108] what is more significant at the moment is how supply chain de-mocracy differs from even the "beneficial" imperialism of an earlier age. Friedman writes, "Unlike Commodore Perry, Wal-Mart did not have to muscle its way into Japan with warships. Its reputation preceded it, which is why it was invited in by Seiyu, a struggling Japanese retail chain desperate to adapt the Wal-Mart formula in Japan."[109] This image corresponds more broadly with the peaceful integration of markets that Friedman argues will emerge from network capitalism. He argues, "No two countries that are both part of a major global supply chain . . . will ever fight a war against each other as long as they are both part of the same global supply chain."[110]

It is this image of network capitalism as a postclass, postcapitalist, post-imperialist, and postconflict stage of production that is most useful for capi-tal today because of the way in which it addresses the surface developments of capitalism—relative growth in cross-border trade, the emergence of out-sourcing as a result of advances in technology and communications, and the formation of international finance treaties—while isolating these develop-ments from the underlying logic of capitalism itself, claiming that whatever happens in the economy—whether it is the re-emergence of global conflict or the rising levels of inequality—is not connected to the exploitation of labor which drives the capitalist engine. That is to say, what Friedman and Castells promote as the "control" over their labor that network capitalism offers more workers than ever is in reality the same control that capital has always offered workers; namely, the "freedom" that is offered under the condition of survival to sell their labor power for a wage. If this form of control is available to more workers around the world, as Castells and Friedman argue, this does not mean that capitalism no longer requires exploitation to generate profit. Rather, it means that capital now exploits the labor of more workers than it ever has before. In contrast to Castells' and Friedman's popular reading of globalization, which promotes the ideology of the "fairness" in the relation between capital and labor, I argue that it is necessary to return to the theory which so many on both the left and the right argue is outdated—namely Lenin's theory of imperialism—because it will enable us to go beneath the surfaces of globalization to counter the first argument that globalization has nothing to do with the imperialism of the past.

Globalization as Imperialism

Imperialism, as Lenin explained, is the competition of transnational capitalists in their attempts to monopolize social resources and to establish their dictatorship of the free market around the world. The monopolization of capital emerges from within the capitalist mode of production as a logical outcome of the division of property between owners of the means of production and owners of nothing but labor power and the private accumulation of capital that this relation engenders. The problem with the idea advanced by network theorists that the relation between capital and labor is transformed through the introduction of new means of production that not only extend the capitalist system across the globe but transform it from an exploitative system to a fluid system of oscillating power relations is that capitalism is defined neither by the kinds of technique used in the production of commodities nor by the geographic distribution of production. These are features of changes in the modes of accumulation used to extract surplus value but not in the underlying logic of how and why labor relations under capitalism result in the production of surplus value. As Marx explains in *Capital*, what differentiates labor power, defined as "the aggregate of those mental and physical capabilities existing in a human being,"[111] from all other commodities is that it "not only produces its own value, but produces value over and above it."[112] In the most basic terms of the free market, capitalists hire workers to work for a set period of time, regardless of the value their labor produces. While on the surface it appears a fair exchange, it is not. Rather, the ability of the worker to produce more than the cost of the wage during the period of his or her daily employment means that the capitalist is able to appropriate the additional value the worker produces in manufacturing new commodities from the raw and semimanufactured materials which the capitalist has purchased. This period of time Marx calls the "working day," the division of time between the period for which the worker produces to reproduce the conditions of labor that is received in the wage and the period for which the worker produces surplus value which is appropriated by the capitalist. As such, it is in the capitalist's best interest to increase the rate of exploitation—the amount of surplus over necessary labor time—so as to increase the production of surplus value. This is accomplished two ways: first, by lengthening the time in which the labor force works ("absolute surplus value") and, second, by increasing the productivity of labor through the introduction and development of new means of production ("relative surplus value"). As the capitalist introduces new technologies, the productivity of labor increases, enabling the capitalist to produce more commodities and, in turn, capture a larger share of the market as long as the relative technological advantage is maintained. When a market is relatively new and the competition among capitals has not fully developed, the rate of profit is high because the amount of capital necessary to establish the production process is low and the amount of labor employed in production is high. However, other capitalists do not remain stagnant and either adopt the technological improvements of their rivals, or are purchased by their more productive and more profitable competitors. As competition increases, each capitalist is forced to introduce new technologies, which, although they drive down the cost of labor by intensifying production, also have the consequence of increasing the costs of production and introduce the simultaneous effect of eliminating the primary source of value—labor.

In fact, the contradictions between labor and capital are actually exacerbated and not lessened by increased technological development because technological advances in production are the means by which capitalism increases the productivity of labor and thus the rate of exploitation. The computer does not change the logic of wage-labor, in other words, merely the speed and productive ability of the workers using it. In addition, it is precisely because the exploitation of labor is the source of surplus value under capitalism that developments in production also enable the geographical reorganization of production—what Castells calls capitalism's "variable geometry"[113]—so as to maximize profits through such labor practices as outsourcing and subcontracting which are designed not only to create competition between workers to prevent them from collectively organizing against capital across national boundaries but to find or create cheaper sources of labor as a means of maximizing profit. Just as the development of capitalism on a "national" scale meant brutal competition to gain monopoly control over production and thus take "more or less complete possession of the industry of their own country,"[114] Lenin's analysis of monopoly capital explains why the increasing development of capitalism means the inevitable drive of capitalists to compete globally for access to cheaper sources of labor and thus to control the rate of exploitation.

Imperialism, as Lenin outlines, is the direct effect of the necessity of capitalism to counter a falling rate of profit through the exploitation of cheaper sources of labor power and securing monopoly prices over social resources. He writes:

> The principal feature of the latest stage of capitalism is the domination of monopolist associations of big employers. These monopolies are most firmly established when *all* the sources of raw materials are captured by one group, and we have seen with what zeal the international capitalist associations exert every effort to deprive their rivals of all opportunity of competing, to buy up, for example, ironfields, oilfields, etc. Colonial possession alone gives the monopolies complete guarantee against all contingencies in the struggle against competitors, including the case of the adversary wanting to be protected by a law establishing a state monopoly. The more capitalism is developed, the more strongly the shortage of raw materials is felt, the more intense the competition and the hunt for sources of raw materials throughout the whole world, the more desperate the struggle for the acquisition of colonies.[115]

If it is to increase profits, capital *must* constantly search for new markets to find cheaper sources of raw materials, increase and develop production, and drive down the costs of labor power. Imperialism is thus the necessary outcome of the development of the productivity of labor under the conditions of private ownership, in which "the uneven and spasmodic development of

individual enterprises, individual branches of industry and individual countries"[116] necessarily leads to an accumulation of "an enormous 'surplus of capital' "[117] in the hands of the ruling class that becomes more profitable by
moving to less developed areas than it does by remaining in highly developed
and monopolized areas of production. In other words, as history has shown,
capital can achieve higher rates of profit by moving to areas in which "capital
is scarce, the price of land is relatively low, wages are low, [and] raw materials
are cheap"[118] than it can by remaining in highly developed and monopolized
areas of production. This goes back to the discussion of surplus value and
what Marx theorizes "the tendency of the rate of profit to fall."[119] As the level
of *constant* capital—the amount needed to invest in production—rises in a
particular industry, the lower the amount of *variable* capital—the amount invested in labor—that is necessary. Marx called this ratio of constant to variable capital the "organic composition of capital." Improvements in the means
of production enable a particular capitalist to (momentarily) undercut his
competitors by producing more for the same price, thereby driving them
from the market and gaining a monopoly share. Yet, at the same time, the
more productive labor becomes and the more the cost of investment in fixed
capital rises, the more commodities the capitalist must sell in order to achieve
the rates of profit that existed prior to intensification of production. Thus,
while any one capitalist may be able to accumulate a larger mass of surplus
value than before by gaining monopoly control of the market, the rate of
profit available in the industry declines overall. Furthermore, when the rate
of profit is high in a particular industry, eventually investment capital comes
flooding in, leading to a leveling of the competitive advantage of the early
adopter of new technologies and a saturation of the market. Both of these
factors combined—the rising organic composition of capital and the direct
competition between capitals over control of the market—ultimately leads to
a crisis of overproduction driven by a reduction in the rate of profit.

This process which requires the holders of accumulated, but unproductive capital, to find new avenues of production—and the accumulation of
new value—has two primary factors. First, as Lenin writes, "The necessity
of exporting capital arises from the fact that in a few countries capitalism
has become 'over-ripe' and . . . capital cannot find 'profitable' investment"
at home and thus must go abroad.[120] Second, it leads to development of
what Lenin defines as "finance capitalism" which is the combination of
banking and industrial capital that results from an increase in the capital

accumulated through advances in production and the need to find new avenues for the profitability of unproductive capital. As Ernest Mandel explains, "The export of capital and the colonialism associated with it are
monopoly capital's reaction to the fall in the average rate of profit in highly
industrialized metropolitan countries, and to the reduction in profitable
fields of investment of capital in these countries."[121] That is to say, having
divided "the home market among themselves and obtained more or less
complete possession of the industry of their own country" capital must expand outside of the home market to find new avenues for profitability
abroad.[122] This expansion is what Lenin defines as the logic of imperialism:

> Imperialism is capitalism at that stage of development at which the dominance
> of monopolies and finance capital is established; in which the export of capital
> has acquired pronounced importance; in which the division of the world among
> the international trusts has begun; in which the division of all territories of the
> globe among the biggest capitalist powers has been completed.[123]

Despite his disagreement with the labor theory of value and the idea that
rising levels of organic capital lead to a fall in the rate of profit[124], Robert
Brenner's analysis of capital expansion in the twentieth century in *The Economics of Global Turbulence* nonetheless demonstrates precisely this logic at
work in spite of his objections. Beginning from the start of the period
known as the long boom, we find that "between 1940 and 1945, the rate of
profit for the private economy was, on average, some 50 percent above its
level in 1929 and 60–70 percent higher than the average for the years 1900–
1929."[125] This "epoch-making" level of profitability, in turn, was driven by
and resulted in the massive investment in developing the means of production, so as to increase the productivity of labor. In fact, "over the years
1938–1950, gross investment in both the private economy and the manufacturing sector grew at an average rate of around 11 percent" meaning that
"output per hour increased 2.7 per cent in the private business economy
and in manufacturing—3.8 per cent and 5.5 per cent for these sectors, re-
spectively, in the four years between 1946 and 1950."[126] In other words, a
high rate of profit at the start of the cycle led to increasing investment
which, in turn, had the effect of increasing the productivity of labor, the
source of new value. Yet, as the labor theory of value and the tendency for
the rate of profit to fall explain, this level of productivity and profit cannot
be indefinitely maintained. First, the massive growth in productivity during

this period and the rising level of investment required to maintain this level of productivity meant that U.S. corporations found less return in investing at home rather than investing in the rebuilding markets of Germany and Japan. As the long boom unfolded, U.S. capital was, according to Brenner, "increasingly attracted to the superior opportunities for profit-making overseas, especially in Europe, where they could combine relatively cheap labour with relatively advanced technology and produce against relatively weak competitors in rapidly growing markets,"[127] leading to an increase in the export of capital abroad and, eventually, the establishment and disbanding of the Breton-Woods agreement in 1973. Second, as the productivity of labor in Germany and Japan grew as a result of the newly imported capital and technology, the corporations in these countries then flooded the market with even cheaper commodities, further driving down the rate of profit. The declining rates of profit globally and the subsequent crisis of overproduction is what ultimately led to the *long downturn*, the period from 1973 to the mid-1990s. From 1973–1984, as Duménil and Lévy show, the rate of profit declined in the United States from 20.6 percent to 15.4 percent, and in Europe from 18.1 percent to 13.8 percent.[128]

The emergence of what is most commonly recognized as globalization in the 1990s is again demonstrating the importance of Lenin's theory of imperialism. The development of new forms of production, communication, and transport has enabled capital to renew its global expansion, while at the same time sharpening the division between classes. This becomes clear when we examine some of the central tenets of network theory and the image of global capitalism as "post-imperialist": the development of supply chain systems of production and the opening of new avenues for the circulation of capital have the effect of displacing global conflict while creating the conditions for decreasing inequality.

The relative rebounds in productivity and the rate of profit which first appear in the middle of the 1980s and reach their peaks at the end of the 1990s is the result of two interrelated factors, both of which support the Marxist theory of imperialism. To take the example of the U.S. economy, which is most often held up as the primary example of profitability of network capitalism, the declining rates of profit and the rise of international competition, particularly from the emerging economies in Asia, required the rethinking of the organization of labor in order to create the conditions for increasing the conditions of exploitation and thus the rate of extracting surplus value. In order to address these conditions, at the end of the long downturn investment begins to shift, and takes a particularly sharp jump in the years between 1978 and 1983, towards the improvement of information technologies in an attempt to solve the economic crisis through an intense rationalization of industry.[129] In other words, capital sought to increase its efficiency in "the capacity to organize production, distribution, and financial operations and to reduce costs."[130] What *efficiency* means here is the process of further streamlining production and to make the most effective (again, profitable) use of labor so as to increase productivity, decrease the costs of labor, and restore rates of profit to precrisis levels. This is where network theory originates. The theory advanced by Ohmae, Friedman, and Castells to organize production around a central hub, with temporary nodes of production positioned in areas where profitability can be achieved, reflects the needs of capital to apply the new technological developments in production in a way that provides the greatest return. In fact, these developments enabled the United States during the period 1990–2000 to claim growth rates in productivity above the 1973 level, as well as above its closest economic competitors in Europe, which achieved significantly lower rates of growth in productivity and output over the same period of time.[131] At the same time, the United States remained attractive to investment because of the attacks on labor that led to a stagnant growth rate in the costs of wages, to the point where the real value of the minimum wage is actually lower in 2005 than it was in the late 1960s, even when adjusted for inflation.[132] As Brenner notes, "US capital had become profoundly dependent on close to zero wage growth inside manufacturing to help counter intense competition from their leading international rivals."[133]

Once again, as explained in Marx's theory of the tendency of the rate of profit to decline, a rising level of profitability resulted in the factors which lead to the concentration and centralization of capital and the monopolization of the marketplace as more productive capital swallowed up their competitors, a reality borne out by the fact that "between 1980 and 1989 there were 31,105 mergers and acquisitions, totaling in value $1.34 trillion dollars."[134] What we see then in the period immediately following is a renewal of expansion of capital abroad to find more profitable avenues for investment, a point that can be traced out in the growth of Foreign Direct Investment (FDI). FDI is defined as "investment in which a firm *acquires a substantial controlling interest in a foreign firm* (above a 10 percent share) or *sets up a subsidiary company in a foreign country.*"[135] Although it is the case that most FDI flows between the industrialized countries,the level of investment in developing countries has nonetheless increased in the period 1990–2000, from a level of 25.4 percent in 1982–1987 to 31.6 percent in 2001,[136] and from $50 billion to a high of $1 trillion in 2000.[137] In this sense, the export of capital increasingly takes on the characteristics of monopoly capitalism. The large amount of capital invested in the so-called developed countries reflects the high organic composition of capital and the higher costs of labor, as well as the ability to produce in relatively stable economic environments, while the lower level of investment in developing economies reflects the increasing productivity of labor in these areas and the attempt to maintain low production costs by locating production in nations which suppress wage levels below that of the home market: "FDI improves the overall efficiency of the resource allocation via the transfer of capital, technology, and managerial and marketing know-how."[138] In other words, as per Lenin's theory, capital can still move production to lower wage areas to achieve at least average, if not above average, rates of profit for lower levels of investment than are required in the home market.

In addition, the idea that FDI results in a "flattening" of the world, or a more "peaceful" integration of capital, is not evident either. The theory of a "peaceful" imperialism actually emerges in the beginning of the twentieth century, when the world market had reached a similar level of integration as the current period. Karl Kautsky, as the most prominent left theorist of the "peaceful" imperialist movement, argued that capitalism had reached a stage of "ultra-imperialism" in which the expansion of capital globally and the development of interconnected networks of production and trade would ultimately require that nation-states would be forced to unite into cartels or federations that would no longer compete with one another. Kautsky writes:

> There is no *economic* necessity for continuing the arms race after the World War, even from the standpoint of the capitalist class itself, with the exception of at most certain armaments interests. On the contrary, the capitalist economy is seriously threatened by the contradictions between its States. Every far-sighted capitalist today must call on his fellows: capitalists of all countries, unite![139]

For Kautsky the need to export capital abroad requires the stabilization of political factors and ultimately the organization of capitals into noncompetitive cartels. He writes, "the result of the World War between the great imperialist powers may be a federation of the strongest who renounce their arms race."[140] While on the surface Kautsky's theory of "ultra-imperialism" would seem to describe the emergence of transnational economic agreements such as the European Union and trade agreements such as NAFTA and GATT, as Lenin demonstrated at the time the ability to export capital to other markets is dependent upon the existence of unequal levels of development, not only between the so-called center and the periphery but also between nations in the center as well. Capital cannot reach a peaceful balance because the creation of new values and the accumulation of capital cannot help but to expand, rather than shrink, the division between nations. "As long as capitalism remains what it is," Lenin argues, "surplus capital will never be utilized for the purpose of raising the standard of living of the masses in a given country, for this would mean a decline in profits for the capitalists; it will be used for the purpose of increasing profits by exporting capital abroad to the backwards countries."[141] The very competition between capitalists towards the monopolization of the market could not but ultimately pit capitalists against one another and, in turn, the nations that represent them, as was manifest in World War I and World War II. To take only one example from the contemporary moment, the rising tensions between France and Germany that emerged in the European Union during the current global financial crisis over the economic instability of the "PIIGS" (the racist term used by economic commentators in the imperialist powers to refer to the countries of Portugal, Italy, Ireland, Greece, and Spain) demonstrates how quickly antagonisms between supposedly unified nations can emerge. As the editors of *The Economist*, who compared prognosticating the EU's future to "staring into an abyss," write, "Will the European Union make it? The question would have sounded outlandish not long ago. Now even the project's greatest cheerleaders talk of a continent facing a 'Bermuda triangle' of debt, demographic decline and lower growth."[142] Under capitalism, the only unity that exists among capitalists is their unified agreement to exploit working people to the fullest extent of their powers.

The state is not magically eliminated by the network because, as Ernest Mandel writes, the state "is a product of the social division of labor."[143] It is the legal manifestation of the mode of production. Under capitalism, the state is the political arm of the owning class that is used to ensure that the exploitation of labor can continue unabated by protecting the property rights of owners. In the age of imperialism it serves as the means by which individual capitalists attempt to control the global market through the use of political and military power. This was recognized by U.S. President Woodrow Wilson at the beginning of the twentieth century:

> Since trade ignores national boundaries and the manufacturer insists on having the world as a market, the flag of his nation must follow him, and the doors of the nations which are closed against him must be battered down. Concessions obtained by financiers must be safeguarded by ministers of state, even if the sovereignty of unwilling nations be outraged in the process. Colonies must be obtained or planted, in order that no useful corner of the world may be over-looked or left unused.[144]

The reemergence of the theory of ultra-imperialism in Ohmae's theory of regionalization or Friedman's theory of supply chain capitalism—and in the theory of network capitalism more broadly—sharply contrasts with the economic realities of the twentieth and twenty-first centuries. Far from integrating markets in a flat or borderless chain, capital remains concentrated and centralized in the hands of a few capitalists who then compete with one another for control of the world markets, while relying upon their national governments to protect their economic interests both at home and abroad. Despite the arguments for a borderless economy, the 2008 *Forbes* list of the top 500 most profitable companies shows that capital accumulations remain centered in the so-called developed countries, as 162 are in the United States, 67 are in Japan, 38 are in Germany, 37 in France, and 33 in the United Kingdom. In addition, while productivity in the developing nations has often increased faster than that of the developed economies, "countries with worse endowments of physical and human capital at the outset might never converge with the more developed economies, which have a greater capital stock, thanks to increasing returns of scale of this stock and the positive externalities derived from scientific and technical knowledge for the rest of their factors of production."[145] This means that the supply chain is not about developing countries, but establishing relative control over labor abroad. This explains why the industrialization of the global South through the export of capital from the global North, while resulting in a relative raise in the level of wages, has nonetheless increased inequality between and within nations. Smaller amounts of capital exported abroad are able to achieve average rates of profit compared to domestic production, but insofar as the primary purpose of this production is for export, the majority of the surplus value produced returns to the company's home country. Network theory provides the theoretical means to effectively organize capital in this manner, while simultaneously representing the exchange between developed countries as fair and equal. Far from being equal, however, the decline of wages in the countries as the center of the global economy (the United States, Canada, and the European Union) and the growing inequality in the peripheral economies (India, Asia, and Africa) demonstrate that what is at the core of network theory is creating a more effective climate for subjugating the workers of the world to the interests of capital in private accumulation.

Productive, Unproductive, and Immaterial Labor

The second aspect of contemporary globalization theory concerns a corresponding development in the organization of labor to the export of capital abroad: the decline of industrial manufacturing in the North and its development in the South. For most commentators on the left and the right, the decreasing levels of industrial manufacturing and the rise of the retail and service sectors in the so-called developed nations serves as another example of the undoing of the labor theory of value, which, I argue, remains indispensible for understanding the digital condition. This premise has been advanced in various forms in the post–World War II period, from the arguments that we are entering a postindustrial service economy which emerged in the 1970s in the work of writers such as Daniel Bell (*The Coming of Post-Industrial Society*) to the arguments that we are now entering a digital economy based upon knowledge proposed in the writings of Richard Florida (*The Rise of the Creative Class*) and Mark Poster (*Information Please*). What is at the core of this argument is that the shift in the forms of production corresponds to a shift in the logic of production. As capital supposedly moves towards a digital economy, what is said to matter most are issues of exchange, representation, and consumption rather than property ownership, production, and exploitation.

The most popular proponents of this argument today are Michael Hardt and Antonio Negri, who draw on network theory and the work of Castells in particular, as the basis of their now foundational reading of globalization as the site of political struggle between the forces of empire and the multitude. They write, "Along with the global market and global circuits of production has emerged a global order, a new logic and a structure of rule—in short, a new form of sovereignty."[146] That is to say, as a result of the way in which "the primary factors of production and exchange—money, technology, people, and goods—move with increasing ease across national boundaries,"[147] they argue that we are witness to the emergence of empire as "something altogether different"[148] from both earlier capitalist relations as well as from the critiques of these relations as imperialism because "the foundation of the classic modern conception of private property is . . . to a certain extent dissolved in the postmodern mode of production."[149] While traditional theories of capitalism assume the division of the world around ownership and control of the means of production, empire is, instead, said to consist of "a *decentered* and *deterritorializing* apparatus of rule"[150] in which "the international divisions and flows of labor and capital have fractured and multiplied so that it is no longer possible to demarcate large geographic zones as center and periphery, North and South."[151] In other words, what is fundamentally "new" about the global economy, they maintain, is that "the assembly line has been replaced by the network as the organizational model of production"[152] and, as a result, "the nature of labor and wealth accumulated is changing."[153] "Today," they conclude, "productivity, wealth, and the creation of social surpluses take the form of cooperative interactivity through linguistic, communicative, and affective networks."[154]

Their theory of globalization-as-empire is premised on the theory of immaterial labor, or labor "that produces an immaterial good, such as a service, a cultural knowledge or communication."[155] The main argument of the proponents of immaterial labor theory is that, unlike labor employed in the production of material commodities, immaterial labor cannot be quantified and therefore falls outside of the framework of the labor theory of value. Instead, capitalism is defined as a primarily political system in which what matters is the control of the "bio-power" of labor rather than its exploitation. The theory of network capitalism as driven by the political control of immaterial labor is most extensively developed in Antonio Negri's reading of Marx's economic notebooks, particularly the passage known as "the fragment on machines." Central to Negri's argument is the idea that in the development of the forces of production—the replacing of living labor with dead labor—central to the capitalist mode of production, the theory of value which explains *why* labor is central to capital as the source of surplus value loses its explanatory force because of the diminishing role of labor in the production process as compared to machines and to science. This conclusion is based upon his reading of Marx's argument:

> To the degree that labour time—the mere quantity of labour—is posited by capital as the sole determinant element, to that degree does direct labour and its quantity disappear as the determinant principle of production—of the creation of use values—and is reduced both quantitatively, to a smaller proportion, and qualitatively, as an, of course, indispensable but subordinate moment, compared to general scientific labour, technological application of natural sciences, on one side, and to the general productive force arising from social combination [Gliederung] in total production on the other side—a combination which appears as a natural fruit of social labour (although it is a historic product). Capital thus works towards its own dissolution as the form dominating production.[156]

For Negri, this passage indicates the process by which capital is self-defeating. According to his reading, through the requirements of technological advances to production as a means of increasing the rate of surplus value, productive capital expands into the process of reproduction and circulation such that the labor theory of value is *reversed* from its original conception. In Negri's words:

> Capital seeks a continual reduction in necessary labor in order to expand the proportion of surplus value extorted, but the more it succeeds individually with workers taken one by one, the more necessary labor benefits the collectivity and is reappropriated by absorbing the great collective forces that capital would like to determine purely for its own account.[157]

Put differently, the shift from an industrial to a postindustrial society is, for Negri, not simply the shift in kinds of labor—from manual to knowledge, or from factory to service. The development of immaterial forms of labor is said to be a reflection of the crisis of capitalism at the level of value itself. According to Negri's reading, what Marx describes as the way in which capital moves towards its own dissolution is actually capital's attempted appropriation of *immaterial labor*—the labor of the reproduction of capital—which can occur only outside of the boundaries of surplus value. He writes,

> when the theory of value can not measure itself by a quantity of labor time or by an individual dimension of labor, when a first displacement leads it to confront social time and the collective dimension of labor, at this moment the *impossibility*

of measuring exploitation modifies the form of exploitation [. . . and . . .] does not suppress the law of value but reduces it to a mere formality.[158]

Once it appropriates immaterial labor, Negri argues, the boundaries of the working day—the division between necessary and surplus labor time—become difficult, if not impossible, to measure. This is because immaterial labor is said to be labor whose primary function is to establish the reproduction of labor elsewhere, thus operating independently of the priority of value that capital establishes. As such, it is precisely by freeing workers from work—through the creation of free time resulting from increased productivity created by technological advances, as well as the growing segment of labor that does not participate in the production process—that Negri argues the law of value is rendered inoperable and capitalism is transformed from an exploitative system to an entirely political system of command and control of labor by capital, in turn leading to the possibilities for revolutionary transformation through the "self-valorization" of the working class. Labor, in short, is no longer bound to capital except through the controlling functions of its policing apparatuses. He writes, "The theory of value, as a theory of categorical synthesis, is a legacy of the classics and of the bourgeois mystification which we can easily do without in order to enter the field of revolution."[159] Thus, to go "beyond Marx" for Negri means understanding that the theory of value works at the level of ideology to bind workers to the forms of labor under capitalism rather than to see that the relationship between capital and labor "*are reduced to a relation of force.*"[160] Instead, he writes, "when production and reproduction are so closely mixed one with the other, we can no longer distinguish productive labor from reproductive labor"[161] and later, with Michael Hardt, "the old Marxist distinctions between productive and unproductive labor, as well as that between productive and reproductive labor, which were always dubious, should be thrown out."[162]

It is on the logic of this theory of immaterial labor as the end of the distinction between productive and unproductive labor that, according to Hardt and Negri, the shift to the postmodern economy of empire from the modern economy of industrial capitalism represents not just a political reorganization of capital but a broader transformation in the mode of production itself. As a result of a shifting focus within capitalism from material production to immaterial knowledge, they argue that the role of labor has undergone a "radical transformation" from the production of material goods to the creation of "relationships and ultimately social life."[163] "The hegemony of immaterial labor," they write, "tends to transform the organization of production from the linear relationships of the assembly line to the innumerable and indeterminate relationships of distributed networks" such that "exploitation under the hegemony of immaterial labor is no longer primarily the expropriation of value measured by individual or collective labor time, but rather the capture of value that is produced by cooperative labor."[164] In this context, they argue that the theory of immaterial labor goes beyond not just the Marxist theories of wage labor, but also the early globalization theories of the 1970s and 1980s which celebrated the rise of "service work, intellectual labor, and cognitive labor" because the theory of immaterial labor is said to recognize the importance of all labor which "produces or manipulates affects such as a feeling of ease, well-being, satisfaction, excitement, or passion."[165] In other words, it includes all aspects of human creativity, whether or not they are productive of surplus value. Since, from their view, resources produced through the new forms of labor (such as "affect") cannot ever be "fully captured" by capital[166] because they exceed the boundaries of the working day, the "multitude" whose labor this represents is becoming "an autonomous agent of production" that is no longer dependent on capital to set it in motion.[167] Thus, the point of contestation is not the extraction of surplus labor but rather the political control of this multitude and their creative powers. For Negri and Hardt, insofar as "proletarian internationalism" represents the "outside" of an earlier, "national" stage of capitalism,[168] the globalization of production means that "there is no longer an 'outside' to capital"[169] and thus workers whose surplus labor is exploited as a collective are no longer the agents of change. Instead, Negri and Hardt posit an "impure politics" of the multitude based on finding "the potential for liberation that exists *within* Empire"[170] and, despite the radical rhetoric, that all that is necessary in the end for the development of what they describe as a "spontaneous and elementary communism" is the formation of a counter-empire that only differs from the current social relations politically but not necessarily economically.[171]

Of course, the argument that capitalism is on the verge of entering a postindustrial, postwork, postclass, postexploitative regime of accumulation in which the free circulation of knowledge and information replaces the exploitative relations of production is not in itself new, and reflects a long-standing attempt within cultural theory to eliminate what was problematic to the ideas of consumer capitalism in reality—the continuing exploitative division between capital and the working class. For example, along with conservative writers such as Daniel Bell and Alvin Toffler, left writers such as Alain Touraine argue in the period of the long boom in the 1970s that:

> In the programmed society, directed by the machinery of growth, the dominated class is no longer defined in terms of property, but by its dependence on the mechanisms of engineered change and hence on the instruments of social and cultural integration. One's trade, one's directly productive work, is not in direct opposition to capital; it is personal and collective identity in opposition to manipulation.[172]

And during the technology boom of the 1990s, Stanley Aronowitz and Jeremy Rifkin separately advanced the theory that labor was being fundamentally replaced by machines in a postwork economy driven by the fact that "knowledge itself, once firmly tied to specific labor processes such as steelmaking, now becomes a relatively free-floating commodity to the extent that it is transformed into information that requires no productive object."[173]

What differentiates network theories of immaterial labor from earlier theories of unproductive labor is the way in which it tries to account for the economic inequality produced by capitalist social relations as structurally inevitable and fundamentality inescapable while opening new avenues of economic opportunity to counter a monopolized global market through a discourse of individualism and entrepreneurialism. Maurizio Lazzarato, in his essay "Immaterial Labor," clarifies this basic premise of the network theory of capitalism. Defining immaterial labor as "the labor that produces the informational and cultural content of the commodity,"[174] he writes, "waged labor and the direct subjugation (to organization) no longer constitute the primary form of the contractual relationship between capitalist and worker"[175] and that "immaterial labor finds itself at the crossroads (or rather it is the interface) of a new relationship between production and consumption."[176] More specifically, Lazzarato argues:

> I do not believe that this new labor-power is merely functional to a new historical phase of capitalism and its processes of accumulation and reproduction. This labor-power is the product of a "silent revolution" taking place within the

anthropological realities of work and within the reconfigurations of its meanings. Waged labor and the direct subjugation (to organization) no longer constitute the primary form of the contractual relationship between capitalist and worker. A polymorphous self-employed autonomous work has emerged as the dominant form, a kind of "intellectual worker" who is him- or herself an entrepreneur, inserted within a market that is constantly shifting and within networks that are changeable in time and space.[177]

Far from representing a system based upon exploitation, according to Lazzarato, capitalism has become an unstable system of power, and as such open, fluid, and reversible. At the core of this theory of labor is the argument that the globalization of production and the expansive telecommunications and service industries calls into existence a regime of social relations no longer based upon production and exploitation, but rather on consumption. The claim of critics such as Castells, Lazzarato, and Hardt and Negri is that immaterial labor represents the elimination of wage labor *from within* capitalism as an effect of capitalism's own drive to eliminate labor through the automating of production, turning both owner and worker into contesting consumers. What emerges from this theory of the social as a series of reversible and fluid acts of consumption that defy the homogeneity of global capital is the idea that it is no longer possible to challenge the central logic of capitalism. Instead, workers are instructed to find and to celebrate the rare moments of discontinuity, in which the ideology of capital and its interests seem to collide, as the only possibility for overcoming the alienation of commodity production.

For example, as an instance of the way in which immaterial labor gives rise to the entrepreneurial resistance of the self-valorizing working class, Hardt and Negri contrast the "oligopolistic" mechanisms of broadcast systems which represent the "centralized production, mass distribution, and one-way communications" of monopoly capitalism[178] with the "democratic" mechanisms of the internet as a space in which "an indeterminate and potentially unlimited number of interconnected nodes communicate with no central point of control"[179] and result in the production of a common set of relationships and knowledges that represents the "incarnation, the production, and the liberation of the multitude."[180] And, it is on similar terms that Castells also locates the possibilities of digital culture as opening a space of agency independent of the economic. It is useful, at this point, to quote Castells at some length:

the new economy cannot be characterized as being centered any longer on multinational corporations even if they continue to exercise jointly oligopolistic control over most markets. This is because corporations have transformed themselves into a web of multiple networks embedded in a multiplicity of institutional environments. Power still exists, but it is randomly exercised. Markets still trade, but purely economic calculations are hampered by their dependency on unsolvable equations overdetermined by too many variables. The market's hand that institutional economists tried to make visible has returned to invisibility. But this time, its structural logic is not governed by supply and demand but also influenced by hidden strategies and untold discoveries played out in the global information networks.[181]

According to Castells, what makes power "randomly exercised" such that it can exceed the economic and ologopolistic control of the market by transnational capital is the innovative power of the individual whose desires cannot be reduced to economists' rigid mathematical equations. He goes on to write, "what characterizes the new system of communication, based upon digitized, networked integration of multiple communication modes, is its inclusiveness and comprehensiveness of all cultural expressions"[182] and it is on the basis of this inclusive culture that the individual becomes the creator (and owner) of symbolic value. Castells argues, "while the media have become indeed globally interconnected, and the programs and messages circulate in the global network," the fact that "not everybody watches the same thing at the same time, and that each culture and social group has a specific relationship to the media system" means "we are not living in a global village, but in customized cottages globally produced and locally distributed."[183]

For network theorists, the significance of the increasing integration of the exchange mechanisms of global society is two fold. First, developments in communications and production technologies have enabled information and commodities to travel, in the words of Thomas L. Friedman, "father, faster, deeper and cheaper than ever before."[184] Second, and more importantly, the technological developments that increase the speed of production and the circulation of commodities and ideas represents a fundamental shift in the framework within which these exchanges occur and in the ways in which the productive forces of society are organized, creating an opportunity to move beyond the corporate stage of globalization through individual customization. Increasing social interconnection is thus represented as the onset of a new stage of capitalism in which the economic, political and cultural forces of what is called informational or knowledge capitalism that emerged in the industrialized nations of the United States, Europe, and Japan in the wake of World War II as a result of the advances in production and communication technologies have begun spreading beyond the boundaries of the nation-state. In the process, network globalization is said to transform the whole of global society from the hierarchical to the individual and, as such, requires a new discourse that substitutes for concepts such as class, labor, production, and imperialism the more fluid concepts of multitude, immaterial labor, consumption, and empire.

Despite their local differences what links all of these theories of globalization is that they represent globalization as largely constituted by cultural processes which, through technological advances, have escaped the determinacy of the economic. In doing so they suggest that the main terrain of struggle and freedom for workers rests in the legal, political, and cultural surfaces of capitalism rather than in changing the underlying economic relations that determine class inequality. The main crux of their argument is to deny the continued existence of exploitation and therefore to deny the historical relation of globalization to class society by making it appear that changes in the culture of the workplace—for example, the shift from the rigid structures of Fordism to the flexible structures of post-Fordism—bring about a fundamental material change in the class position of workers.

Digital Capitalism and the Labor Theory of Value

The debate over productive and unproductive labor is not new, but is central to understanding the limits of the theory of immaterial labor. It is important because this distinction is necessary if one is to understand the mechanisms by which capital not only accumulates value, but requires productive labor to produce new values to accumulate. As Marx explains in the second volume of *Capital*:

> The transformation of the forms of capital from commodities into money and from money into commodities are at the same time transactions of the capitalist, acts of purchase and sale . . . Just as the circulation time of capital is a necessary segment of its time of reproduction, so the time during which the capitalist buys

and sells and scours the market is a necessary part of the time in which he functions as a capitalist, i.e. as personified capital. It is a part of his business hours.[185]

The significance of buying and selling is that the circulation of capital—M-C-M' (Money–Commodity–Money Plus Return)—requires that the capitalist sells the commodities produced by the labor he has purchased in order to buy new materials to restart the cycle. However, what is also significant is that the value of the commodities does not reside in this exchange. Marx writes, "To effect a change in the state of being [from commodity to money or from money to commodity] costs time and labor power, not for the purpose of creating value, however, but in order to bring about the conversion of value from one from into another."[186] It does not matter whether the capitalist is able to sell for above or below the average price, this exchange does not change the amount of surplus value available. It changes only the distribution of this value and the amount of profit realized by the capitalist. The role of the merchant or retailer is to facilitate the ability of the capitalist to realize a portion of the surplus value produced as profit and to return part of this acquired value to the production process. That is to say, insofar as "a certain amount of labour power and labour time must be expended in the process of circulation"[187]—since the capitalist must sell the commodities produced in order to realize the accumulated surplus value as profit—it is in the interests of the capitalist to shorten this time as it constitutes part of the costs of circulation that will have to be deducted from any potential future profits. This is where the merchant or retailer comes into the process by agreeing to purchase the commodities from the capitalist for a share of the surplus value contained in the commodity. While the retailer is able to pressure the capitalist into selling below what he might have been able to achieve on the market, it is still less expensive than if the capitalist had to run this part of the production cycle. The retailer therefore reduces the circulation costs of the capitalist and allows the capitalist to return newly acquired capital back into the production process faster than if the capitalist were required to sell the commodities directly. In fact, in mapping out the relationship between the productive and distributive wings of capitalism, Marx's analysis anticipated the development of the major retail chains such as Wal-Mart:

> If by a division of labor a function, unproductive in itself although a necessary
> element of reproduction, is transformed from an incidental occupation of many

into the exclusive occupation of a few, into their special business, the nature of this function itself is not changed. One merchant . . . may, by his operations, shorten the time of purchase and sale for *many* producers.[188]

Insofar as the labor theory of value explains the economies of scale that correspond to the rise of monopoly capitalism, it also explains why a business can also monopolize a particular aspect of the reproduction process. However, this does not mean that Wal-Mart dictates the direction of the economy. Rather, the retailer "should be regarded as a machine which reduces useless expenditure of energy of helps to set production time free."[189] A business like Wal-Mart dominates the market because it uses an economy of scale to drive down the costs of reproduction to the commodity producer, but it could not exist without them. It is in a similar context that Marx talks about the growth of banking capital. It renders the "relation between the capital originally advanced and the capitalized surplus value" more intricate, but does not create new value except, perhaps, indirectly as it becomes the means by which a new production cycle might begin. It emerges when, as a result of increases in production, there develops a "hoard" of accumulated, yet unproductive capital that cannot be reinvested into production because of its effect on the rate of profit. This capital thus becomes available for investment elsewhere. As Marx explains:

> For instance from not having sufficient capital of his own at the very outset for this purpose, A borrows from banker C a portion of the productive capital with which he starts in business or continues it during the year. Banker C lends him a sum of money which consists only of surplus value deposited with the Banker by Capitalists D, E, F, etc. As far as A is concerned there is as yet no question of accumulating capital. But with regard to D, E, F, etc., A is, in fact, nothing but an agent capitalizing surplus value appropriated by them.[190]

The role of the retail and financial industries are thus extensions of the circulation cycle in which surplus value is capitalized and made available for investment in new commodity production. While appropriating part of the surplus value that the initial capitalist has extracted from the surplus labor of his workers, neither industry can add new value. If, for example, the banker is able to charge a high interest rate, this is paid as part of the costs of production by the borrowing capitalist based upon the expectations of future profits. If the capitalist does not realize these profits, then the money is not repaid and the bank is out whatever money was lent.

This addresses one aspect of the argument that unproductive labor has replaced productive labor as a source of value in network capitalism. As we saw in arguments of Thomas L. Friedman, the growth of Wal-Mart into the world's largest company in terms of generated revenues and employees is said to mark a new kind of profitable enterprise, in which value comes from exchange rather than production. However, Marx's main point here is that both retail and banking are dependent upon the existence of productive labor in that they take over aspects of the production process initiated by productive capital in return for a share of the surplus value that is created. The capitalists invested in these enterprises expect the average rate of profit, and often institute the same mechanisms for ensuring that their workers spend more time capturing the surplus value in the form of profit than wages, but whatever profit is generated comes out of the original surplus value that was created when the commodity was produced. Even insofar as it does not distinguish between profits based upon production and those based upon services, according to the 2008 *Fortune* 500, profits in the general retail industry rank significantly lower (38th) than those achieved in the extraction of raw materials (1st), pharmaceuticals (2nd), network and communication equipment (4th), household products (16th), and farm and industrial equipment (21st) to name only a few. In addition, the appearance of so many financial services points precisely to the falling rate of profit and the contradictions of overproduction that have plagued capital since the 1970s. As Duménil and Lévy write, "During the 1980s finance more directly took back the initiative concerning competition . . . giving rise to a vast movement of restructuring of the productive system, of concentration, of takeovers, and, in a more general way, of strengthening property networks."[191] Even as productivity increased, capital has not been able to achieve the rates of profit that existed prior to the period of the long downturn and so increasing amounts of capital have become unproductive and available for investment, which strengthens the finance industry devoted to managing this hoard of unproductive capital. In fact, even during the current global financial crisis when billions of dollars of public monies were channeled worldwide to the banking industry to make up for the loss of expected profits, it has been reported that "nonfinancial" U.S. corporations are sitting on $1.8 *trillion* dollars of cash and liquid assets rather than lending them to banks or putting them into the stock market only to receive less than average rates of return from the new production that would result from such investment.[192] The point is, if capital were to shift entirely to services, there would be no commodities produced, and therefore no surplus value to realize. Likewise, if capital completely ignored services, then the surplus value in the commodities might not be realized without additional circulation costs and a lower rate of profit. As such, Marxism does not deny that unproductive labor plays an important role in the circulation of capital, only that it cannot produce new values simply by changing the state of the commodity into money or money into a commodity. On these terms, instead of viewing the growth of the immaterial sectors of the economy as the displacement or erasure of productive labor, or the blurring of the boundaries between productive and unproductive labor, Mandel offers a counter-reading which explains the explosion of such industries in the world's economic centers. According to Mandel:

> As long as "capital" was scarce, it normally concentrated on the direct production of surplus-value in the traditional domains of commodity production. But if capital is gradually accumulated in increasingly abundant commodities, and a substantial part of social capital no longer achieves valorization at all, the new mass of capital will penetrate more and more into areas which are non-productive in the sense that they do not create surplus-value.[193]

The point is that one cannot simply look on the surfaces of capital—in this case, the shift in the division of labor between manufacturing and services—and assume that the underlying logic of capital has changed. The growth of the services and retail industry corresponds to the tremendous growth in the productivity of labor in the post–World War II period and a decline in the rate of profit over the same period. Rather than the class equalizer that Friedman portrays it as, Wal-Mart is an expression of the fundamental contradictions of capital that result from the private ownership of the means of production. The problem, to be clear, is not the consumer habits of working people—the problem, as some ethicists portray it, is not whether or not to shop at Wal-Mart. The problem is exploitation. Wal-Mart is a manifestation of the growing productivity of labor which is put towards the private accumulation of capital rather than the meeting of needs.

The second aspect of the debate over productive and unproductive labor concerns the forms of labor that play a part in the reproduction of capital. Commentators often point to the declining numbers of manufacturing workers in relation to service workers as indicative of a shift towards a service or immaterial economy as well as the transformation in the law of value as outlined in the discussion of Negri's *Marx Beyond Marx*. As Guillermo de la Dehesa points out, "In 1950, the average for industrial employment in Europe stood at 41 percent of the total. By 1998, this figure had fallen to 28 percent" whereas the developing economies in Asia "have moved in the opposite direction and increased their percentage of industrial employment, from 14 percent to 27 percent."[194] The same process is occurring in the United States, as the number of manufacturing workers declined from 30 percent in 1950 to 15 percent today.[195] In response to these numbers there are two important points that need to be made. First, it is often the case that the relation between manufacturing and services are blurred in such accounts, as software and utility companies are many times combined with retail workers under the banner of service. Second, and more importantly, as Chris Harman points out, "Marx's distinction was not between material production and 'services'" but rather between productive and unproductive labor.[196] In his introduction to the second volume of *Capital*, Mandel explains:

> When Marx classifies certain forms of labour as productive and others as unpro-
> ductive, he is not passing moral judgement or employing criteria of social (or
> human) usefulness. Nor does he even present this classification as an objective or
> a-historical one. The object of his analysis is the *capitalist mode of production*, and
> he simply determines what is productive and what is unproductive for the func-
> tioning, the *rationale* of that system, and that system alone.[197]

In this context, productive labor is defined as "*labour productive for capital as a whole*" and thus as labor that "*increases the total mass* of surplus-value" whereas "no new surplus-value can be added in the sphere of circulation and exchange, not to speak of the stock exchange or the bank counter; all that happens there is the redistribution or reapportionment of previously created surplus-value."[198] For example, while a doctor might be socially "productive" in the sense of maintaining the health of the community, it is "unproductive" labor from the point of view of capital. On the other hand, the production of "dum-dum bullets, hard drugs, or pornographic maga-zines" might be socially "useless" in terms of "morality," but as commodi-ties "the surplus-labor in them is realized" when they are purchased "and capital is reproduced and expanded."[199]

The implications of this distinction for understanding the limits of the theories of immaterial labor for understanding the economic logic of con-temporary capitalism are perhaps best reflected in the debates over the role of so-called intellectual workers in the digital economy and, more specifically, the status of teachers in the knowledge factories of the global North. While there is no shortage of books detailing the ways in which institutions of higher education have increasingly taken on the corporate logics of global capitalism—from *The Knowledge Factory* by Stanley Aronowitz to *The Last Professors* by Frank Donoghue to *How the University Works* by Marc Bousquet, to name but a recent few—there remains an underlying assumption that the pressures on higher education are a reflection of a structural transformation in the very logic of capitalism away from productive labor towards the further incorporation of unproductive and immaterial labor under the control of capital. For example, in the introduction to their collection *Knowledge Workers in the Information Society*, Catherine McKercher and Vincent Mosco argue that while "the social relations of production, if increasingly organized around communication and information, remain distinctly capitalist" the "enormous and accelerating capacity to create communication and information networks challenges capitalism's capacity to manage and contain them"[200] and that "the meaning of knowledge labor is not measured simply by external criteria, but by how it is subjectivity experienced by the workers themselves."[201] In his essay, "Value production and struggle in the classroom: Teachers within, against, and beyond capital," David Harvie consolidates these assumptions in arguing that while "Marxists have long recognized that educators play a key role in the reproduction of capitalist relations of production in general, and of that special commodity, labour power, in particular,"[202] the new economic structures of digital capitalism, which are characterized by "the rise of *immaterial* or *affective* labour,"[203] mean that the labor theory of value as theorized by Marx is unable to "recognize the ways in which teachers' existing practices already rupture, and even go beyond or transcend, the capital relation."[204] Instead, what Harvie proposes is that under the emerging structures of digital capitalism, the division between productive and unproductive labor is not determined by its relation to the production of surplus value, but rather by whether or not labor struggles against the conditions of control imposed by corporate interests. This argument is premised upon a theory of labor power in which labor power is not defined, as Marx proposes, as the ability to do work but as "the willingness to do so under another's control, regardless of whether this control is direct or indirect, and whether it is exercised

by a private capital or by a social capital."²⁰⁵ In this way, despite his acknowledgment that it "may not even be possible" to prove the Marxist distinction
between productive and unproductive labor as it relates to the primary
status of the production of surplus value to capitalist economies to be
"somehow wrong or incorrect,"²⁰⁶ Harvie nonetheless argues that the limit
of the Marxist distinction between productive and unproductive labor is
that it focuses the discussion of value too much on "one of its common
forms of appearance, money"²⁰⁷ instead of realizing that the expansion of
capitalist economic conditions into every aspect of life means that value is
better understood as "lived experience" and, following the arguments of
Hardt and Negri, that capitalism is "a specific social form of imposing work,
rather than as simply a system geared towards profit-making."²⁰⁸ He states:

> In some labor powers, the ability to kill other human beings efficiently is a desir-
> able characteristic, while others call for tenderness and caring abilities. Although
> all of these characteristics have always existed in human beings, one cannot say
> that capital has simply appropriated certain of them without changing and devel-
> oping them.²⁰⁹

Drawing upon the work of Mariarosa Dalla Costa and Selma James (*The
Power of Women and the Subversion of the Community*) and Leopoldina Fortunati (*The Arcane of Reproduction*), who argue that Marx's theory of productive
labor excludes the social contribution of immaterial labor such as domestic
work, Harvie is proposing that it is the work training labor for the marketplace which incorporates teachers and other intellectual laborers into capitalism. In other words, by incorporating the issue of control into the
definition of labor power, Harvie is proposing that *labor power* is not an
essential or inherent quality, but is dependent upon the labor of teachers to
shape it into the socially appropriate form, thereby explaining its importance
to the production process.

Harvie goes even further and argues that to fully understand the importance of teachers, it is necessary to expand the concept of value. More specifically, he declares that what he calls "teaching labor" is "directly value-
producing" because value should be determined not by the productivity of
the worker, but rather by the extent to which the labor a worker does is
"abstract" and "alienated."²¹⁰ He writes, "Value is embodied labour that is
also abstract labour" and, if "abstract labour is the substance of value," then
"we can say that any labour in capitalist society that has a two-fold nature,

being a unity of abstract labor as well as concrete labour, is also productive labour."²¹¹ But, according to Harvie, what makes it productive is that it is both "abstract" *and* "alienated," or work that "appears to the worker as an external power, outside his or her direct control."²¹² Thus, insofar as teachers are forced to work increasingly generalized tasks under conditions that they don't define for themselves, he concludes that they become part of the capitalist structure.

At first glance, it might seem to some that in revising *value* as an effect of "abstract" and "alienated" labor, Harvie effectively expands the concept of the working class to account for new social formations by opening the concepts of labor and value. However, I argue that by erasing the distinction between productive and unproductive labor, he actually obscures the very framework of what defines capitalism as an economic system—namely, the exploitation of labor—and, in turn, presents a solution that extends, rather than challenges, the fundamental logic of capitalism. This becomes clear when he suggests that teachers operate "beyond capitalism" by being "unproductive as a result of the struggles of teachers themselves: against neoliberalism; to resist measure; to create alternative educational practices and relationships."²¹³ According to Harvie, being "unproductive" includes not only teacher strikes and student walkouts,²¹⁴ but also "individual and invisible" forms of struggle such as "teaching from a textbook" rather than developing dynamic lessons that take a lot of time and "refusing the labour of writing comprehensive and reliable student references."²¹⁵ In other words, "productive" and "unproductive" are entirely separated from the question of exploitation and instead become "more or less" measures of the extent to which one "struggles" against the control of capital over one's life.

But capitalism is not simply about control; it is based upon exploitation. Or, rather, the control that capitalism enacts is based upon what Marx described as the "dull compulsion of economic relations [which] completes the subjection of the labourer to the capitalist."²¹⁶ What gives the capitalist control is ownership over the means of production. In this sense, differentiating between productive and unproductive labor is central, I argue, because it gets to the core logic of the capitalist system and what is necessary to transform it; namely, ending the private accumulation of surplus value through the exploitation of labor. In other words, the distinction between productive or unproductive labor is not a matter of morality or lifestyle, nor does it define who is really a member of the working class, as the critics of

Marxism charge. It is about the basis of capitalism in the production and extraction of surplus value and the need to change this relation if capitalism is to be transformed. If we revise capitalism from an economic system to a system of control, we move away from ending exploitation and towards modes of resistance that ideologically extend the very logic of capitalism. When Harvie states that classes are defined by the extent to which they struggle against capitalism, it remains entirely unclear what they are struggling against and why. The problem is that by privileging independence from control as the measure of productivity, Harvie, Negri and other immaterial labor theorists essentially replicate the very ideology of capitalism which promises the worker freedom in their everyday life in exchange for the wage. Virtually all of the rhetoric surrounding the digital condition replicates this same version of freedom in the promise that new technologies will give the consumer more control than ever over what they watch, wear, eat, or drive. In fact, it is this very logic which is now being used by digital evangelists such as Mark C. Taylor to argue that tenure should be abolished because it offers "no leverage to encourage a professor to continue to develop professionally or to require him or her to assume responsibilities like administration and student advising" and instead universities should act *even more* like corporations by imposing mandatory retirement and seven-year contracts which "reward researchers, scholars and teachers who continue to evolve and remain productive while also making room for young people with new ideas and skills."[217] The more technology gives teachers freedom in the classroom, this argument goes, the more restrictive the institutional system of controls such as tenure become. Of course, corporate theorists like Taylor can openly call for the end of tenure because their endless defenses of the system mean that they need no protection from political retribution. However, for the numerous teachers, retail and service workers, domestic workers, and other forms of immaterial labor working under increasingly precarious and restrictive conditions without the kinds of backing that Taylor has, the issue is not gaining limited freedom from management. The fact that private schools are primarily concerned with turning a profit, while public universities are turning towards corporate logics as a way of coping with less and less financial resources because of regressive tax policies that favor the rich over the poor, does not reflect a change in the relation of productive and unproductive labor. Instead, these changes are a reflection of the fact that all aspects of life are being turned towards realizing as much of the surplus value expropriated during production into capitalists' profits as possible. As such, it is not new technologies or control over how one works that will change this. The solution is transforming the economic relations which create these conditions. What is necessary for real transformation, in short, is freedom for all from a system driven by the private accumulation of surplus value.

Returning, then, to the role of technology in relation to the production of surplus value, it is precisely the role of technology under capitalism as a means of increasing the rate of exploitation that is at the basis of Marx's analysis in "the fragment on machines" that Negri opportunistically uses as the source of the theory of immaterial labor. That is, contrary to the conclusions Negri presents, what Marx outlines in this passage is the way in which technological development *appears* to reduce the role of labor by ideologically representing the social division between capital and labor as an increasingly technological relation between labor and machines. In other words, how technological development, because of the division of labor at the point of production, ideologically appears to mediate the relation between labor and capital while actually expanding the commodification of daily life that the profit motive of capitalism requires.

Following the passage that is central to Negri's analysis—that through technological developments capitalism "works towards its own dissolution as the form dominating production"—Marx explains *why* technological development in itself cannot overturn the labor theory of value but rather comes to take on the appearance of a force independent of labor as a reflection of the role of the capitalist who owns it. He writes that as a result of the way in which capitalism must, in the interests of profit accumulation, develop technologies that shorten the portion of the working day paid in wages, "the transformation of the production process from the simple labour process into a scientific process, which subjugates the forces of nature and compels them to work in the service of human needs, *appears* [emphasis added] as a quality of *fixed capital* in contrast to living labor."[218] In other words, the appearance of technology as becoming the driving force of social relations in spite of labor, which, Marx writes, "ceased altogether to *appear* [emphasis added] as productive" and "posited as external to labour and as existing independently of it" is an ideological effect of the division of property between the capitalist and the worker.[219] Instead, as Marx explains:

Fixed capital, in its character as means of production, whose most adequate form [is] machinery, produces value, i.e. increases the value of the product, in only two respects: (1) in so far as it *has* value; i.e. is itself the product of labour, a certain quantity of labour in objectified form; (2) in so far as it increases the relation of surplus labour to necessary labour, by enabling labour, through an increase of its productive power, to create a greater mass of the products required for the maintenance of living labour capacity in a shorter time.[220]

In other words, technological developments produce value only in the sense that they are products of labor and therefore contain an amount of extracted surplus value, and that they are used to increase the productivity of labor within the working day, thereby indirectly contributing to the production of future surplus value. Machines do not produce value in themselves but only as instruments of human labor. As Marx explains, "Nature builds no machines, no locomotives, railways, electric telegraphs, self-acting mules etc. These are products of human industry; natural material transformed into organs of the human will over nature, or of human participation in nature. They are organs of the human brain, created by the human hand; the power of knowledge, objectified."[221] Technology, in short, is not an autonomous object body, but a product of labor and thus whose use is determined by the historical mode of production. As such, while Negri is correct in drawing from Marx that the contradiction between the forces and relations of production, in the words of Marx, "are the material conditions which threaten to blow [the limited] foundation [of capitalism] sky high,"[222] this transformation cannot occur from *within*, in the renegotiation of the terms of the market or through the independent development of technology, as the development of the forces of production is tied to the interests of profit. As Marx explains, "Capital employs machinery, rather, only to the extent that it enables the worker to work a larger part of his time for capital, to relate to a larger part of his time as time which does not belong to him, to work longer for another."[223] Rather than being judged on the priority of social necessity, technological advancements are judged on their ability to valorize capital. By denying the exploitation of labor as the source of the capitalists' wealth, network theory acts as a negative knowledge of capitalism by cleansing from globalization its historical and material relation to capitalism, thus blocking the production of a red theory of globalization necessary for organizing the collective struggles of the international working class.

Postcyberpunk and the Hip Ideology of Middle-Class Values

The growing popularity of the network theory of globalization can be seen in the way in which it is reflected not only in high theory, but also in popular cultural forms. That is to say, theoretical reflections of production ultimately find their way into the discourses of the everyday. By analyzing an exemplary cultural representation of the network theory of globalization—William Gibson's *Pattern Recognition*—I will show why, in contrast to the theoretical accounts of network culture as overcoming the capital-labor relation, network theory in actuality works at the level of ideology to secure the social contradictions of capitalism by representing a free-market agenda as a challenge to the corporate model of globalization.

Cyberpunk fiction emerged in the 1980s as a literary movement committed to combining the theoretical insights of postmodern theory with the technological developments that would lead to the digital economy of network capitalism. Initially organized around the figure of the alienated antihero lost in the new technological world, cyberpunk writers were linked by the assumption that the development of digital technologies were blurring social binaries between high and low art, reality and fiction, and production and consumption. In the introduction to *Mirrorshades*, the foundational collection of short stories which set the terms through which cyberpunk was to be read, Bruce Sterling writes, "Traditionally, there has been a yawning cultural gulf between the sciences and the humanities: a gulf between literary culture, the formal world of art and politics, and the culture of science, the world of engineering and industry. But the gap is crumbling in unexpected fashion."[224] Through the work of writers such as William Gibson, Bruce Sterling, and Neal Stephenson, cyberpunk quickly established the discursive framework through which the emerging digital society was to be read—introducing concepts such as the *matrix* and *cyberspace* into the popular lexicon—to the point that Frederic Jameson famously declared cyberpunk "the supreme literary expression if not of postmodernism, then of late capitalism itself."[225] Cyberpunk was thus situated as the manifestation of a "global point of view" and part of an era of "reassessment, of integration, of hybridizing influences, of old notions shaken loose and reinterpreted with a new sophistication, a broader perspective" that privileges "decentralization" and the in-between play of "interzones" over "hierarchy."[226]

What is particularly interesting in the relationship between the theories of globalization and immaterial labor is the current transition from cyberpunk to so-called *postcyberpunk*, a term first introduced by Lawrence Person in his 1998 essay "Notes Towards a Postcyberpunk Manifesto."[227] In this essay, Person argued that cyberpunk no longer reflected the developments of the new global economy. Instead of the alienated antihero who sought to "topple or exploit corrupt social orders," postcyberpunk was focused on the middle-class who "seek ways to live in, or even strengthen, an existing social order, or help construct a better one."[228] This view of the world is, according to Person, what enables postcyberpunk to "explore themes related to [a] world of accelerating technological innovation and ever-increasing complexity in ways relevant to our everyday lives" without losing the "sense of wonder that characterizes science fiction at its best."[229] What is particularly interesting here is not only the underlying narrative about radicalism being an adolescent interest that one gives up in order to grow up into adulthood, which is itself a kind of cliché of ideology. More significant is the way in which postcyberpunk reflects the managerial logic of network capitalism and, in turn, translates this narrative into a new discourse that can both address the growing inequalities of the economic system while simultaneously separating these inequalities from issues of exploitation and class.

In the United States, culture is largely geared towards the production of a middle-class reality. By *reality*, I do not mean the actual conditions in which people live. Rather, I am referring to the ways in which the economic conditions that shape people's lives are made to appear in popular culture as transhistorical, without reason, and thus natural, inevitable, and beyond social transformation. The image of the middle-class that one finds repeated endlessly in films, television shows, novels, and music until it becomes the sign of the "real" is premised on the idea that the middle-class represents a postcapitalist space in-between the class antagonisms of owners and workers. That is to say, the "in-betweenness" of the middle-class lifestyle—the ability of working families to afford (a few) commodities previously accessible only to the wealthy, from homes and cars to DVD players and iPods—is taken as proof that as technological advances increase the productivity of labor, "there is a lessening of class polarization and class contradictions."[230] The function of middle-class culture is, in other words, ideological. Its purpose is to make the exploitation of wage labor under capitalism appear to be a fair and free exchange. In this sense, the ideology of the middle-class represents the consumerist framework of the so-called American way of life—democracy as shopping.

Globalization, technology, and consumption are at the center of William Gibson's postcyberpunk novel *Pattern Recognition*. Described by *The Economist* as "the best exploration yet of the function and power of product branding and advertising in the age of globalization and the Internet,"[231] *Pattern Recognition* has become in a short period of time a canonic cultural reading of the cultural changes occurring as a result of globalization. The novel tells the story of a knowledge worker who has become disillusioned with corporate brand culture. What has made Gibson's novel so appealing, I argue, is the way in which it is able to translate the complex economic theories of writers such as Peter Drucker, Daniel Bell, Antonio Negri, and Manuel Castells into a more popular discourse and to establish this discourse as the correct representation of the real by filtering it through a postpolitical, postideological, postcyber reading of the contemporary, giving the conditions of exploitation a "postcool" digital edge.

Immanently speaking, the novel, set in the contemporary moment, represents a slight shift in Gibson's work. One of the founders of cyberpunk fiction,Gibson, instead, turns in this novel to the present. *Pattern Recognition* is an attempt to find meaning in the heightening contradictions of globalization in the period immediately following September 11, an event described in the novel as "an experience outside culture."[232] The central character in the novel is Cayce Pollard, a freelance "coolhunter" whose job is to travel the world in search of emerging cultural trends before they reach the mainstream for advertising agencies that use these trends for developing new ad campaigns. At first glance, it would seem that as a knowledge worker who has reaped all of the benefits of the supposedly postindustrial world of immaterial labor, Cayce represents precisely what both left and right theorists of globalization such as Thomas L. Friedman (*The World Is Flat*) and Antonio Negri and Michael Hardt (*Multitude*) celebrate as the cultural engine of the new global economy. That is to say, her job in reading and interpreting the quickly changing cultural landscape of globalization—part of the "pattern recognition" of the title—means that she not only works within the up-to-the-minute reality of network capitalism, but serves as one of the primary cultural architects who enable corporations to "pivot into the new century."[233]

However, as the novel opens and Cayce arrives at her music video directing friend's stylish apartment in Camden Town, the market district of London, where she has taken a job with a "post-geographic" corporation called Blue Ant to review a new sneaker logo, we get a very different reading than that of a group of cyberhipsters working at the boundaries of culture. Unlike early cyberglobalization novels such as Douglas Coupland's *Microserfs*, *Pattern Recognition* does not celebrate technology and consumer society. The protagonist, Cayce, is described as feeling trapped in globalization's "dire and ever-circling wolves of disrupted circadian rhythm" and, despite staying in an apartment full of the very kind of consumer goods she helps advertisers to market more effectively, Cayce finds that this commodity-filled apartment is unable to meet her "reptilian demands for sex, food, sedation."[234] That is to say, although the apartment appears to be filled with the kind of commodities that are supposed to represent the full freedom of choice available to Western consumers—a "German fridge," an "Italian floor lamp" and "electric kettle," and an "imported Californian Tea Substitute"—they are said to be "as devoid of edible content as [their] designers' display windows in Camden High Street."[235] Rather than representations of the exciting life of the new global elite, the accoutrements of consumer society she is surrounded by are described as "very clean and almost entirely empty,"[236] unable to fulfill the promises of maintaining the comfortable life through consumption that has come to be associated with the middle-class lifestyle. Furthermore, in what is described as "an experience outside culture,"[237] we later learn that Cayce's father disappeared on September 11— having been there "for no known reason"[238] and is presumed killed in the attack on the World Trade Center. Thus, at the time of her arrival in London,

> her mortal soul is leagues behind her, being reeled in on some ghostly umbilical down the vanished wake of the plane that brought her here, hundreds of thousands of feet above the Atlantic. Souls can't move that quickly, and are left behind, and must be awaited, upon arrival, like lost luggage.[239]

By opening the novel with the sense of unease and cultural dislocation that marks Cayce's relationship to the images of a consumer society that have seem to have lost all meaning after 9/11, Gibson establishes that she is a character who is out of step with the commodified culture of globalization.

The contrast between the apartment which is *full* of all of the signs of consumer society and the spiritual *emptiness* these signs are now said to represent is symptomatic of a reading of the contemporary in which the images of the middle-class as a leisurely life of consumption no longer seem to correspond to the actual conditions of economic insecurity and political alienation that most readers are now facing.

The irony of the opening is that despite the fact that her job depends upon her ability to read the new cultural trends, what differentiates Cayce from other coolhunters, and what has made her one of the most successful, is precisely her inability to read the changing signs. Although she describes her job as trying to "recognize a pattern before anyone else does,"[240] she has succeeded as a coolhunter not by reading the codes but, instead, by harnessing a kind of subliminal counter-response to brand names, described in the novel as "a morbid and sometimes violent reactivity to the semiotics of the marketplace."[241] Gibson writes,

> She is, literally, allergic to fashion. She can only tolerate things that could have been worn, to a general lack of comment, during any year between 1945 and 2000. She's a design-free zone, a one-woman school of anti whose very austerity periodically threatens to spawn its own cult.[242]

In one scene, Cayce has an allergy attack after being confronted by a Tommy Hilfiger display while walking through the menswear department at Harvey Nichols, forcing her to face the possibility that globalization means an increasingly virtual world in which the soul is obscured under levels of simulacra. She states,

> My God, don't they know? This stuff is simulacra of simulacra of simulacra. A diluted tincture of Ralph Lauren, who had himself diluted the glory days of Brooks Brothers, who themselves had stepped on the product of Jermyn Street and Savile Row, flavoring their ready-to-wear with liberal lashings of polo kit and regimented stripes. But Tommy surely is the null point, the black hole. There must be some Tommy Hilfiger event horizon, beyond which it is impossible to be more derivative, more removed from the source, more devoid of soul.[243]

Although Cayce's outrage that others cannot see that contemporary culture is nothing but a diluted version of what has come before is meant to mark her as different from the existing overly commodified culture, it is significant that this outrage does not mean much more than taking an ethical approach to shopping. That is to say, even though she is described as an "anti-consumer" who literally vomits at the sight of certain logos,[244] Cayce's primary complaint about contemporary culture is that it is derivative. It is such that she does not so much as turn away from consumer society, but rather retreats into what is represented as its more *authentic* past. Her difference, in other words, is really not that different. It is simply a change in terms. In her desire to avoid one commodified reality, she chooses another, less familiar (because it is out-dated) form of commodified reality. In fact, she is not even allergic to all of contemporary culture. For example, upon her arrival in Japan, she "remembers" that "the way certain labels" such as Gucci and Burberry "are mysteriously recontextualized" in Japanese culture means they "have no effect on her"[245] because of what she describes as the "Japanese way" of production that makes "an imitation more real somehow than that which it emulates."[246] Furthermore, in a flashback to a day spent in the former East Germany, communism is described as "manifestly cruel," "nasty," and "petty," because, she "protests," it was not as aesthetically pleasing as the cultural bounty available in the West.[247] It is through such examples that the reader begins to learn that it is not consumption that is actually the problem, but the choices you make as a consumer. It is, in a variation on Ritzer's *Globalization of Nothing*, a question of cultural values. The binary that Gibson establishes with Cayce's decidedly modest outrage—you are a good consumer if you purchase outdated or hard-to-find fashions and a bad one if you don't—assumes that it is consumption and not class that defines your position in society. What is presented as antifashion and a means of resisting consumer society actually reproduces the ideology of consumer society with a vengeance.

Cayce's retreat from the hyper-market of globalization into an older market semiotics leads her to what is represented as the "other" of the derivative consumer culture: a series of video and still-image fragments that are being mysteriously posted on various websites and internet newsgroups without any indication of who is producing it, whether the scenes are old or new, or why. Known as "the footage," what makes these images so appealing to Cayce is that unlike contemporary culture, which is represented as semiotically *empty*, the footage is semiotically *neutral* in that it appears to lack any context. In one fragment, for example, the lack of visual cues mean that it is impossible to know whether the actor is "stepping onto a submarine in 1914" or is "a jazz musician entering a club in 1957."[248] Because the footage seems to resist any singular interpretation, Cayce finds it to be completely "masterful."[249]

Neutrality, however, is an ideological fiction. It erases the fact that the meaning of any sign is determined historically, by the level of development of production. By proposing that meaning is produced through the individual act of reading—reading as consumption—the image of neutrality maintains the idea of culture as an in-between space of personal desires that corresponds to the ideology of a middle-class lifestyle. On the surface, in other words, whereas the emptiness of the commodity form is attributed to the reduction of all interpretations to the same one meaning through corporate advertising, the neutrality of the footage appears more open and democratic because it allows anyone to read (consume) it however they want. In this way, interpretation becomes a metaphor for the free market and the idea that consumption, rather than production, determines meaning. It is for this reason that Cayce, an anticonsumer who is really a more sophisticated consumer in disguise, becomes so obsessed with the footage. It allows her the appearance of momentarily escaping the contradictions of consumer society into an alternative community that is like going to "a familiar café that exists somehow outside of geography and beyond time zones."[250] *Pattern Recognition* has become so popular because it makes the world appear strange, but never different, and thus maintains the illusion that reading, like consumption, is a personal act of meaning-making without any reliable connection to reality.

Because the footage appears to Cayce to be irreducible to any one reading, it comes to represent a new form of consumption with *values* and it is on these terms that she accepts the offer by Hubertus Bigend, the owner of the "post-global" advertising firm Blue Ant, to finance her search for the maker of the footage. It is telling that during the search for the producer—a search that takes her across the historical terrain of capitalism: from England to Japan to Russia—Cayce also begins to confront the reasons for her allergies as well as possible solutions. That is to say, as she gets closer to discovering the creator of the fragments, she begins to realize that she "is, and has long been, complicit . . . in whatever it is that gradually makes London and New York feel like each other, that dissolves the membranes between mirror-worlds."[251] However, this feeling of complicity is short lived—it is immediately dismissed as "a mood"—and thereafter Cayce begins to meditate on the meaning of life. While commodities can be easily replaced, lives, she concludes, cannot: "However odd things seem, mustn't it be to exactly that extent of oddness that a life is one's own, and no one else's?"[252] As Cayce has been firmly established in the narrative as the anti-consumer, the reader is thus led to believe that despite whatever Bigend's intentions are Cayce's desires are pure. As opposed to corporate figures such as Bigend who seek to define the commodity for the consumer, she refuses to impose any reading and thus embraces everyone's individual desires as they are. Her acknowledgment of complicity in that which makes her ill is simply intended to mark her as a realist and thus, in spite of her illness, a trustworthy reader of the contemporary. In an ideological twist, then, Cayce's search for the creator of the footage offers readers the illusion that (even more) consumption is the only means of restoring lost values to a world that previously had been criticized as having been emptied of value by (too much) consumption. In other words, although Cayce is represented as a defender of the "old" values, the dismissal of her momentary questioning of her role in expanding capitalism—the real effect of a politics of consumption—as a "mood" is the effective elimination of any alternative to capitalism. There is no revolution, in short, simply a new way of reading the same. In this, *Pattern Recognition* turns consumption into an act of resistance and makes anyone who thinks that a more fundamental social change than changing one's shopping habits is necessary to transform an unequal and unjust economic system appear to be too out of touch with the new reality.

The novel concludes with the discovery that the producer of the footage is a young woman, Nora, who is a former filmmaker who has lost all ability to communicate as the result of being injured during a mafia bombing in Moscow. Cayce learns that the footage is taken from the closed circuit cameras in the hospital where the woman stayed while recuperating and that it is rendered for Internet distribution by the inmates of a prison established and run by her oligarch uncle, described as "the richest man in Russia." What makes the footage so special is that it has been Nora's only form of communication since a small piece of a claymore mine originally produced in America became embedded in her skull. Gibson writes,

> this one specific piece of ordinance, adrift perhaps since the days of the Soviet's failed war with the new enemies, had found its way into the hands of Nora's

uncle's enemies, and this one small part, only slightly damaged by the explosion of the ruthlessly simple device, had been flung into the very center of Nora's brain. And from it, and from her other wounds, there now emerged, accompanied by the patient and the regular clicking of her mouse, the footage.[253]

In the end, Cayce learns that the footage is being used by Nora's uncle and Hubertus Bigend to develop an information distribution network, created in part by the role Cayce has played in testing its security as she tracked down the maker of the footage. What is significant about this is that despite the fact that she has directly contributed to the opening of post–Soviet Russia to the global market, something which might have previously contributed to her anxiety because it ultimately means the further "branding" of local and spontaneous forms of culture, Cayce nonetheless loses her allergies and regains her "soul."[254]

Cayce regains her soul because she recognizes in Nora's silence the possibility of a playful space in-between the daily routine of the working class and the cultural homogeny of corporate globalization. Like Cayce, Nora does not create anything new, but rather works within the existing to repackage the everyday in unfamiliar ways. However, whereas Cayce's resistance was ultimately limiting because it could only ever be a nostalgic return to the past, Nora's silence—essentially a more severe form of Cayce's allergy that places her entirely outside of the semiotics of the marketplace—is meant to be taken by the reader as the purest form of meaning-making because its meaning is entirely *personal*. The footage is thus intended to represent a more ethical form of capitalism for the twenty-first century in which the meaning of a commodity is not imposed unilaterally through corporate advertising but rather created individually by each consumer to fulfill his or her personal desires. Cayce's easy reconciliation with the system that previously had made her violently ill reflects the fact that what the novel is proposing does not actually challenge the underlying logic of capitalism—the exploitation of labor by capital. Instead, it teaches the middle-class reader that the problem is not capitalism but advertising and thus that all we need to do to resist corporate globalization is to adopt a more individual approach to consumption. That is, what matters are not the things we own, but the values we have. By arguing that you can change the world through shopping, *Pattern Recognition* is a lesson in finding moments of resistance within the logic of the market.

According to Jameson in a recent speculative meditation on the text, "Fear and Loathing in Globalization," Gibson's narrative of the footage is written in the terms of Bloch's "conception of the novel of the artist,"[255] which "projects the Utopian anticipation of a new art premised on 'semiotic neutrality,' and on the systematic effacement of names, dates, fashions and history itself, within a context irremediably corrupted by all those things."[256] He argues, "the footage is an epoch of rest, an escape from the noisy commodities themselves, which turn out, as Marx always thought they would, to be living entities preying the humans who have to coexist with them."[257] However, while Jameson concludes that "Unlike the footage, however, Gibson's novel gives us homeopathy rather than antidote,"[258] I argue that it is precisely in the idea of a "homeopathic" treatment—finding resistance only from within the very logic of exploitation—that *Pattern Recognition* presents globalization as inescapable except through momentary eruptions of subcultural agency. In other words, it is a lesson in recognizing the ways in which the "soul"—a code for a reading of value as not determined within the working day, but rather in the affective work of immaterial labor—can exceed but never fully escape the logic of the market. It is based upon the assumption that capitalism has formed an encompassing global network in which the only possible means of resisting are from within through cultural reappropriation. As such, it becomes clear that for Gibson, the significance of the footage is that it ultimately cannot be commodified—it cannot become a source of surplus value except through the secondary networks created to distribute it— because it is entirely affective. It is created, we are told, only for the appreciation of the artist, regardless of whether there is an audience. Cayce's cynical romanticism in searching for the "maker" thus becomes the nostalgic search for a capitalist market that is not monopolized, but remains open and free. In this sense, the fact that she cannot help but extend the capitalist network, despite her best intentions, is a reflection of the fact that what is being proposed does not actually challenge the underlying logic of capitalism—namely, the exploitation of labor—but rather seeks to find new, ethical ways of resisting the more oligarchic aspects of monopoly capitalism by locating, as Castells and Hardt and Negri advocate, the spaces from which information always leaks in unexpected ways from the network.

The End of the Network

What has ultimately made the theory of networks so popular, I argue, such that the concept of the *network society* is embraced by a politically diverse range of globalization theorists from Thomas L. Friedman to Manuel Castells to Michael Hardt and Antonio Negri—and thus reaches the level of ideological obviousness that places it beyond the common sense differences that traditionally define the boundaries of left and right—is precisely because by substituting the form of the organization of capitalist production for its underlying logic, network theory works to *make natural* highly unnatural conditions and thus keeps in motion what Marx calls the social metabolism of capitalism—the extraction of surplus value from the labor of the working class.

The dominance of the technological in contemporary social theory is an index, then, of the reality that advances in the means of production have made the class struggle over whether developments in the forces of production will be used for the production of profit or for meeting the needs of all an issue impossible to ignore. That is to say—as the massive layoffs of the workers in the dot-com sector following the 1990s tech boom in the United States have demonstrated—it is through the development of the forces of production that the laborer comes face to face with the objective fact that their means of survival rests solely on their ability to sell their labor power. As the editors of *The State of Working America 2008/2009* indicate, the end of the dot-com boom meant not only recession, but a future in which increased productivity heightened the competition between workers and thus a lever for the capitalists to further restrict or drive down the growth of wages. They write:

> The recession of 2001 was followed by nearly two years of continued job loss, and it took an unprecedented *four years* to re-attain the number of jobs the economy supported prior to the recession . . . The resulting lower rates of employment and consequent lack of upward pressure on wages translated into lost output and foregone increases in living standards. Poor job growth is one of the important factors underlying the ongoing divergence of overall economic growth and the wages and income of working families.[259]

And, we see the same pattern repeated in acknowledgments that the latest economic recession will mean extended stagnation in the job market for several years after the recession is supposedly to have come to an end.[260] In other words, while the development of industry lowers the socially necessary labor time, enabling more commodities to be produced, and creates the potential for meeting the needs of all, under the capitalist system the impetus of new machinery contradicts this possibility and, in the words of Marx, "dispels all fixity and security in the situation of the laborer . . . constantly threatens, by taking away the instruments of labor, to snatch from his hands his means of subsistence . . . and in the devastation caused by a social anarchy . . . turns every economic progress into a social calamity."[261]

Contrary to the objective contradictions of capitalist relations, the dominant readings of network society in both popular media as well as cutting edge theory represent the process of increasing productivity through the intensification of the production process—in which capitalists accumulate tremendous profits while workers are subjected either to increased domination by machinery or to the poverty of the industrial reserve army—as the transformation from a system based upon the exploitation of labor to a network of social relations in which work has been "liberated" through the introduction of technology: a postcapitalist, postproduction era of endless "free time." By locating the solution of capitalist exploitation in consumption, network theory naturalizes the exploitation of wage labor that occurs in the production of the commodity, privileging distribution and individual consumption practices as the focus of analysis. Marxism, on the contrary, by locating the fundamental basis of society in production, thus makes clear that issues of distribution cannot be solved solely through the redistribution of commodities because the cause of the initial inequality has not gone away. Without transforming the system that produces inequality, no amount of redistribution of social wealth will prevent inequality from returning.

In this context, I argue that it is necessary to return to Marx's theorization of the labor theory of value and Lenin's theory of imperialism in order to understand globalization because it explains why capitalism does not reach its limit either in the contraction of a noncapitalist outside with which to trade—which is the presupposition of the network as the elimination of geographic and economic boundaries—nor in terms of a cultural remaking of the politics of oppression from within the logic of capital. More importantly, it explains why the working class remains the agent of social transformation—the capitalist system depends on the exploitation of their labor and this exploitation cannot be eliminated through technological development. The limit of capitalism is that it is a system based upon a fundamental and unequal relation to property in which some own and control the means of production and others own nothing but their labor power, and, as Marx and Engels write, capital "cannot increase except upon condition of begetting a new supply of wage-labour for fresh exploitation."²⁶² Thus it is in the interests of ensuring higher rates of accumulation that capitalism becomes a universal system, driven to conquer every corner of the globe.

As Lenin argues, "The export of capital greatly affects and accelerates the development of capitalism in those countries to which it is exported" and thus "while, therefore, the export of capital may tend to a certain extent to arrest development in the countries exporting capital," as evident for example in the crisis of public education, health care, housing and the environment in the United States, "it can only do so by expanding and deepening the further development of capitalism throughout the world."²⁶³ In other words, to propose that the technological developments that have enabled the network expansion of capitalism across the globe will, by themselves, eliminate the exploitative relations between owners and workers without having to change the underlying property relations which define capitalism is not simply historically naïve or politically foolish, it is an ideological defense of global capitalism that works in the interests of the status quo. Imperialism, in other words, represents "that stage of development in which the domination of monopolies and finance capital has established itself; in which the export of capital has acquired pronounced importance; in which the division of the world among the international trusts has begun; in which the partition of all the territories of the globe among the great capitalist powers has been completed."²⁶⁴ It is the attempt by capital to overcome the contradictions that result from increasing costs of production and decreasing rates of profit at home by finding underdeveloped sectors abroad, regardless of whether this occurs through political annexation or by the financial indebtedness of the policies enforced by the World Bank and the IMF. It is in the context of finding new avenues of productivity that network theories of globalization provide the theoretical resources for expanding the use of technology to further the relations of exploitation. What is presented as *decentralization* and *individualization* of the market—what Castells and Hardt and Negri promote as the ability of cultural formations to act as a space of resistance to the oligopolistic mechanisms of the market—does not actually represent a challenge to the underlying logic of the market—the "freedom" of the wage laborers to sell their labor power for a wage—merely the terms upon which this exchange occurs. As such, because Castells and Hardt and Negri draw the conclusion that there is no outside to capitalism and that property relations can be "blurred" through the redistribution of resources, rather than undermine market relations, such images reflect what Lenin calls the small producer's "dream of taking a step backward, of a return to 'free,' 'peaceful,' and 'honest' competition."[265]

What is particularly telling about the ideological aspects of this theory is how a number of critics on the left critique Hardt and Negri for not going far enough in eliminating the concepts of class and imperialism from radical discourse. John Holloway, for example, writes that "there is a tendency to treat capital as an economic category, reproducing in this . . . the assumptions of the Marxist orthodoxy which they so rightly attack."[266] In turn, the primary problem, according to Holloway is drawing class boundaries too finely, when what is necessary is recognizing that "class struggle is a conflict that permeates the whole of human existence," that "we do not 'belong' to one class or another,'" that the class divide is an antagonism that "exists in all of us, tearing us apart."[267] Similarly, Mark Poster writes that "Hardt and Negri, beholden to a Marxist opposition of labor power and information technologies, attempt to attribute to labor the qualities at play in new communication systems"[268] and that, "a critical theory of globalization . . . must look not for a revolutionary subject but for a matrix of dispositifs."[269] However, the failure of Hardt and Negri is not that they still believe in class, but, as Paul Thompson writes, that class becomes "power" in Hardt and Negri's autonomous theory of labor and, as such, independent of the economic mechanisms of capitalism. Thompson argues, "at one stage we are told that the biopolitical sphere is like a great hive in which 'the queen bee continuously oversees production and reproduction.' As to who the queen is and how she does it, we are none the wiser."[270] In this respect, what becomes clear is the relationship between Hardt and Nergi's theory of empire and the managerial theory that emerges in the 1970s and 1980s to develop new ways of organizing production to maximize the extraction of surplus value from labor, not to eliminate it. As Thompson argues,

> what is striking is the similarity between Hardt and Negri's arguments and those of hyperglobalizers such as Ohmae (1990), who speak of boundaryless worlds.

Despite the different language and gloss, both reify the market and posit a new world order in which there are no intermediary institutions, no public space or politics outside the power of the market.[271]

The problem is that even many on the left who are critical of the limits of Hardt and Negri's rejection of the Marxist theory of imperialism often accept the premise that if we are to talk about imperialism today it means moving beyond, or at least revising, the labor theory of value. The limits of contemporary "radical" left thinking on imperialism are perhaps most evident in David Harvey's recent critique of Hardt and Negri's conclusion to their "Empire" trilogy, *Commonwealth*. In a recent exchange in *Artforum*, Harvey advances a useful immanent critique of Hardt and Negri's declarations that "overthrowing capitalist rule is not, in our view, the only mode of revolutionary activity" and "there is a relative autonomy to the different axes of domination and exploitation."[272] such that there is little value anymore in class analysis. As he points out, their turn towards Spinoza and his belief in "*experientia sive praxis*, the principle of a truth formed by the activism of subjects who want to live a common life"[273] provides an idealist solution to the material contradictions of capitalism. Harvey writes, "it is precisely because Spinoza did not have to be concerned with such mundane things [as the economic contradictions of global capitalism] that his formulations are so attractive [to them]."[274] He further goes on to argue that their defense of the "love" of the "multitude" against the "evil" of the "Empire" essentially echoes the empty rhetoric of Dick Cheney's declaration that "we don't negotiate with evil, we defeat it."[275]

Hardt and Negri, for their part, offer an extremely weak response in which they attempt to push Harvey to their side against other critiques of their revisionist approach to Marx. They write, "Marxists are renowned for reserving their severest criticism for other Marxists, often proving their points by twisting their opponents' arguments or triumphantly pulling out as trump cards technical terms that those uninitiated in the arcane of Marxology find baffling" and thank Harvey for his "attentive reading" and "praise."[276] Of course, it is precisely by representing the core theorizations of Marxism as arcane technical terms in favor of theoretically empty but "feel-good" concepts that has made Hardt and Negri's theory of empire so influential among business pundits and cultural theorists alike. If Spinoza's theorizations of nature are less arcane than Marx's theorization of the labor theory of value, it is only because what Spinoza calls "substance" is the idealist logic of a reality that cannot ever be "totalized" or fully "determined" that one finds written throughout almost all of cultural theory today. At the time of his writings, Spinoza's critique of Cartesian idealism and in favor of materialism represents a radical intervention and reflects the developments in labor through which the world was being transformed. However, to return to Spinoza's theory of substance today as a revolutionary theory of the contemporary, as Hardt and Negri do, reflects the limited logic of capitalism, which represents wage labor as a fair exchange and, through the process of commodity fetishism that separates production and consumption, turns the materiality of labor into the matterism of "things." This is what governs their arguments about control over the commons having replaced exploitation as the driving engine of capitalism—by isolating consumption from production and thus transforming reality into substance, they accept the historical conditions of production as given and only open a space for debating how it should be distributed. This is the value of a Spinozan critique of capitalism—it displaces labor as a revolutionary force and, instead, attempts to make sense of reality as existing independent of labor, thus bracketing the conditions of production from transformation.

At the same time, even though Harvey argues for the primacy of class in understanding the contradictions of capitalism and that "no matter how important race, gender, and sexual identity may have been in the history of capitalism's development, and no matter how important the struggles waged in their name, it is possible to envisage the perpetuation of capitalism without them—something that is impossible in the case of class,"[277] he nonetheless accepts Hardt and Negri's thesis that something has changed within capitalism such that the concept of value has to be redefined to include the immaterial and nonmarket aspects of life and, ultimately, that class, too, has to be understood in broader terms of power and control. He writes, "What is certainly true, however, is that, as the market for things becomes saturated, capitalism switches to immaterial forms of production . . . Hence the turn to the commodification of affects, spectacle, information, images, experiential moments, and the like."[278] In addition, he also indicates that he "can easily agree" with their argument that "value is created when resistance becomes overflowing, creative, and boundless and thus when human activity exceeds and determines a rupture in the balance of power."[279] Like Hardt and Negri, Harvey redefines exploitation to include not only the extraction of surplus value, but the control and command of what he calls the "urban commons" or "the social world of the city" which is created through people's "daily activities."[280]

At the core of Harvey's thesis is the proposal, which he expressed in the 2006 introduction to the recent reprint of his central theoretical work *The Limits to Capital*, that Marx's theory of "the falling rate of profit" doesn't fully account for the "deeper problem" that explains capitalism's inherent drive towards crisis, what he calls "the tendency towards overaccumulation." According to Harvey, overaccumulation represents "the ever increasing quantities of surplus value that capitalists produce" which "cannot profitably be absorbed" and, as he makes clear, that when he uses the term "profitably" that it "has nothing directly to do with the supposed law of falling profits."[281] More specifically, in *The Limits to Capital*, Harvey advances a theory of the economic contradictions of capitalism in which he states that there are what he describes as three "cuts" in the capitalist process—the drive to decrease socially necessary labor time through technological advances that creates the conditions of the falling rate of profit as the "first cut,"[282] the financial and monetary affairs involved in the "realization *and* consumption *and* distribution" of capital after production as the "second cut,"[283] and the contradictions which emerge within the geopolitical organization of space as the "third cut,"[284]—an argument that is key to understanding his influential readings of the broad economic transition in the twentieth century from "Fordism" to "flexible accumulation" (*The Condition of Postmodernity*) as well as his more recent analyses of the economic and cultural contradictions of globalization (*The New Imperialism*). What Harvey is ultimately suggesting, in other words, is that the extraction of surplus value at the point of production is only one of three avenues through which capitalists accumulate value. He writes, "The concept of value as embodied labour time is not be construed . . . as a fixed and immutable building block on which an analysis of the contradictions of capitalism can be founded, but as a concept that undergoes perpetual modification in its meaning the more we grasp what the socially necessary characteristics of capitalism are."[285] By rhetorically shifting the discussion of surplus value in this passage from "socially necessary labor time" to "socially necessary characteristics of capitalism," Harvey here turns the discussion of capitalism away from the exploitation of labor and towards a theory of accumulation as a multifaceted process that includes other forms of accumulation besides exploitation. In this sense, although he agrees with Marx that exploitation is central to the capitalist economy, he ultimately expands the concept of accumulation to include "rent" and "interest" as equivalent forms of generating surplus value. For example, he argues that "far from the 'euthenasia of the rentier' that Keynes envisaged, class power is increasingly articulated through rental payments" and "the emergence of a global property market and urbanization as an expanding conduit for capital accumulation has allowed certain dynamic centres of capitalism, such as Hong Kong, to survive on the basis of property development and rent extractions . . . as anything else."[286]

It is on this basis that Harvey claims to make his most important contribution to Marxist theory, what he calls the "spatial fix." Arguing that "the role of imperialism and colonialism, of geographical expansion and territorial domination, in the overall stabilization of capitalism is unresolved," Harvey proposes:

> The central point I have sought to hammer home . . . is that the production of spatial configurations is necessarily an active constitutive moment in the dynamics of accumulation. The shape of spatial configurations and the means for the annihilation of space with time are as important for understanding these dynamics as are improved methods of co-operation, the more extended use of machinery, etc. All of these features have to be assimilated within a broad conception of technological and organizational change. Since the latter is the pivot upon which accumulation turns as well as the nexus from which the contradictions of capitalism flow, then it follows that spatial and temporal expressions of this contradictory dynamic are of equal import.[287]

In other words, equivalent to the mechanisms upon which capitalism extracts surplus value from labor are the physical, geographical spaces in which this extraction takes place. Harvey's articulation of the "spatial fix" advances a theory of imperialism that draws more upon Luxemburg's *The Accumulation of Capital* and Arendt's *Imperialism* than Lenin's foundational work. According to Luxemburg, "Accumulation is . . . primarily a relationship between capital and a non-capitalist environment"[288] in that it is through the appropriation of resources and markets of a "non-capitalist" periphery that the capitalist "center" is able to overcome what she argues is the primary crisis of capitalism, namely a crisis of "underconsumption." She proposes that in this way, "imperialism is the political expression of the accumulation of capital in its competitive struggle for what remains still open of the non-capitalist environment" and that "the more violently, ruthlessly and thoroughly imperialism brings about the decline of non-capitalist civilizations, the more rapidly it cuts the very ground from under the feet of capitalist accumulation."[289] That is, the ultimate crisis of capitalism emerges when there are no longer any "non-capitalist" areas of the world for capitalists to exploit through colonial and other means for the direct appropriation of resources. Similarly, Arendt argues that what initiated the era of imperialism was an awareness on the part of the bourgeoisie that "the original sin of simply robbery, which centuries ago had made possible the 'original accumulation of capital' (Marx) and had started all further accumulation, had eventually to be repeated lest the motor of accumulation suddenly die down."[290] Although Harvey challenges Luxemburg's theory of "underconsumption" as the reasoning for capitalism's outward expansion,[291] he nonetheless accepts the premise of both Luxemburg and Arendt that Marx's theory of the primacy of accumulation through the extraction of surplus value effectively relegated "accumulation based upon predation, fraud, and violence to an 'original stage' that is no longer considered relevant" and that, instead, "a general re-evaluation of the continuous role and persistence of the predatory practices of 'primitive' or 'original' accumulation within the long historical geography of capitalist accumulation is . . . very much in order."[292] Harvey calls this process "accumulation by dispossession" and argues that it includes a range of alternative forms of capital accumulation from "the commodification and privatization of land and the forceful expulsion of peasant populations" and "the suppression of the right to the commons" to "usury, the national debt, and ultimately the credit system as radical means of primitive accumulation."[293]

Marx, however, is clear as to why these forms of accumulation are secondary to what Harvey reduces to the "first cut" of three. In the third volume of *Capital*, he writes that one of the limits of classical economy is that "it has never even considered profit in its pure form as distinct from its different, self-established components, such as industrial profit, commercial profit, interest, and ground rent."[294] In theorizing the tendency of the rate of profit to fall, Marx argues instead that "we intentionally present this law before going on to the division of profit into different self-established categories" because "the profit to which we are here referring is but another name for surplus value itself" and thus that "the drop in the rate of profit, therefore, expresses the failing relation of surplus value to advanced total capital, and is for this reason independent of any division whatsoever of this surplus value among the various categories."[295] In other words, it is not, as Harvey claims, that Marx was too caught up in classical economics and thus failed to consider the implications of these other forms of accumulation. Rather, Marx focuses on the production of surplus value at the point of production because he is arguing that it is the central mechanism by which capitalism produces new value to accumulate. In turn, it is the exploitation of labor that thus comes to define the limits and possibilities of all of these other modes of accumulation, which become dependent upon the surplus value produced in production as the basis of their share of profits.

The consequence of this difference becomes clear when we turn to the question of social transformation. Insofar as Harvey, like Hardt and Negri, extends the theory of value to include forms of accumulation as equal to the exploitation of labor, he proposes that "struggles against dispossession (of land rights, of welfare, pension and healthcare rights, of environmental qualities, of life itself) are of a different character to struggles around the labour process that have long dominated Marxist politics"[296] and that "the class relation between capital and labor . . . is merely a starting point from which to analyze the production of far more complicated class configurations unique to capitalism."[297] In other words, despite his hesitancy to embrace Hardt and Negri's theory of the multitude by "expanding" the concept of value as operating beyond production,[298] we move away from an economic analysis of class towards a theory of new social formations that, I argue, actually fractures the basis of unity rather than generate new forms of solidarity. As Lenin explains, capitalism in its monopoly stage represents the expansion of capitalist relations not only across the globe but "into every sphere of public life, regardless of the form of government and all other 'details.'"[299] The commodification of even the most basic social resources such as water, food, healthcare, education, and shelter that mark the economic reality of globalization has brought about a growing crisis that spans across all social levels, making clear that the growing contradictions of capitalism are indicative of the inequalities that, as Marx and Engels argued over one hundred fifty years ago, systematically arise and place the entire capitalist system on trial. The declining social net of education, health care and housing, the spread of diseases such as AIDS and tuberculosis, the constant daily threat of starvation of almost one billion people, the potentially irrevocable damage to the environment, and a growing permanent population of un- and under-employed people are the social background against which a new series of inter-imperialist wars to re-divide the boundaries of control over the global labor market are now being launched. What unites the working class is not a fractured framework of multiple identities, but rather the fact that every aspect of life is being subsumed to the profit motive. As Lenin's theory of imperialism makes clear, the problem with the fuzzy concepts of a postimperial, postcapitalist, postclass network capitalism is that while globalization is pronounced as a new stage of capitalist development, the ongoing failure of capitalism to address the material needs of the majority of the world's population has not only become increasingly difficult to ignore but, more importantly, is impossible to solve without bringing about the transformation of a society based upon private accumulation of surplus value to one founded upon meeting the needs of all.

THREE

Reading and Writing in the Digital Age

One of the main arguments in cultural theory today is that the transition from what is described as a closed print-based culture to an open digital culture is part of a broader shift in how culture is produced and consumed. It is argued that digital technologies turn consumers and readers into producers and writers by giving them access to the necessary tools for remixing and remaking culture for themselves. In this chapter, I locate the question of cultural production within a broader historical debate over the status of mimesis and propose that the theory of nonmimetic reflection, in which culture is understood as shaped by social relations, provides the most effective framework for the study of digital culture.

Knowing versus Understanding

With the development of the digital economy, the contradiction between what the productivity of labor makes possible and the property relations that confine all possibilities to the profit motive has never been sharper. In the heightening of this contradiction, capitalism increasingly divides *know-ing*—asking *how* things work—from *understanding*—asking *why* they work the way they do—privileging the first over the second. This is because, on the one hand, the complexity of living and working in the digital economy requires the development of knowledge that provides the labor force with the skills needed for working in a system of global production and exchange. On the other hand, the growing division of labor serves as the basis for an expansion of the negative knowledge described by Marx as "commodity fetishism," in which the social relations between people appear as the social relations between things and the irrational economic relations of capitalism come to seem "normal" and "everyday."[1] In this context, what has emerged in the academic institutions of the North as most effective for capital is a highly sophisticated but local and historically empty discourse that displaces the understanding of social relations and replaces it with a mode of knowing that can maneuver in the global economy without having any need to un-derstand why it works the way it does.

The knowledge that has proven most effective for capital in this respect have been the theories that, since the end of the long boom, have focused attention on the intricacies of language, representation, and meaning while situating this process as an endless series of questions without conclusions. This discourse, which originated in the post–World War II era as postmod-ernism but which has since become the commonsense of the digital age and thus no longer requires a distinct nomenclature, has proven so useful to capi-tal because of the way in which it takes the economic contradictions of capital-ism and turns them into texts that can be poured over, studied, debated, disassembled, and deconstructed without any possibility of reaching a conclu-sion. In other words, it is so effective for maintaining the ideology of the wage as a "fair" exchange for labor power precisely because it does not ignore social conflict and contradictions, but rather appropriates them and turns them into spaces for interminable analysis that prove again and again the impossibility of understanding their underlying economic logic. It turns class divisions into divisions of power, and then represents power as that which "always reconsti-tutes itself,"[2] erasing the possibility of any alternative to the existing.

This "knowing" discourse is nowhere clearer than in the emerging theo-rizations of the so-called digital text. In the most basic sense, the digital is a binary logic in which all actions are reduced to one of two positions, on or off, and which serves as the basic language of all computing. In contemporary cultural theory, however, new technologies of reading and writing are taken to mean more than what the digital makes possible in the ways in which information is written, stored, and transmitted. As the editors of *The Literary Text in the Digital Age* argue, in the "twilight of the Age of the Printed Book," we *are* at the beginning of a time of profound change, one that will forever alter our notions of 'literature'" as "fixed, linear, noninteractive, and, most restrictive of all, essentially confined to a single medium."[3] In this sense, the ability to *digitalize* text has become a sign for historical difference—the idea that the present is unlike the past and, furthermore, that the complexity of the present makes both itself and the past unreadable. The digitalization of the text does not eliminate the binary, but renders the binary indecipherable and makes this indecipherability the space of pleasure. According to the work of prominent literary and cultural theorists working within digital textual studies, such as N. Katherine Hayles (*Writing Machines*), Avital Ronell (*The Telephone Book*), George P. Landow (*Hypertext 3.0*), Alan Liu (*The Laws of Cool*), and Jerome McGann (*Radiant Textuality*), the digital text means nothing less than a fundamental transformation in the very structure of social life, requiring a move from an analytics of *depth* to a postanalytic play of *surfaces* that complicates all binary relations, including the relation between writer and reader, past and present, inside and outside, production and consumption. For example, Alan Kirby writes in *Digimodernism* that the digital text represents "a new form of textuality characterized in its purest instances by onwardness, haphazardness, evanescence, and anonymous, social, and multiple authorship"[4] such that what he declares "digimodernism" goes beyond postmodernism in denying the relevance of history. Kirby writes that whereas postmodernism "emphasized a new sense of history construed in the present" the "apparently real and digimodernism are by contrast lost in the here and how, swamped in the textual present; they know nothing of the cultural past and have no historical sense."[5]

The digital, in this context, is no longer defined as the difference between on and off, but between open and closed. In this pairing, *closed* is the sign of totality, of objectivity, of history, of understanding, and of critique. The closed system is "a static and determined value which would inform and enclose the genesis of Being and meaning" and thus prevent the play of endless interpretation.[6] In contrast, *open* is defined as the space of the "bastard, hybrid, grafted, multilinear, and polyglot."[7] Knowing, in this sense, is "the infinite opening" that seeks out the eruptions of pleasure in the "irreducible incompleteness" that renders closure impossible.[8] It is a form of knowing that assumes "what I can never understand, in a structure, is that by means of which it is not closed."[9] The binary, according to this logic of open and closed, is not erased, but rendered unreadable and without conclusion by positing that it is the excessive space of both/and/neither without determination. It is, in short, the textualization of the digital, the turning into narrative the historical conditions which produce the digital economy and which limit its development, that is at work in this logic.

However, what is necessary today is a different reading of the digital, one that begins not in terms of the surfaces of digital culture, but, following Marx, "from the contradictions of material life."[10] While theorists such as George P. Landow argue that with the digital text "we must abandon conceptual systems founded on ideas of a center, margin, hierarchy, and linearity, and replace them by ones of multilinearity, nodes, links, and net-works"[11] which have "no primary axis of interpretation" and "no center,"[12] the relationship between the emerging digital economy and its cultural representations can only be understood by connecting what is *inside* the digital text with what is *outside* of it. That is to say, what is necessary if we are to understand the relation between the virtuality of digital representations and the actuality of class inequalities is to return to the Marxist theory of nonmimetic reflection, which approaches cultural developments not simply in terms of their overt forms but their underlying social logic. It is on this basis that I propose that by employing the theory of nonmimetic reflection one can understand why the argument that culture has become open and postreferential—that is, not antireferential, fictional, or illusion, but always plural, renewable, and without any determination—is itself a *reference* to both the possibilities of digital culture and the contradictions that capitalism finds itself in today. Through this analysis, one can begin to understand why the digital condition is read as the eruption of space of an "in-between-ness" that requires no finality, no theorization beyond *how* it works. It is a response to the crisis of a falling rate of profit that has plagued capitalism since the emergence of the long downturn by providing capital with new ways for conceptualizing the organization of production globally. In other words, the contradictions of capitalism are not the effect of closed narratives. Whether culture appears open or closed, is not determined inside the text, but outside it in the class struggle over the relations of production. The textualization of the digital, however, is the way of explaining the contradictions of network capitalism—between the increasing productivity of labor across the globe and the restriction of the productivity of labor to the profit motive, which itself depends upon the fundamental contradiction between those who own and control the means of production and those who are forced to sell their labor-power to survive—as the effect of something other than the inherent inequality of capitalist property relations. By rendering indecipherable the connection between the economic relations of society and its cultural representations, I argue that the dominant theories of the digital text actually *fix* history rather than open it to the plays of language by reducing the contradictions of reality to a narrative without materiality—an opening without closure that is the "condition of possibility and a certain impossibility of every structure"[13]—and thus work to extend the economic relations of exploitation rather than against them.

The Open Ideology of Digital Textualism

In the theoretical tradition of the postmodern criticisms of Barthes, Derrida, Foucault, and Lyotard, digital theorists who take a textual approach to social contradictions seek to destabilize history by positing that a fundamental break has occurred which undoes all previous assumptions about history itself. In literary studies this break has come to be defined as the shift from a culture based around the logic of print to a postprint culture of the screen. According to this reading, *print* represents not just the material means by which information is transmitted, but the broader cultural logic that reduces writing to the recording of reality, and thus a pale copy of the real. In this sense, print is defined as that which seeks to *fix* the play of meaning by situating the objective as the source of meaning and the subjective as the site of passive reflection. As such, the logic of print culture is said to be the effect of the metaphysics of presence spanning the history of Western philosophy from Plato to Hegel in which the text is assumed to be "merely a pure and simple 'copy' of *another* existence, situated in an extra-structural field, the 'real.'"[14] That is to say, print here is understood to signify a stable relation between text and reality in which what is inside the text is an unmediated reflection of what exists outside of the text. In contrast, the emergence of the digital text is said to represent a turn away from what Derrida describes in *Paper Machine* as "a certain totality" of the book,[15] and what Baudrillard portrays as the referentiality of "the map, the double, the mirror, or the concept,"[16] towards what Peter Lunenfeld outlines in *The Digital Dialectic* as "an era hostile to meta-narratives, a climate that resists the urge to totalize."[17] Or, to put this differently, the digital text is what in the contemporary *resists* conceptualization and exceeds all attempts to finalize the meaning of any narrative. As Samuel Weber writes in describing the "virtuality" of the writings of Walter Benjamin and thus of their relevance for the modern age,

> What defines the world in its heterogeneity—divine, human, non-human—is precisely the diversity of translatability, which in turn entails the ability to impart: to partition, to take leave of oneself in order to transpose a part of that self elsewhere, thereby altering it. The world, thus described consists not of a single, continuous medium, nor even of different media that resemble one another, but rather of a network of media whose sole shared trait is the ability to "part with" in im-parting. "Differentiation," perhaps, but not one that produces anything like "global integration." Rather, global disintegration.[18]

The digital is understood to be the expression of a culture of surfaces: a culture that is posthistorical, postpolitical, and postanalytical and which can no longer be understood as shaped by any metanarrative of progress, class struggle, or social transformation that is claimed to take place "outside the text."

It is on these terms that the digital text is said to require a new mode of analysis that, according to the editors of *Digital Media Revisited*, is detached from the "grand narrative of modernity"[19]—which means abandoning concepts such as production, causality, totality, and referentiality when making sense of the text—and, instead, embraces a new way of reading in which, "the name of the game is tearing apart and weaving together, decoupling and recoupling, analyzing and synthesizing, diverging and converging" without appealing to any final or definable outside of the text, whether this outside is the "author" or "reality."[20] As Robert Markley writes, "to historicize and theorize virtual realities . . . is to enter into a wide-ranging investigation of technology, mathematics, economics, gender politics, and psychology that resists any simple narrative or conceptual closure."[21] In other words, the digital text is taken to be the sign of an *open* culture that resists the *closure* of analysis and critique. It is a culture of tissues, traces, and *ghosts* without any determination.

It is not coincidental that what is now represented as the newness of the digital text first emerges in the 1960s, at a time when the economic structures which had been established to regulate the global economy in the post–World War II period began to conflict with the need for capital to expand globally. The Bretton Woods agreement, which pegged international currency rates to the U.S. dollar in an attempt to stabilize them as the European and Asian markets recovered from the war, no longer made sense in a world in which the economies of Germany and Japan had not only recovered, but began to outpace manufacturing in the United States while at the same time offering cheaper sources of labor, resulting in a higher rate of profit.[22] The decline in profit rates by 40.9 percent and 29.3 percent in the manufacturing and private business sectors in the United States during the period 1965–73, combined with the desire of capital to move to areas with more profitable rates of return—marked by 50 percent faster growth in international investment by U.S. corporations as opposed to domestic investment in the period 1958–1965[23]—were a reflection of the fact that Fordist ways of thinking about the organization of production were increasingly in conflict with what had become materially possible with the advances in labor productivity that had only begun to be realized during the long boom. What begins to emerge at this time are new ways of thinking about the economy as needing to be more open and flexible than the closed economic structure of Keynesian economics had allowed. At this time, the so-called open society philosophies of Henri Bergson and Karl Popper, in which it is argued that the closed social and philosophical systems that are collectivist and place the needs of the group over the needs of the individual need to give way to "open societies" in which "individuals are confronted with personal decisions" and "strive to rise socially, and to take the place of other members,"[24] begins to return to prominence in the form of the monetarist policies of Milton Friedman. At the same time, one sees at the level of cultural theory the beginnings of the postmodern logic in which the contradictions of society become the restrictions between closed and open readings of the text and the focus is on examining the processes of reading rather than the conclusions of analysis. In other words, capitalism had reached a historical limit that needed to be overcome. It is in this context that theories of openness and fluidity became useful as ways of making more effective (that is, profitable) use of technological developments as well as for thinking globally as the economic markets in Europe and Asia rebounded.

In the contemporary moment, the theory of the digital text corresponds to the renewed global expansion that begins to take place in the 1990s, but which first started with the restructuring of capital during the 1970s and 1980s in response to the crisis of a falling rate of profit that led to a crisis of overproduction and lower rates of economic growth. Once again, the conflict is defined as the end of the closed society (that is, the Soviet Union) and its philosophy (Marxism) and the emergence of the new open global order (neoliberalism). Just as in the theories of the open society, what underlies this new theory, in which the digital becomes text and therefore indecipherable, is the broader assumption that we have entered a fundamentally new moment in history in which concepts such as class and production can no longer account for the informational realities of network capitalism because network capitalism operates on a new economic logic in which knowledge replaces labor. Because knowledge is represented as an inexhaustible resource that cannot be owned in the traditional sense of private property, it is posited that what defines an individual's social status is not production but consumption—the ways in which individuals exchange and make use of digital culture as it flows through the Internet. For example, as Henry Jenkins argues, in the new digital economy "each of us constructs our own personal mythology from bits and fragments of information extracted from the media flow."[25] Similarly, Mark Poster writes, "the art of network computing brings forth a culture that highlights its future transformation" and "rather than confirming the completeness of the real . . . insists on the virtuality of the real, its openness to possibility."[26]

According to this logic, by having access to the means of representation rather than control over the means of production, it becomes the responsibility of the individual to create the reality that he or she desires to live in regardless of their class status. This "responsibility," which ultimately turns all social issues into private troubles, is said to be the effect of a new regime of cultural freedom from the homogenizing cultural structures of modernity. As Silvio Gaggi states in *From Text to Hypertext*, "Books, stories, poems, essays, or articles may no longer be conceived as primary units, more or less complete and self-sufficient statements of one kind or another. Instead, there will simply be a textual network that one enters, through which one moves, and from which one exits."[27] Whereas print assumed a particular, determined relationship between the text and the real, in the age of the digital text Gaggi argues, "there is no source of values or priorities which tell the reader which direction or path he or she *should* choose."[28] Similarly, as Christian Vandendorpe writes in *From Papyrus to Hypertext*, "while reading a book is marked by duration and a certain continuity, reading hypertext is marked by a sense of urgency, discontinuity, and constant choices."[29] In other words, in spite of the fact that we are said to be moving into an age of information, the availability of the digital text supposedly means *less* understanding of its meaning. The digital has, instead, become the sign of ambiguity, uncertainty, and openness. Thus, becoming recognized as a "subtle" and "sophisticated" reader who knows and can navigate the pluralities of the new forms of digital reading and writing—what might be called the *shuffling* of the text in which multiple narratives exist simultaneously, playing endlessly against one another to undermine any singular meaning of the work—depends upon accepting the impossibility of understanding the world with any kind of certainty.

One of the more influential versions of this reading of the digital text within cyber-cultural studies is Richard A. Lanham's *The Electronic Word: Democracy, Technology, and the Arts*. According to Lanham, the unspoken assumption of print is that it is an essentially noiseless—in the sense of cultural or social interference—reproduction of reality and the promise that the truth of any reading is justified by the ability of writing to accurately reflect reality. He thus describes reading in the print age as concerned primarily with "looking THROUGH" the text: "Look THROUGH a text and you are in the familiar world of the Newtonian Interlude, where facts were facts, the world was really 'out there,' folks had sincere central selves, and the best writing style dropped from the writer as 'simply and directly as a stone falls to the ground,' precisely as Thoreau counseled."[30] According to this reading, what matters is not the text, but the world outside of the text. The text is read as a mimetic reflection of the truth of life, or what Henry James calls "a direct impression of life"[31] and "the sense of reality."[32] On the contrary, in the digital age, Lanham argues, it has become impossible to ignore the mediations of the screen. He writes, "when the text moves from page to screen . . . the digital text becomes unfixed and interactive."[33] What this means is that in becoming digital, and thus able to be manipulated endlessly by both reader and writer in ways that the fixity of print supposedly does not allow, the text becomes *interminable*—there is no longer any "final cut" and thus "no conventional endings, or beginnings, or middles either."[34] As such, we can no longer just "look THROUGH" the text. As readers we are forced to confront the impossibility of moving from the inside of the literary to an understanding of the outside of reality. Instead, Lanham posits that we are to "look AT" the text, in its (temporary) manifestation on the screen. It is by looking "AT" the text, rather than projecting an outside "THROUGH" the text, that "we have deconstructed the Newtonian world into Pirandello's."[35]

The emergence of a digital text—in which the form of scientific understanding of the relation between the outside (reality) and inside (literary) represented by the figure of Newton is blurred and becomes the oscillating, postreferential writings of Luigi Pirandello (*Il Turno, Suo Marito*)—is positioned as a direct challenge to the theoretical principles which Lanham locates as the foundation of modern society up until the digital age. He writes, "The center of Western culture since the Renaissance—really since the great Alexandrian editors of Homer—the fixed, authoritative, canonical text, simply disappears into the ether,"[36] which, in turn, means that "the definitive and unchangeable text upon which Western humanism has been based since the Renaissance, and the Arnoldian 'masterpiece' theory of culture built upon it, are called into question, put into play."[37] To "look AT" the text is for Lanham to take into account the mediations of form, the plays of language, and the ways in which, this argument goes, what is *outside* the text is really put there by what is *inside* the text. In short, that what the text produces is not reliable knowledge of the world, but rather what the literary critic Paul de Man calls "negative knowledge" in which we accept the idea that the text "is a reliable source of information about anything but its own language."[38]

There is both a local and a global contradiction in this argument. To establish a historical boundary between AT and THROUGH, print and postprint, and analog and digital is to assume a theory of referentiality that can effectively understand the development of society independent of historical narratives. That is to say, even as it denies the possibility of looking beyond the screen, Lanham's theory nonetheless depends upon a reading of history as progressive and moving towards a more democratic reality through the development of new technologies. In this sense, to what extent is "looking AT" the text fundamentally different from "looking THROUGH" it? If we accept the argument that the AT undoes the THROUGH then it becomes impossible to see why history should be divided into a past and a present at the moment at which the computer screen emerges. AT and THROUGH, print and postprint, analog and digital are all binaries, and thus the problem is clearly not with thinking in binaries, nor in selecting one as the true reflection of reality. The problem that Lanham cannot account for directly is that his history ignores that history *is* divided, but this division is not reducible to the narratives of history in a kind of self-reflexive information feedback loop or to developments in technology in a weak form of technological determinism. It is the social relations of production that shape history. In other words, the problem is not simply that Lanham has not escaped the metaphysics of presence. Rather, the problem is an objective division between the owners of the means of production and the property-less workers that cannot simply be reduced to language. In this way, what Lanham is proposing *is* a theory of history which addresses class conflicts, but redefines it as the control over meaning before promising that with the new developments in technology everyone will have the opportunity to redefine the text (and thus take temporary control over the property of the text). This is another name for the spiritualism, which, as Marx argues, is the "inverted consciousness" of an "inverted world."[39] In other words, it emerges from actual social conflicts—in this case, the conflict over whether digital technologies will be put to use for meeting the needs of all, or whether it will continue to be used destructively in the interests of private accumulation of capital—but turns away from reality and towards the idea, solving in the realm of the spiritual what can only really be solved by transforming the material reality which produces the contradiction.

Mimesis, Nonmimesis, and Nonmimetic Reflection

The representation of the digital as resisting conceptualization and requiring "playful" modes of analysis that operate "beyond the metaphysics of truth and appearance of the utopian imagination informing the revolutionary ideas of modernity" because they "cannot be planned or even thought in advance"[40] has its roots in the postmodern critical writings of Roland Barthes, Jacques Derrida, Julia Kristeva, Michel Foucault, and Jean-François Lyotard. Although *postmodernism* has become a term that has fallen out of style because it could no longer effectively be used to justify growing inequalities and thus has been swept aside with the "end

of theory" pronouncements, postmodernism "lives on" after its death because it still provides an effective spiritual solution to material contradictions of contemporary capitalism. In the guise of opening a space for the
freedom of the individual from so-called closed structures of reason and
rationality, postmodernism provides ideological cover for capitalism by
denying that there is any understandable connection between the structures of meaning and culture (where individual freedom is said to reside)
and the exploitation of labor that the capitalist system is based upon.

What in particular makes these theories socially conservative is that they
put forward a worldview that severs the economic from the cultural and in
doing so propose that what is ultimately necessary is not social transformation but cultural refiguration. The exploitative relations of capitalism are
held in abeyance, protected from social criticism by the notion that it is
impossible to say with any certainty whether there is any connection between the material relations that determine the structure of people's lives—
whether, for instance, they must sell their labor on the market or whether
they purchase the labor power of others—and the cultural representations
of these relations because *certainty* has been declared suspect and a sign for
being a crude and not a subtle or fun reading of the text. The distinction I
am referring to here is between what Walter Benjamin describes as "coarse
thinking" or thinking that "dispense[s] with illusion"[41] on the one hand,
and, on the other, the blissful reading that Barthes describes as "the dialectics of desire, of an *unpredictability* of bliss" that avoids judgment or critique
but instead seeks to continually reconfigure a text in new ways.[42] Unlike the
"coarse thinking" that seeks to sharply uncover the relation between culture
and society, the blissful reading denies that contemporary culture has any
history that can be known with certainty and therefore any ability to be
fundamentally changed. It is assumed that what exists now has always existed and will always exist, regardless of what happens, because the operations of power that structure every text—whether literary or social—means
that the play of the text cannot help but refigure itself in essentially the
same ways even after having been deconstructed. In this way, it is the blissful reading that ultimately projects forever into the future the relations of
inequality and oppression that are said to constitute any social system. The
idea that capitalism will exist in perpetuity operates as the underlying assumption of a blissful reading and is smuggled in under the guise of power.

The writings of Jacques Derrida have been particularly influential in establishing the theory of the digital-as-text and therefore as an excessive sign that always exceeds closure, determination, and conclusion. He has become, in many ways, the "master" theorist of the global network economy because through his arguments that the purpose of analysis should not be to "destroy structures from the outside," but to find moments of pleasure from within by "inhabiting those structures" and demonstrating how the structures can become spaces of "play" even if they can never be fully overturned or transformed by exposing the slippages of meaning,[43] he ultimately dismisses the possibility of transformative critique and replaces it with the playful and desireful logic of the "in-between." One of the central texts in which Derrida advances this thesis is "The Double Session." In this essay, Derrida provides a close reading of Plato's *Philebus* and Mallarmé's *Mimique* in order to challenge what he argues is the basis of all Western thought in mimesis, or the theory that the meaning of the signifier is determined by a direct connection to a stable referent independent from itself. Instead, through his reading of Mallarmé, Derrida proposes what is essentially a politics of immanence in place of a politics of critique in arguing for the necessity of reorienting theory away from the mimetic toward what he calls *dissemination*, the displacement of the search for truth and the "abandoning of all depth"[44] in favor of the "affirmation of the non-origin, the remarkable empty locus of a hundred blanks no meaning can be ascribed to, in which mark supplements and substitution games are multiplied *ad infinitum*."[45] The "double" in the "double session" is thus about the impossibility of moving beyond the binary—including the binary of class—and instead celebrating the pleasure that the temporary suspension of the system can provide before it restructures itself. In positing the irreducibility of the binary—the simultaneous logic of both/and/neither—the "double session" has become so influential because it responds to the contradictory needs of capital to provide working people with a skillful mode of reading that can deal with the intricacies of a global, digital economy that requires the ability to think in terms of a transnational network of production and exchange, while representing what is ultimately a form of know-how for the digital age as "sophisticated" and "daring." What Derrida calls the "double session" is precisely the theoretical framework for the textualization of the digital—the suspension of analysis and the play of surfaces that blocks understanding of the economic laws of contemporary capitalism.

The "double session" is initiated by the placing of a text within a text; specifically, Derrida begins by "cutting and pasting" an excerpt of Mallarmé's *Mimique* into a passage from Plato's *Philebus*, such that the latter surrounds the former. What Derrida refers to as the formal "play" of the text is intended to be read as the first example of the "double session" and to draw the reader's attention to the surfaces of the text. It foregrounds the playfulness of text and, in many ways, is a precursor to the digital logic that interlinking one text with another renders meaning indecipherable because there is no longer any way to determine which is primary and which is secondary. It turns the text into a side-by-side and nonconfrontational logic, in which two arguments exist simultaneously in a post-dialectical frame without resolution, hierarchy, or synthesis. He writes, "a short text by Mallarmé, *Mimique*, is embedded in one corner, sharing or completing it, with a segment from the *Philebus*, which, without actually naming mimesis, illustrates the mimetic system and even defines it, let us say in anticipation, as a system of illustration."[46] For Derrida, Plato's mimetic system of reference is based upon the presupposition that writing is simply the recording of an independent referent, and thus that the truth or falsity of writing depends upon its accuracy in reflecting what is external to it. In this context, he writes, "true history, the history of meaning, is told in the *Philebus*."[47] What Derrida means by "true history" is an ontological theory of meaning which depends upon the "presumed possibility of a discourse about what is, the deciding and decidable *logos* of or about the on (being-present)."[48] On the contrary, Mallarmé's text is read by Derrida as exposing the fallacy of ontology as a reliable basis of truth. He states, "Mallarmé . . . preserves the differential structure of mimicry or mimesis, but without its Platonic or metaphysical interpretation."[49] This is because, Derrida explains, Mallarmé's theory of nonmimesis assumes "no total message located in some imaginary order, intentionality, or lived experience" and thus that "the text is no longer the expression or representation (felicitous or otherwise) of any *truth*."[50] By placing Mallarmé's text inside of Plato's, the reader is meant to see that their relationship is one in which Mallarmé's theory of nonmimesis is at work within Plato's theory; in fact, in his reading of Plato, he implies that the theory of nonmimesis is actually prior to Plato's theory of mimesis and what Plato's theory has to suppress in order to function. On these terms, Derrida is proposing that what is posited as truth and which is said to secure the meaning of writing is actuality an effect of writing itself. In contrast to this, what Derrida advances in "The Double Session" is a counter-reading of writing to challenge what he argues is the fallacy of truth in all writings, a fallacy which he believes closes off the play of meaning and restricts the possibilities for thinking difference without antagonism or synthesis.

In the excerpt from Plato's *Philebus* cited by Derrida, Socrates is engaging in a dialogue with Protarchus regarding the relation between representation and reality, specifically the basis upon which an image that emerges in the mind can be characterized as true or false. Socrates begins this section of the dialogue by establishing that the inner workings of the mind (opinion) are equivalent and in fact prior to what is expressed by the spoken word (assertion), and that when alone a person will "continuing thinking the same thing [as if they were speaking aloud]."[51] The purpose of the ordering of "opinion" (thought) and "assertion" (speech) is to show that the illustration of the idea—its manifestation in speech—comes after it first arises in the mind. Following this, Socrates argues a person's thoughts, which are compared to writing a book "on the soul," can be classified as true or false depending upon whether they correspond to the truth of *logos*. He states, "when this experience writes what is true, the result is that true opinion and true assertions spring up in us, while when the internal scribe that I have suggested writes what is false, we get the opposite sort of opinions and assertions."[52] I will return to the issue of "reality" as it is defined here; what is central to this passage is the understanding that the truth value of a statement is determined not within itself—that is, it cannot be decided on its own terms—but in relation to something outside the statement. That there is an outside to thought within Plato's writings can be seen in his definition of the idea, which is described as "the conjunction of memory with sensations, together with the feelings consequent upon memory and sensation."[53] According to this definition, any idea about the world consists of a relation between internal reason and external reality. That is, on the one hand, the idea consists of "the conjunction of memory with sensations," or the history of past experiences combined with the experiences of the present and, on the other hand, "the feelings consequent upon memory and sensation," or the ways in which we respond to our past and present experiences of the world. In other words, the basis of the idea and, at the same time, the means by which it is possible to determine whether or not one's understanding of the world is true, is the existence of a reality outside and independent of the idea. According to Derrida, it is here that Plato establishes "the history of meaning,"[54] by which he means the assumption in virtually all of Western thought that ascribes the very possibility of *meaning* to the ability to "see through" language to reality. He writes, "the very concept of history has lived only upon the possibility of meaning, upon the past, present, or promised presence of meaning and truth."[55] It is this mimetic system—the idea of the truth of history residing elsewhere—which, for Derrida, is at work in all of history, literature, and science and which, he argues, represents the fallacy of truth at the center of Western thought.

According to Derrida, Plato's theory of meaning is based upon an internal division in which what is assumed to be outside of language is an effect of language. He argues that in Plato's definition, writing is presented as a kind of dialogue between the individual self and the other. Yet, it can be described from the beginning as an illusory dialogue because "the need for the book or for writing in the soul is only felt through the lack of presence of the other . . . the object is to reconstitute the presence of the other by substitution."[56] In other words, writing is defined here as a substitute for what is missing from reality and it is on this basis that it can become a substitute for reality itself. When one does not have access to the outside reality represented by the true dialogue with the other, one recreates this reality internally and in turn judges the validity of this representation based upon its accuracy in reproducing that which is missing. Derrida explains, "It is through recourse to the truth of that which is, of things as such, that one can always decide whether writing is or is not true, whether it is in conformity or in 'opposition' to the true."[57] That is, insofar as Plato situates the book as either a true or a false substitute for reality, it must be possible to compare what has been written with the absent reality it supplements. It is on these terms, Derrida argues, that "writing *in general* is interpreted as an imitation, a duplicate of the living voice or present *logos*."[58]

More specifically, Derrida defines the Platonic theory of mimesis as follows:

> There is thus the 1 and the 2, the simple and the double. The double comes *after* the simple; it multiplies it as a *follow-up* . . . First there is what is, "reality," the thing in itself, in flesh and blood, as the phenomenologists say; then there is, imitating these, the painting, the portrait, the zographeme, the inscription or transcription of the thing itself.[59]

What is particularly troubling in this passage, according to Derrida, is the articulation of writing as imitation, which presupposes a relation of "repetition, resemblance (*homoiōsis*), doubling, duplication"[60] between reality and writing; specifically, the idea that the purpose of writing is to come after reality as its transparent illustration. Instead, Derrida argues that it is precisely the supplemental status of writing as described by Plato—in which "truth or falsity only declares itself at the moment the writer transcribes an inner speech, when he copies into the book a discourse that has already taken place and stands in a certain relation of truth (of similarity) or falsity (dissimilarity) with things in themselves"[61]—that essentially inverts the relationship between what is and what is written, undermining the assumption that the validity of what is written is dependent upon the existence of what *is*.

To demonstrate this, Derrida turns to Plato's dismissal of painting, which is described in the *Philebus* as coming after writing and in *The Republic* as "having no serious value" insofar as it is simply a copy of what is without "knowing whether what [the painter] has produced is good or bad."[62] Derrida explains that in Plato's theory of mimesis, "either [the mimetic reproduction] hinders the unveiling of the thing in itself, by substituting a copy or a double for what is," as in the case of painting, or "it works in the service of truth through the double's resemblance (*homoiōsis*)," as in the case of writing.[63] However, despite the fact that painting is described as following writing and is thus positioned as a "degenerate and somewhat superfluous expression"[64] of what has already been determined to be truthful by having been written, he argues that even in Plato's discourse it is "what gives us the image of the thing itself, what communicates to us the direct intuition, the immediate vision of the thing, freed from discourse that accompanied it, or even encumbered it."[65] Painting is the image of what is *prior* to its illustration in language and yet, despite the fact that it is closer to *logos* because it illustrates truth as it emerges in thought prior to language, Plato still positions painting as coming *after* writing, as supplementing what is already known. But, having shown that writing is supplemental to *logos* in that *logos* cannot be known except through writing, Derrida declares that contrary to the idea that painting comes after writing, Plato is dismissive of painting precisely because it is no less, and is perhaps even more, a direct reproduction of reality. Painting is, in fact, the very logic of the *logos* that Plato must suppress because it exposes the supplemental, and therefore unreliable, nature of writing. Specifically, although *logos* is the means by which the truth of reality becomes known, if it emerges first within the individual mind prior to its utterance in language then *"logos* is first and foremost a faithful image of the *eidos* (the figure of intelligible visibility) of what is . . . a sort of primary painting, profound and invisible."[66] That is, if *logos* is itself only a representation, a redoubling of a truth which emerges before writing but which can only be recognized as such after it has been written, then the internal division in Plato's theory of mimesis, and thus of the entire history of Western philosophy, is that what is known to be true and what is false that only becomes truthful after it has been illustrated. Truth, in other words, is what happens *after* writing, not before it. For this reason, Derrida proposes that "what is imitated is more real, more essential, more true, etc., than what it imitates."[67] Or, put differently, if truth can only be known through its illustration after the fact, the imitation is more true than what it imitates because it is only through the redoubling of the image that the truth of the original can be uncovered. In short, the original is dependent upon the imitation for its existence while, at the same time, because the imitation exists only where the original is not, the imitation does not depend upon the original for its existence. In fact, it is precisely the absence of the original that calls the imitation into being. This, according to Derrida, is "the closure of metaphysics."[68] It is the "presumed possibility of a discourse about what is, the deciding and decidable *logos* of or about the *on* (being-present)"[69] which places the ontological outside of language, as the basis for deciding the truth or falsity of a statement, and yet relies upon language to supplement and replace the ontological when it is not there. Thus, what Derrida concludes is exposed in the relationship between painting, writing, and truth that the Platonic theory of mimesis must suppress is precisely that the ontological does not come before language but that, by its very nature as the supplement to the ontological, it is language that *produces* the ontological ground upon which it rests.

In order to demonstrate that writing cannot be judged true or false based upon its relation to an ontological outside, Derrida counterposes to the Platonic theory of mimesis as a reflection of what *is* with what he argues is Mallarmé's postreferential theory of the nonmimetic. His purpose is to reveal that at the center of all writings is not, as Plato proposes, an ontological truth but rather that all writing operates as a kind of miming of reality which "does not allude, but alludes to nothing, alludes without breaking the mirror, without reaching beyond the looking-glass" to something beyond language.[70]

Mallarmé's *Mimique* is an account of a pantomime, *Pierrot Murderer of his Wife*, in which the eponymous character imagines the murder of his wife, Columbine, considering and discarding several options (strangulation, stabbing, poison, shooting) before deciding that he will "tickle [his] wife to death."[71] At this point in the narrative, a double mime occurs. In acting out what Pierrot imagines the death scene to be, "the Mime plays the roles of Pierrot and Columbine alternately,"[72] thus portraying Pierrot tickling himself as he imagines tickling his wife. During this scene, Pierrot "is overtaken, incoercibly, by 'Columbine's tickle, like a contagious, avenging ill'" which forces him to collapse in a painful ecstasy onto their bed.[73] Despite his attempts to escape, the painting of his wife that hangs over the bed comes to life, laughing at him before "Pierrot is again overcome by trepidation and tickling, and finally he dies at the feet of his 'painted victim laughing still.'"[74] What actually happens, in other words, is a kind of suicide, in which Pierrot becomes his wife and suffers her fate in the act of miming her murder.

For Derrida, the challenge to the Platonic theory of mimesis comes from two aspects of the play. The first is the question of authorship. Mallarmé's account of the play is based upon the second edition of a published account of the play, "issued four years after the first, five years after the performance itself."[75] Derrida recounts the history of the play in the following terms:

> a mimodrama "takes place," as a gestural writing preceded by no booklet, a preface is planned and then written *after* the "event" to precede a book written *after the fact*, reflecting the mimodrama rather than programming it. The preface is replaced four years later by a note written by the 'author' himself, a sort of floating outwork [*hors-livre*].[76]

He argues that what is significant here is not only that Mallarmé's account is a reproduction of another text in a series of attempts to describe what occurred, but that the very act described, the "mimodrama," was acted out without direction. That is to say, it was "prescribed . . . to the Mime that he not let anything be prescribed to him but his own writing, that he not reproduce by imitation any action (*pragma*: affair, thing, act) or any speech (*logos*; word, voice, discourse). The Mime ought only to write himself on the white page he is; he must *himself* inscribe *himself* through gestures and plays of facial expressions.''[77] Thus, while there is a real object that Mallarmé is addressing—the booklet recalling the performance—the performance itself has not been directed, or, rather, has been directed not to refer to any known gestures. Furthermore, any accounts of the event—including the preface to the text—were written well after what took place. For Derrida, this means that the actions of the mime, the initial author of the text that Mallarmé is reproducing in his text, "represents nothing, imitates nothing, does not have to conform to any prior referent with the aim of achieving adequation or verisimilitude.''[78] Instead, he writes, "the plays of facial expression and the gestural tracings are not present in themselves'' and "don't represent anything that comes before or after the mimodrama.''[79] Insofar as the mimodrama itself describes "an orgasm-crime that has never been committed and yet turns into a suicide without striking or suffering a blow,''[80] the actions of the mime are said to not reflect or represent anything outside of the performance. His actions are a writing that refers only to itself. For this reason, Derrida concludes that the writing of the play "no longer belongs to the system of truth, does not manifest, produce, or unveil any presence; nor does it constitute any conformity, resemblance, adequation between a presence and a representation.''[81] Given the repetition of the narrative—Mallarmé writes about a pamphlet which describes a play that depicted in a spontaneous and undirected form a crime that did not take place—it becomes impossible to determine where the truth of the text should be located because there is no originary event being recounted. It is the inscription by the mime of what is not there that marks precisely the absence of an original. Derrida writes, "We are faced then with mimicry imitating nothing; faced, so to speak, with a double that doubles no simple, a double that nothing anticipates, nothing at least that is not itself already double.''[82] It is, in short, described as an open system of representation for which "there is nothing prior'' to the actions of a mime whose movements "form a figure that no speech anticipates or accompanies'' and thus challenges any attempts to enclose it within a system of writing because it is "not linked with *logos* in any order of consequence.''[83]

The second aspect of the text that Derrida addresses is Mallarmé's account of the play. In particular, Derrida focuses on the following line:

"The scene illustrates but the idea, not any actual action, in a hymen (out of which flows Dream), tainted with vice yet sacred, between desire and fulfillment, perpetration and remembrance: here anticipating, there recalling, in the future, in the past, *under the false appearance of a present*. That is how the mime operates, whose act is confined to a perpetual illusion without breaking the ice or the mirror: he thus sets up a medium, a pure medium, of fiction."[84]

Derrida raises two points about this passage, which is placed in quotation marks in the original text. First, it appears in Mallarmé's text as a citation. However, Derrida marks that *Mimique* is actually the third version of the text, and insofar as the citation changes with each version, he writes, "on comparing these three versions, we can draw a first conclusion: the sentence in quotation marks is indeed a simulacrum of a citation . . . Aside from the fact that such a 'citation' is nowhere to be found . . . the fact that it changes slightly in the course of the three versions would suffice to prove that we are dealing with a Mallarméan fiction."[85] For Derrida, this "simulacrum of a citation" is another example of the way in which Mallarmé's text exposes the operation of writing: as a citation to a referent that does not exist, but rather comes into being after its own illustration.

Second, and more importantly, Derrida argues that what is at the center of the text is a slippage in meaning in the signifier of the *hymen*. Described as the source "out of which flows Dream," and therefore from which meaning emerges, the hymen is nonetheless situated as an in-between space, both "sacred" and "vain," "desire" and "fulfillment," "perpetration" and "remembrance." Derrida writes, the hymen "is an operation that *both* sows confusion between opposites *and* stands *between* the opposites 'at once.'"[86] That is to say, he proposes that the hymen becomes in this passage the signifier simultaneously associated with both what has occurred in the past and what may occur in the future. It is for this reason caught perpetually between meanings and thus, because "the hymen differs (defers) from the present, or from a present that is past, future or eternal, then its sheet has neither inside nor outside, belongs neither to reality nor to the imaginary, neither to the original nor to its representation."[87] It is a reflection of the nonspace of meaning, which refers to no stable or reliable referent. Instead, it always gestures towards reference without ever realizing itself as one or the other. By operating within the space of the in-between the hymen is a code for what disrupts all systems of understanding and replaces them with the pleasureful knowing that one cannot ever reach understanding and thereby stop the play of meaning. On these terms, the hymen operates as that which undoes the meaning of the text from within. As it cannot be reduced to any referent or presence, it thus defers both the possibility of ever reaching conclusion as well as being located as the result of any origin.

The figure of the blank space on the page functions in the same terms. Derrida writes that what appears to act as "the polysemic totality of everything white or blank *plus* the writing site (hymen, spacing, etc.) where such a totality is produced"[88]—in other words, as the virtual possibilities for the numerous and infinite readings of a text which can be constructed over the blank, erasing the emptiness of white space with the plenitude of the sign—in actuality, "re-marks itself forever as disappearance, erasure, non-sense."[89] That is to say, Derrida argues that the blank, contrary to its common representation as the empty space on which the presence of the text is constructed, instead "marks everything white . . . [and, at the same time] . . . allows for the mark in the first place"[90] thereby producing "a tropological structure that circulates infinitely around itself."[91] For this reason, interpretation is not a matter of a multiplicity of equally valid meanings. On the contrary, what writing multiplies is the absence of meaning. Writing here is understood to be the supplement to the blank; it takes the place of the blank but cannot be said to eliminate it. It is neither reality nor the absence of reality, but that which marks the boundaries of reality without fully enclosing it. Writing always has to suppress precisely that it cannot ever fulfill the absence over which it is transcribed. It is in this sense that Derrida defines writing as an act of desire—the wish of collapsing the signifier and the signified into a reality that in the act of being written prevents any such realization. Whereas the mimetic theory of writing presupposes the ability of writing to fulfill the need of presence by taking the place of what is absent, Derrida argues that nonmimetic writing defers and delays presence. In other words, writing is that which calls further attention to what Derrida calls the "non-sense of spacing."[92] In attempting to describe and to take the place of that which is not there, writing only multiplies the signifiers without connecting them to any meaning. The process of multiplication of reference without referent is what Derrida calls *dissemination* and what, he argues, "forbids us to seek a theme or an overall meaning in an imaginary, intentional, or lived domain beyond all textual instances."[93]

In order to address the limits of Derrida's theory of dissemination, it is necessary first to engage the false binary he establishes between mimesis and nonmimesis. According to Derrida's reading, the fallacy of writing as it operates within the history of Western philosophy from Plato to Mallarmé is the presupposition of a metaphysical outside to writing which serves as both the source of meaning and as the final guarantee of truth. Although not directly stated, the implication of this reading is that the mimetic system serves as the means by which power is established and maintained. That is to say, insofar as mimesis is defined as the transparent and unmediated replication of what *is*, the effect is to displace the way in which power operates by fixing the play of meanings so that they reflect the interests of the powerful while appearing natural, thereby maintaining the appearance that what *is* cannot be read differently. By unleashing the play of meaning, deconstruction becomes the primary means for disrupting power and exposing its claims of truth as nothing but the effects of the system of ideas upon which power is based. In other words, power here is read as the effect of the control over ideas, a control which is established and maintained by the ideas themselves.

What appears, at first glance, to be a "radical" theory of social change is, I argue, highly conservative. What makes Derrida's nonmimetic theory so appealing, particularly in the digital age, is that it appears to open a space within the existing culture from which to challenge dominant assumptions without ever having to suffer the consequences of taking a side. It is a desiring politics of the "side-less" and the "in-between." However, while he is not incorrect in marking the instability of ideas and the semiotic means by which they are communicated—that is, in the simplest sense, signifiers change their meaning—insofar as his analysis goes no further than describing this instability he occludes the possibility of explaining *when* and *why* signs lose their natural appearances and become the site of conflict. The meaning of signs are the site of conflict because what they reference—the material relations of production—is a site of conflict; namely, the conflict between the few that own the means of production and the many that own only their labor power. If we assume, as Derrida does, that the signifier is always supplemental to the ontological, we can reach only two possible conclusions. First, that the arbitrary nature of language is not determined by its relationship to the social. Regardless of the historical conditions, then, the arbitrary nature of the signifier will always act as a space for the eruption of desires that result from the suppression of semiotic play. In this context, even the most progressive or revolutionary society is assumed to operate within the same system of power as the most regressive or conservative.

Second, the play of the signifier requires no social transformation in order
to be realized. If semiotic play is unrelated to exploitation, then exploitation
does not have to end for the emergence of (individual) desire. On these
terms, the theory of dissemination provides an effective worldview for an
expanding global capitalism. It denies that there is any connection between
the exploitative relations of production and political, cultural and social formations while, at the same time, promoting the idea that social change is
unnecessary because social relations do not alter the inherent violence of
language. Instead, the only change which can occur is on the surfaces of
capitalism; namely from within culture. It privileges a slow and subtle reading that pours over the text, looking each time to make it new so as to
extend the play of language. As such, dissemination actually corresponds to
the dominant economic theories which argue that it is consumption and not
production, ideas and not labor, which determines meaning.

Derrida accomplishes this by reducing all theoretical positions outside of
his own to the same logic, to what he defines as mimesis. Immanently speaking, Derrida is not incorrect in reading the Platonic theory of mimesis as
a static theory of representation and, ultimately, of social change. If one
approaches the theory of mimesis historically, rather than textually, one
begins to see why the development of the theory of mimesis—in which
knowledge of the world is assumed to be reliable and quantifiable—reflects
both a society for whom mathematics and the sciences had become increasingly important and, at the same time, why the Platonic theory of mimesis
nonetheless turns reality into a static entity. According to Plato, reality is
assumed to be the manifestation of the truth of the transcendental ideal, the
eidos. As such, the conditions of history are read as the unfolding of the ideal
in the world which, in turn, has the effect of naturalizing unequal social
relations by denying that inequality is the effect of any material causes. As
Ellen Meiksins Wood writes, Plato "elevates the division between ruling
and producing classes to a philosophical system" in which "the first principle" and "the key to both ethical and epistemological truths" is "a hierarchical organization of classes in which the ruling class is fed by the ruled."[94]

However, it is precisely such a historical reading that Derrida's theory
erases. In this sense, although Derrida positions deconstruction as the
"other" of Platonic idealism, by dehistoricizing the concepts of truth,
meaning, and power he ultimately reproduces the very idealist logic he

claims to critique. Or, to put this in slightly different terms, the disconnection between social relations and the shifts in signification means we are to assume that "play" is ahistorical and at the center of language throughout time. Thus, while it is different from Plato in the sense that it does not assume the existence of a transhistorical ideal, the presupposition of an endless series of reversals between *jouissance*, or what Derrida refers to as "the heights of pleasure,"[95] and repression is similar in reaching the conclusion that the existence of exploitation and oppression is impossible to change.

There is, I maintain, an alternative to both the Platonic theory of mimesis and the Derridean theory of nonmimesis; namely, the historical materialist theory of nonmimetic reflection. I will provide a more extended explanation of this concept later in this chapter; for now, suffice it to say that the theory of nonmimetic reflection does not deny that the relation between the signifier and signified can, at any moment, become a site of confusion and disagreement. However, in contrast to Derrida, it does not assume that the arbitrary nature of the sign prevents us from understanding the relationship between the meaning of a text and the history of social relations. Rather it locates the contradictory nature of the sign as an effect of the conflicts over the material conditions of life. It is social life that determines the meaning and value of representation and as social life under capitalism is a site of class conflict, so is language.

In this understanding of the relation between language and the actual relations that language represents, I am drawing upon the dialectical analysis of society and culture as developed by Marx and Engels. As Marx and Engels write, "man's ideas, views and conceptions, in one word, man's consciousness changes with every change in the material conditions of his existence, in his social relations and in his social life."[96] In other words, how we *see* the world is an effect of how we live in the world. In the history of human society, which to this point is a history of class struggle, as society develops the forces of production and thus expands the possibilities for social life, the old relations and the old ideas which defend them come into conflict with new relations and their new ideas, thus drawing attention to the historical limits and contradictions of the prior modes of representation. That is to say, it does not assume that ontology the conditions of our social reality are transhistorical, nor does it assume that ideas simply change. If, as Marx and Engels write, culture appears to contain an unending struggle between play and repression, as Derrida proposes, it is because, "the social consciousness of past ages, despite all the multiplicity and variety it displays" has been shaped by "the exploitation of one part of society by the other."[97] To put this even more sharply, conflicts over meaning are a reflection of the class conflicts over the productive forces in society.

In his essay "Art and Objective Reality," Georg Lukács provides a useful example of how the theory of nonmimetic reflection approaches the relationship between culture and reality. Lukács argues, "the artistic correctness of a detail has nothing to do with whether the detail corresponds to any similar detail in reality."[98] In fact, he suggests, "the artistic truth of a detail which corresponds photographically to life is purely accidental, arbitrary and subjective."[99] Instead, Lukács writes, "The detail in a work of art is an accurate reflection of life . . . when it is the accurate reflection of the total process of objective reality, no matter whether it was observed by the artist in life or created through imagination out of direct or indirect experience."[100] What Lukács is proposing is that the reality depicted in a cultural text is determined not by the more-or-less mimetic qualities of the text, but by the extent to which the text has been shaped by the totality of social relations. A picture, for example, might be a mimetic reproduction of the real, but it tells us nothing about the history of what it depicts. If taken as a substitute for actual conditions, it becomes a one-sided representation that naturalizes the existing. At the same time, the fact that the meaning of what the photograph depicts changes, which is what follows from Derrida's theory of dissemination, also tells us nothing except that throughout history the semiotics of meaning do not stay the same. Again, what matters, I argue, is an examination of *why* meanings change and, further, that the reasons why such changes take place must be sought in the roots of society; that is, in the relations of production.

Based upon this counter-reading of the play of the signifier, it becomes possible to reread *Mimique* as a nonmimetic reflection of the material conditions that existed at the time it was written and which continue into the period that Derrida deconstructs the text. For Derrida the mime's "gestural writing" represents "a reference without a referent"[101] because it has not been directed either by a prior writing or by an actual event insofar as the crime itself does not take place. He writes, that the mime "follows no preestablished script, no program obtained elsewhere."[102] As such, when the mime "illustrates" the crime, Derrida posits that he is not following a "model" based upon "ontology" or "any dialectic."[103] He is a mime miming nothing. Instead, he states that by "tracing" the events of the play "upon the white page he himself is, the Mime does not allow his text to be dictated to him from any other place."[104] What I argue, however, is that contrary to Derrida's reading the whole event *has* been "dictated . . . from another place," in the sense that the "intelligibility" of the play, in the most basic sense, requires the existence of an entire series of historical relationships. What Derrida represents as a spontaneous act of writing without reference is a decidedly historical gesture that, while not mechanically dictated, cannot be understood independently of the history of social relations. The basic plot of the mimodrama—a husband who plans to kill his wife, but kills himself in the process—presupposes, to take only one example from the narrative, an audience who knows what marriage is. By *is*, I do not mean that marriage is a transcendental signifier without its own history. Instead, what I am referring to is the fact that the mime and the audience both live within a set of historical relations in which marriage *is* understood to be a particular kind of relationship between two individuals. The mime does not have to explain to the audience the relationship between Pierrot and Columbine—what it means that they are married—because it is simply assumed to be part of the normal functioning of everyday life. In fact, on this point, it is telling that Derrida also does not feel it necessary to explain this, nor does he comment on the events leading up to the play (the meaning of the alleged "unfaithfulness"), because it can be said that at the moment we also share the same set of historical relations in which the meaning of marriage has not fundamentally changed. It *goes without saying* what Columbine's actions are supposed to signify. Thus, even if the mime chooses to represent the relationship in a way that is new, it nonetheless does not fundamentally challenge the material relationship of marriage as to require explanation. By focusing our attention on the staging of the play, Derrida limits the possibilities for inquiry to variations on a theme which exist within a particular set of historical limits. It can be a new representation on an old theme, but the theme itself remains the same. He suspends any analysis of the play and the way in which it is both shaped by and comments on the material conditions of marriage under capitalism, thereby positing that these conditions are, in a basic sense, eternal.

However, marriage is not a transhistorical condition of being. Marriage is, in fact, a property relation with a long history of changes corresponding to developments in production. As Engels writes in his historical study of the family, the singular family structure depicted in the play, "was the first form of the family based not on natural but on economic conditions, namely, on the victory of private property over original, naturally developed, common ownership."[105] Under capitalism, the social purpose of marriage is further concentrated to "a contract, a legal transaction" regarding the distribution and inheritance of private property.[106] If we even briefly begin to analyze the play from such a historical perspective, it becomes clear that the basic elements of the plot are not unfamiliar but reflect a particular moment in the history of marriage. While Derrida's analysis is an attempt to suspend the possibility of reaching any conclusions about Pierrot's actions, the play is a narrative about a patriarch planning to murder his wife because she has been unfaithful. In other words, insofar as the monogamous family arises with private property and "is based upon the supremacy of the man" and "its expressed aim is the procreation of children of undisputed paternity" for the purposes that "these children may in due time inherit their father's wealth as his natural heirs,"[107] then Columbine's alleged infidelity has threatened the patriarchal lineage central to the laws concerning the inheritance of property and thus her actions represent a challenge to the established order. Far from being an undirected event, what Mallarmé describes is, in actuality, an all too familiar narrative in the history of the oppression of women. It is the cultural expression of a social relation in which the ownership of property by some means the exploitation and subjugation of others.

Of course, a reader might argue that, immanently speaking, the husband's intent to murder his wife backfires with his unintended suicide under his wife's laughing portrait. Does this not undo, as Derrida suggests, the authority of the husband by exposing that his patriarchal status within the relationship is itself the product of the impossible desire to control the meaning of marriage-as-text and not any ontological reality? Isn't it the case that Columbine's Nietzschean laughter marks precisely Pierrot's inability to establish the terms upon which his actions will be read? Are we not trapped within the postreferential space of the undecidable in that both Pierrot and his wife are dead and not dead at the same time? First, it is important to note that Columbine does not actually appear in the play except as an image. The entire narrative unfolds from the perspective of Pierrot, who relays the events to the audience. Thus, although he commits suicide in the play, he nonetheless remains alive to explain what happened. In other words, it remains entirely *his* narrative. In addition, even if we accept that his narrative is undone in the blurring of his identity with Columbine's, we are again within the terms of a conservative theory of social change. Given that the basis of his authority is established in terms of the control of the image and not his property rights, the material conditions which created the conflict to begin with are not transformed. Thus, while it can certainly be argued that his account of the mimodrama reflects the social changes which are occurring at the time Mallarmé is writing—in which, as Engels explains, developments in the means of production meant that for the first time, full and real equality based upon "the passage of the means of production into common property" could be realized[108]—it can be argued that by placing the entire narrative within Pierrot's voice the play is actually about restoring the control over the meaning of marriage at a time of social upheaval. In other words, in situating the entire episode as an issue of representation rather than property, it takes the material possibilities of labor and rewrites them so that they effectively extend the relations of capital.

It is the same with Derrida's theorization of the concept of the hymen. While Derrida, following Mallarmé, argues that the hymen, "undoes, outwits, under the rubric of the present . . . the assurance of mastery"[109]—that is, the ability to say with certainty the meaning of any signifier—it is significant that the entire theory of writing as desire is framed in decidedly masculine terms. When he writes that "in a hymen depending upon the verse, blank once more, composed of chance and necessity, a configuration of veils, folds, and quills, writing prepares to receive the seminal spurt of a throw of the dice,"[110] what is presented as an undecidability reflects a theory of desire that is written from the perspective of Pierrot. That is to say, in theorizing desire in masculine terms, Derrida reproduces the assumption that the feminine is the other of reason. What is an ideological theory of gender which emerges within capitalism to explain the economic inequalities that exist between men and women in terms other than the relations of production becomes in Derrida's text the essential condition of writing. This is the ultimate effect of the theory of dissemination—the naturalizing of social inequalities and the displacement of any transformative critique of the existing.

The Economic Reality of Digital Postreferentiality

Despite the "death" of postmodernism, Derrida's influence remains the guiding framework of digital textualism. One of the key books in digital theory on the status of the relation between representation and the referent "after print" is David Jay Bolter's *Writing Space: The Computer, Hypertext, and the History of Writing*. What has made it particularly popular is its adaptation of the postmodern attack on understanding for the digital age. According to Bolter, "The shift from print to the computer does not mean the end of literacy . . . but the literacy of print."[111] Whereas "in the age of print, it is permanence and fixity that is valued,"[112] the digital text differs because, "electronic writing is the first text in which the elements of meaning, of structure, and of visual display are fundamentally unstable."[113] What this means, for Bolter, is that the text is no longer ever singular, but always already plural. He writes, "An electronic book is a fragmentary and potential text, a series of self-contained units rather than an organic, developing whole."[114] In a more extended passage he argues,

> Today, we cannot hope for permanence and for general agreement on the order of things. . . . What we have instead is a view of knowledge as collections of (verbal and visual) ideas that can arrange themselves into a kaleidoscope of hierarchical and associative patterns—each pattern meeting the needs of one class of readers on one occasion.[115]

According to this reading, the digital text is understood as marking a break with past structures of referentiality—in which the signifier could be traced, even if contingently, to an outside—into a new moment of postreferentiality, in which signifiers can never be traced to any stable referent but instead are always already linked to a plurality of possible interpretations without conflict or resolution. To put this on slightly different terms, the digital text is said to usher in a new mode of representation in which it is no longer an issue of engaging with reality but rather refiguring reality itself through the play of signification.

The impact of postreferentiality on the production of culture is particularly evident for Bolter in the ways in which it has changed the function of the author. He argues that the definition of cyber-culture is marked specifically by the shift from an analog author bound to the age of print to a digital author of hypertext. He argues:

> The conceptual space of the printed book is one in which writing is stable, monumental, and controlled exclusively by the author. It is the space defined by perfect printed volumes that exist in thousands of identical copies. The conceptual space

of electronic writing, on the other hand, is characterized by fluidity and an inter-active relationship between writer and reader.[116]

It is necessary to point out that the concept of the author, in this context, is not only conceived of as the source of meaning but becomes also a code word for the possibility of causality and for connecting the meaning of a text to a structure of determinacy. Bolter argues, "the traditional view of literature as mimesis (imitation) is also troubled by electronic writing and for the same reason, the active participation of the reader. Because the text changes with each reading, the electronic author cannot simply capture a replica of nature in his or her text and offer that replica to the reader."[117] Instead, "no single definition can triumph at the expense of all others."[118] That is to say, the idea of tracing the meaning of a work back to an author operates in Bolter's account not only as an expression of the humanist mode of textual interpretation, but also to the possibility of relating a text to *any* outside. There is, in other words, no true reading because there is no possi-bility of determining what relation exists between reality and representa-tion. The digital text, on these terms, is taken as the becoming of Derrida's famous declaration "there is nothing outside of the text."[119] If there is one concept to define the digital text, he concludes, it is that it exists "in a perpetual state of reorganization" and is "in constant danger of breaking down and combining into new patterns"[120] because of any text that has been digitalized is now defined by the possibility of multiple authors. The text is forever left open to endless future reinterpretation and reappropriation in (supposed) contrast to the closed readings of the past.

In defining the digital text as "a fluid network of verbal elements"[121] within which each "reader calls forth his or her own text out of the network, and each such text belongs to one reader and one particular act of read-ing,"[122] Bolter is arguing that the digital text is marked not only by an in-creasing difference from the original, but that the digital text undermines the idea of the original entirely through the ability of anyone to produce a seemingly endless multiplication of copies that continuously alter the origi-nal in unpredictable ways. According to this reading, just as the text multi-plies the mediations of that which it refers to until it becomes impossible to distinguish what was original and what came after, it also questions the very possibility of locating an original that was not always already influenced by something else.

In this sense, Bolter is challenging, on the one hand, the possibility of writing as access to a stable referent that defines the humanist approach to writing, for instance in the work of theorists such as Henry James, F. R. Leavis, Eric Auerbach, and I. A. Richards, in which it is assumed that the literary text is an expression of the relationship between the author and the world that, in turn, enables the text to assume the ability to communicate between two independent individuals. In other words, the idea that it is the ability of the writer to represent the sense of reality—the emotional impact of reality as generated by the individual's unique narration—that gives the text its value. For example, in defining a humanist theory of referentiality, I. A. Richards argues, "the very structure of our minds is largely determined by the fact that man has been engaged in communicating for so many hundreds of thousands of years, throughout the course of his human development, and beyond that."[123] What he means by communication is, however, deeply connected to a faith in the ability to relate the truth of reality to others independently of the mediations of language. Richards writes, "the arts communicate experiences, it has been said, and makes states of mind accessible to the many which otherwise would be only possible to few" and thus serve as "an occasion for a collectedness and concentration difficult to attain in the ordinary cause of life, and the means by which human effort may acquire a continuity analogous to but more subtle than the continuity of science."[124] *Interpretation* on these terms is the interpersonal means by which the ideal, and therefore distinct from the mediations of a changing reality (science), can be transferred from one consciousness to another.

Postreferentiality, on the contrary, is based precisely on the impossibility of any direct, reliable relation between the text and reality and, instead, the free play of the sign in opposition to any singular or closed interpretation. It assumes a plurality of meanings which cannot be transferred from one consciousness to another because of the fact that those who participate in any exchange of signs are subsequently changed, even momentarily, by the exchange itself. Bolter, on these terms, argues that contemporary culture is marked by the increasing mediation between signs by layers of technology that provide the reader with images on a screen, but which lack any materiality or depth. Bolter writes, "there has never been anything behind the text, the process of reading and interpreting has always taken place in front of the text—in the eye and the mind of the reader."[125] Rather than two free and autonomous individuals who participate in the exchange of ideas, the exchange of ideas shapes the identity of those who participate and, in turn, becomes the basis upon which each can play with reality itself without the pressure of worrying that it will have any consequence in the actual world precisely because it locates the real as the product of the text itself.

In fact, in drawing conclusions on the meaning of "post-referential" culture, Bolter claims to go further than what Derrida writes in "The Double Session," in the sense that it is characterized as still too interested in defining the limits of the social rather than the possibilities of the open society that the digital economy supposedly represents. He argues that while "electronic writing does not permit a return to traditional assumptions of stable and monumental texts" and thus that we "cannot return to the comparatively unself-conscious literature before modernism," it nonetheless "takes us beyond the paradox of deconstruction, because it accepts as strengths the very qualities—the play of signs, intertextuality, the lack of closure—that deconstruction poses as the ultimate limitation of literature and language."[126] He continues, instead, "the Author must be ready to accept for his or her electronic text the conditions that deconstructionists have claimed for printed texts. An electronic text that remakes itself for each reader and for each act of reading is not incoherent, even if it does embrace its own contradictions."[127] According to this argument, the plurality of the digital text through the redistribution of the means of representation will allow everyone to have a voice in the new economy of signs. Freedom, in other words, now exists entirely at the level of cultural exchange as a substitute for the freedom from necessity that is determined at the level of the economic. On these terms, the idea that the digital text does not position people in any sort of fixed relation is based upon the presupposition that it can no longer be said that who we are—what class we belong to—is anything other than a fluid and temporary lifestyle defined more by the culture we consume than where we are located in the division of labor. Bolter writes, "just as our culture is moving from the printed book to the computer, it is also in the final stages of the transition from a hierarchical social order to what we might call a 'network culture.'"[128] In place of political, cultural, social, religious, and above all, economic hierarchies, "a powerful leveling force is at work in our society."[129] It is particularly important to take notice here of what Bolter argues is the status of class in the digital economy:

The only great hierarchical force left is money, and today the possession of money creates and depends upon no other distinctions . . . we use money to play at class, at hierarchical organizations that no one now takes seriously.[130]

What this means for Bolter is that the outside of society (class) is defined by the playful possibilities made possible by the increasingly availability of money (consumption). He concludes:

> The point here is that our culture of interconnections both reflects and is reflected in our new technology of writing. With all these transitions, the making and breaking of social links, people are beginning to function as elements in a hypertextual network of affiliations. Our whole society is taking on the provisional character of a hypertext: it is rewriting itself for each individual member.[131]

At the center of these assumptions, in short, is the idea that network capitalism defies all class relations and social inequalities by suspending the opposition between owner and worker in the marketplace. Individuals are presumed to operate as an independent agent who can determine for themselves the meaning of their lives by accessing the primary means of self-interpretation—the wage. As such, what Bolter is offering is a variation on ideology of the fairness of the wage in which it is argued that capitalism today no longer depends upon the exploitation of labor, but rather is primarily driven by consumption and desire. According to this narrative, the transition of the major industrialized countries to service and knowledge economies means that there is no longer any division between those who own and control the means of production and those who own only their labor power. Instead, insofar as capitalism is said to depend upon the generation of knowledge, it is no longer based upon a resource—labor—that can be controlled or exploited. As the reserve of knowledge cannot be exhausted, it is simply a matter of time before every individual has the same access to knowledge, regardless of his or her class status. In turn, because ideas cannot be owned, class can no longer be defined in strict terms of property relations. Capital and labor are simply complimentary binaries without conflict or antagonism. Network capitalism is thus represented as an entirely open system in which the binaries of class are not erased, but forever suspended by the play of finance.

In contrast, Marxism begins from the premise that life is determined by the social relations of production. That is to say, it starts from the position that culture—the ways in which individuals make sense of the world around them and the ways in which this sense becomes a material force through labor—is a reflection of the developments of the mode of production. In the supposedly open society of the postprint, digital culture of global capitalism, the possibilities for truly radical advances in productive forces that would eliminate all forms of social inequality are restricted by the contradiction between private ownership and accumulation of capital and the propertyless workers whose labor is the basis of private accumulation. In other words, what is established through continual representation across all sites of culture—from television, music, the Internet and film, to the social structures of education, church, family—as open and possible is what Marx calls "commodity fetishism"; that is, those ideas that take as their starting point the logic of capitalist production—that the exploitative relation between capital and labor is really free and the basis of all possible future forms of freedom—and represent this as the boundary of all discussion that cannot be crossed. Culture, in this context, takes on the dimensions of class struggle because it is the space in which people become conscious of their class interests in the conflict over the means of production and the organization of society and begin to "fight it out."[132] For this reason, it is not an coincidence that cultural theory has taken the position that network capitalism represents a fundamentally new social relation in which "anti-capitalist oscillations have lost their grounding in the once clear opposition between capitalism and socialism,"[133] "new identities and social movements cannot be reduced to class,"[134] there is "no longer an outside to capital,"[135] and that "the free market offers opportunities for new emerging identities."[136] What is represented as open thinking in refusing to "believe that all forms of power can be explained by capitalist relations"[137] is in actuality the argument that there is no alternative to capitalism, that we must accept the existing property relations, and that the enjoyment of consumption and culture is a fair substitute for ending the exploitation of labor that occurs under wage labor. That such arguments can be represented as a challenge to existing power relations in any sense of the term would be ridiculous if not for the fact that capitalism requires such challenges in order to eliminate constantly ideological concepts that no longer assist in the organization and accumulation of profit while continuing to represent an exploitative system as open, fair, and just. In contrast, if the full potential of labor is to be realized and not just put to use in the interests of profit, what is necessary is a mode of analysis in which the study of culture is a study of the ways in which our sense of the world is not natural but historical and, in a class society, the site of a conflict that has its basis in the relations of private property.

Senses, Surfaces, and Reflection

In *The German Ideology*, Marx and Engels establish a framework through which the study of culture can become a material force for understanding and for transforming social relations by connecting culture as a sense of reality to developments in the formation and reformation of the mode of production. History, they write, is the dialectical process by which "definite individuals who are productively active in a definite way enter into these definite social and political relations" and these definite social and political relations in turn "are continually evolving out of the life-process of definite individuals."[138] What distinguishes Marx and Engels' analysis from either print or postprint or digital theories of representation and referentiality is that it seeks to begin the investigation of all social phenomena "not as they may appear in their own or other people's imagination, but as they *actually* are, i.e., as they act, produce materially, and hence as they work under definite material limits, presuppositions and conditions independent of their will."[139] In other words, in order to determine whether we live in an open or closed society, a society that has suspended class relations or one that has exacerbated them, it is necessary to examine culture in relation to the material conditions in which people *actually* live, not how they might *appear* to live. This is one of the central tenets of materialism and why it is more than ever necessary for examining the contradictions of the network society which promotes the ideology that digital culture suspends class inequality by providing access to the means of representation—what has been called "the increased integration of the aesthetic in economic production"[140]—and instructs people in ever more sophisticated ways of "getting the job done." A historical materialist analysis of culture is not just concerned with knowing *how* things work—that is to say, with the immanent intricacies of the text required to find work on the global labor market that have become the mark of sophistication and subtlety—but *why* they work the way that they do.

Culture and ideas are always effects of material relations. All of the developments that are described as culture—everything from leisure time activities, to global advances in science, and the local ways in which people cook their food and where they go to work—are predicated upon the ability of society to produce the conditions necessary for maintaining its existence. In arguing that "the satisfaction of the first need, the action of satisfying and the instrument of satisfaction which has been acquired, leads to new needs,"[141] Marx and Engels locate the development of social resources, including advances in science and technology, in terms of the meeting of needs and it is in the process of meeting needs that society drives to increase its knowledge of the world and its ability to expand production. In other words, as society progresses through the division of labor, it not only creates new ways of meeting the old needs, but in fact also creates the conditions for new needs to develop.

To address social relations in their totality, as Marx and Engels propose, means understanding that the relationship between culture and the economic is a dialectical relation, but with determination. That is to say, culture and the economic are not simply binary states of being. They exist in a hierarchical relation in which developments at the level of production make possible developments at the level of ideas. This is, of course, an unpopular reading in the academies in the North because it calls into question the dominant ideology that acts of consumption—whether in real life or in the construction of virtual avatars—suspend class inequalities by providing people with the opportunity in which, as Stuart Hall claims, to "play the game of using things to signify who they are."[142] It is usually dismissed as too reductive and turning all consumers into "dupes" of capitalist ideology. This is not what the historical determination of culture means, however, and is an easy way of not having to address the fact that capital *does* have an interest in circulating knowledge that obscures issues of exploitation and replace them with narratives of equality and fairness. To presuppose that people have a clear and complete understanding of the world around them simply by participating in it is to eliminate entirely the necessity of science and going beyond the surface appearances. But the spontaneous and the obvious are, as the French Marxist philosopher Louis Althusser argues, among the most ideological sites in capitalism and require that the development of scientific ways of examining culture if one is not to remain at the level of ideology.[143] To go beyond the surface appearances of digital culture thus requires taking up the unpopular notion that "a certain mode of production . . . is always combined with a certain mode of co-operation, or social stage [and as such] the 'history of humanity' must always be studied and treated in relation to the history of industry and exchange."[144] To analyze culture is to understand that it is a product of a particular stage of development of the productive forces of society. By examining the ways in which any society develops within a set of definite conditions of production, "we thus see that the *social relations within which individuals produce, the social relations of production, are altered, transformed, with the change and development of the material means of production, of the forces of production*" and, at the same time that, "*the relations of production in their totality constitute what is called the social relations, society, and, moreover, a society at a definite stage of historical development*, a society with peculiar, distinctive characteristics."[145] What Marx calls "peculiar, distinctive characteristics" is precisely the way in which the relation between production and consumption, culture and the economic are not mechanical, but dialectical. In fact, it is capitalism, not Marxism, which promotes the idea that people have no agency in transforming their conditions of existence by constantly circulating the idea that there are no alternatives to the market. On the contrary, it is precisely the consequence of Marx and Engels' theory of culture as an effect of the economic that enables people to understand history as the history of human labor power and, therefore, able to be changed by those whose labor actually creates the conditions of existence.

Within this framework, developments of culture are shaped by the material conflicts over the organization and ends of social production. For this reason, the study of culture needs to distinguish between "the material transformation of the economic conditions of production" and "the legal, political, religious, aesthetic or philosophic" forms in which class struggles are fought out.[146] This is another way of saying that, although class relations shape the cultural, culture is never a transparent reflection of class—it is never simply a mimetic reflection but a site of conflict. In fact, the work of a materialist cultural critique requires the explanation of why the diverse forms of cultural life are complex reflections of underlying class relations. This mode of analysis is based on the fact that the appearances of social life are not self-evident, particularly under capitalism, because the very process through which the labor of some in society is appropriated by the few produces ideological forms of consciousness that mystify and invert the actual relations of production. The division of labor under capitalism, in other words, produces ways of thinking that treat the fundamentally unfair and unfree relations—which force working people to work to survive under conditions that involve the expropriation of their surplus labor—as free and fair. As Marx argues in the first volume of *Capital*, in the relations of the market, the transformation of the products of labor into commodities "converts every product into a social hieroglyphic" and that to understand the social requires that "we try to decipher the hieroglyphic, to get behind the secret of our own social products."[147] What this means for the study of culture is a mode of analysis that assumes neither that culture is a pure reflection of the social ideal, as in the case of traditional humanism, nor the postreferential slippages of digital textualism, but rather what can be called a nonmimetic reflection of the relations of production. The historical materialist theory of nonmimetic reflection is a critical practice which works to uncover in cultural practices the unseen laws of motion which shape them.

In defining culture as the space for the "training of sensibility" in the "delicate organizations of feeling, sensation and imagery," as F.R. Leavis writes,[148] traditional humanism takes the surface to be a symbol of depth; but its depth is not actually *under* but *above* the surface. It dehistoricizes the senses and turns them into structures of feeling that can "check and control the blind drive onward of material and mechanical development"[149] by locating the source of the senses above the messy contradictions and conflicts of class society. This is another way of saying that what is presented as depth is actually the space of the spiritual, holy, and divine. Althusser addresses the effects of the humanist theory of referentiality when he writes "neither Balzac nor Solzhenitsyn give us any knowledge of the world they describe, they only make us 'see,' 'perceive,' or 'feel' . . . the world."[150] In this way, classic theories of mimesis focus on the sensuousness of the world, as if senses were spontaneous and independent from history. Traditional humanism thus makes the same mistake the German philosopher Ludwig Feuerbach made: "he does not conceive sensuousness as *practical*, human-sensuous activity."[151] For Marx, our senses—the way in which we come to understand and interact with the world around us—are the effect of the abstract relations of labor. Sensuousness is the praxis by which people work on and change nature and in the process change themselves.

But if traditional humanism spiritualizes sensuousness, the new nonmimesis tropologizes life as an archive of representation, memories, and signs. It substitutes for the humanist articulation of the senses as spirit with what

Roland Barthes calls the "linguistic sensuality" which comes from the suspension of meaning and the endless play of the text.[152] It is the pleasure of finding the "in-between" of the text, the moment when the text is caught between the "both/and" where the senses reside. Postreferential theories, and chief among them Derrida's theory of dissemination, call for interrupting the relation between depth and surface and for the dismissal of all abstract relations in the social as essentialist. Postreferential theory, in other words, alibis its rejection of abstract relations through its antiessentialism. But, what is antiessentialism except a theory of what I call "de-understanding" the social? In turning the sensuous into the suspension of meaning, nonmimetic theory renders impossible any theory that seeks to draw conclusions from analysis. In this sense, it provides the perfect theory for a capitalism caught in the contradictions of overproduction, in which the most effective sense is that which constantly renews the commodity as a space of desire without consequence.

Both the humanist theory of mimesis and the postmodern theory of nonmimesis are a poetics of surfaces that correspond to the historical needs of capital to isolate what our senses perceive from what the material conditions make possible. What unites both, in other words, is the way they dematerialize the cultural forms in which this conflict is fought out. They either invert the relation between culture and the economic—between the material basis of society and the level of ideas—treating consciousness itself as the driving force of history or in a more complex move reduce consciousness to the material suggesting that there is no basis on which to distinguish one from the other.

On the contrary, the historical materialist theory of nonmimetic reflection is the analytics of the social relations of production that are made invisible by the inversions of the market. For example, in the same way that, in the political realm, capitalism gives rise to not just one but numerous political formations, from constitutional democracies to fascism to nonelected transnational organizations such as the World Trade Organization and the World Bank, depending upon what provides the most effective means of organizing production for profit, cultural forms also are a reflection of the economic conditions from which they emerge.

Bertolt Brecht, the Marxist cultural critic and playwright, provides a clear articulation of the ways in which developments in production shape cultural forms; specifically, how the refining of oil transformed social life. He writes, the extraction and refinement of petroleum spirit represents a new complex of subjects, and when one studies these carefully one becomes struck by quite new forms of social relationships. A particular mode of behavior can be observed both in the individual and in the mass, and it is clearly particular to the petroleum complex. But it wasn't the new mode of behavior that created this particular way of refining petrol. The petroleum complex came first, and the new relationships are secondary.[153]

In other words, the development of new ways of refining petroleum transformed people's ability to travel, to heat their homes, to cook their food, to work and to enjoy leisure time . . . and these changes are reflected in new forms of art that emerge. By using this example, I am not suggesting that technological developments such as the refining of petroleum constitute the mode of production. Rather, new ways of refining petroleum do have a material impact on the forces of production and, in turn, change the ways in which people view and act in the world because both are the effect of advances in the productivity of labor. As Brecht argues, the changes at the level of ideas are dependent upon the same development of productive forces that enabled the discovery of petroleum, which necessitated the attempts to find more effective ways of refining it for manufacture, and which provided the material basis upon which new ideas could emerge. Culture is nothing other than a product of human labor.

Marx and Engels, to be clear, do not deny that our knowledge is mediated or that new advances in science and technology can transform our thinking about the world around us in ways that we cannot yet imagine. Their work, in fact, is premised upon putting the most advanced developments in production, which necessitate an increasingly complex understanding of the world, to the most productive use by meeting the needs of all. What they do criticize, however, is that the very fact that knowledge is mediated by change means that the world is unknowable, or that the increasing complexity of scientific knowledge in any way effectively disconnects that knowledge from the social relations from which it develops. According to Marx and Engles,

the sensuous world . . . is not a thing given direct from all eternity, remaining ever the same, but the product of industry and of the state of society; [It is] the result of activity of a whole succession of generations, each standing on the shoulders of the preceding one, developing its industry and intercourse, and modifying its social system according to changed needs.[154]

In other words, the extent to which knowledge of the world is mediated is determined historically, and is a reflection of the level of development of the productive forces of society. Knowledge, in short, is a product of human labor power (what, in this passage of the *German Ideology* is called the "sensuous" activity of individuals). It is on these terms, for example, that Marx and Engels discuss the development of the natural sciences such as biology and physics which, because they describe what appears to be unchanging, seem to be unmediated by historical developments. However, they write, "even this 'pure' natural science is provided with an aim, as with its material, only through trade and industry, through the sensuous activity of men."[155] Engels provides a useful concrete example of the relationship between labor and knowledge in *The Dialectics of Nature*. He writes:

> If, after the dark night of the Middle Ages was over, the sciences suddenly arose anew with undreamt-of force, developing at a miraculous rate, once again we owe this miracle to—production. In the first place, following the Crusades, industry developed enormously and brought to light a quantity of new mechanical (weaving, clock-making, milling), chemical (dyeing, metallurgy, alcohol), and physical (lenses) facts, and this not only gave enormous material for observation, but also itself provided quite other means for experimenting than previously existed, and allowed the construction of *new* instruments.[156]

Knowledge, in other words, is a product of the ability of human labor power to constantly develop new means of production, which require new ways of thinking about the world, which in turn lead to new developments that expand our understanding.

In the contemporary moment, theories of culture that privilege knowing over understanding have become dominant in both high theory and popular culture precisely because they reflect the ruling class's stake in the material developments of digital capitalism. Their dominance is reflected in the funding and resources which are continually provided despite the fact that that economic reality calls into question their conclusions about a postclass, consumer-driven, digital economy almost every day. They respond to the contradictions of digital capitalism by preparing a work force who are excellent readers of the local and the contingent and who can quickly adapt when corporations move productive facilities overseas, purchase controlling interest in a foreign manufacturing plant, or when stock and commodity prices rise or fall on the stock market on the basis of future projected earnings, but who have little understanding of the underlying logic of the system in the private accumulation of surplus value. It is a consciousness, as Ernest Mandel writes, that is divided by a *"contradictory combination of partial rationality and overall irrationality"*[157] and, in this sense, comes to reflect the very logic of the market and, therefore, cannot help but reproduce it everywhere.

On the contrary, to say, as Marx does, that culture is historical and thus shaped by the conflicts of history is, therefore, also to retheorize the very question of openness. Unlike the textualist notion of openness, which focuses on the immanent plurality of texts and language, *openness* for Marxism is the historical possibility conditioned by labor relations. True openness is neither a textual effect, nor something that exists immanently within the human spirit. It is predicated on the transformation of the relations that allow humans to live off of the exploited labor of other humans. It is "the positive transcendence of private property as human self-estrangement, and therefore as the real appropriation of the human essence by and for man."[158] This is another way of saying that only when the right to private property, which capitalism formalizes into law because it is the basic structure of capitalist economic relations, is eliminated and no one has the right to exploit another person can a truly open society be developed. Private property relations are necessarily closed relations. They restrict access to socially produced wealth and the means of its production to the few, and subject the many to relations in which they are controlled by their own products (and are thus alienated from their labor, from themselves and from each other).

It is thus by connecting culture—whether print, postprint, analog, or digital—with the organization of the productive forces in society that Marx and Engels enable the uncovering of the ways in which culture reflects the material realities of class inequality and thus provide the means for knowledge of the social to become the understanding denied by bourgeois culture. As culture is part of the totality of productive forces in society, they do not understand *culture* as somehow exceeding the inequalities of society and thus operating as a cross-class, universal space beyond the limits of social production. They write:

> The ideas of the ruling class are in every epoch the ruling ideas: i.e., the class which is the ruling *material* force of society is at the same time its ruling *intellectual* force. The class which has the means of material production at its disposal, consequently also controls the means of mental production, so that the ideas of those who lack the means of mental production are on the whole subject to it.

The ruling ideas are nothing more than the ideal expression of the dominant material relations, the dominant material relations grasped as ideas.[159]

What is at the core of this passage are the ways in which culture, as a product of social relations, necessarily *reflects* the ways in which those relations are structured. This means that culture is not an autonomous zone, but rather part of the social totality and thus a space in which the class conflicts occurring at the point of production also come to the foreground. The resources that people have available to them—whether they have a job, a place to live, access to health care, or means of transportation—are determined both by the level of development of the productive forces of society, as well as by the relations of production in which some own and control the means of production and others own only their labor-power as a means of survival. In other words, it is not possible to separate the ideas that people have about the world from the accumulated history of the society in which they live and the ways in which the society around them is organized. By approaching culture as the history of the formation and reformation of modes of production, cultural studies becomes, I argue, a means of analyzing developments in culture to discover the root cause of social contradictions. It turns cultural studies from a witness to social transformation into an active force for change that enables people to understand the complexity of the world around them as an integral aspect of social agency.

It is in this context that the idea that the digital text represents a radical break from the past because the complexity of interactions which shape and transmit digital culture has fundamentally reversed the relationship between the world and ideas, such that ideas no longer are shaped by social relations but rather that social relations are now shaped entirely by ideas. What, for example, are the consequences for thinking about digital culture if one separates the advancements in science and technology that have resulted in the development of a global system of communication and exchange from the human labor power that created it? What does it mean to erase, or at the very least minimize, the role of labor in the production process? Arguably, it means to shift cultural studies away from acting as a material force for social change and to turn it into a support system for the global expansion of capital.

Rather than representing a new literary theory for reading and writing in the age of network capitalism, digital culture theorists are instead keeping up with the new technological developments through which capital increases exploitation. In other words, they are taking what is really a very one-sided view of technological change—which does provide the benefits of increased cultural openness for some—and presenting it as if it were a universal condition, available to all. The one-sidedness of such a theory is so useful to capital because in order to advance its thesis, it must bracket off the actual conditions of deepening economic inequality which shape the global world. While the textual theories of the digital claim to be a theory of open networks and connections, they are founded instead upon a closed disconnection—the disconnection between the exploitation of labor and commodity production. Only by reconnecting the study of culture and class will literary and cultural studies be able to grasp the contemporary and act as a material force for social change by freeing the productivity of human labor from the restrictions of private accumulation.

FOUR

The Ideology of the Digital Me

In this chapter, I investigate the argument that we are entering the age of the cyborg, which is said to represent the opening of a space for the pluralizing of identity and difference beyond past social divisions of class, race, gender, sexuality, and (dis)ability. I argue that by positing knowledge as the basis of reality—for example, by proposing that social divisions such as class are the effect of an instrumental logic of classification—cyborg theory obscures the fact that knowledge is always shaped by class relations. Instrumental reason is itself not disembodied from the social, but deeply implicated in capital's drive to increase the rate of profit. In developing my argument, I advance a labor theory of digital culture that resituates the social, economic, and cultural changes that are said to define the cyborg in terms of the organization of capitalism since the end of the long boom and thus open a new direction for digital theory by reading class back into the study of culture.

Capitalism as Difference Engine

Capitalism is a dynamic system in which the competition between capitalists results in the continual development of the means of production. This pressure requires that capital continually recruit new concepts and new ways of thinking that can both work with and expand the conditions of production that have emerged while simultaneously limiting these developments to the furthering of the profit system. The digital condition is the most recent version of this contradiction between progress in the forces of production, on the one hand, and the restriction of this progress to a system of private accumulation, on the other. It is in moments such as this that capital turns to cultural theory to establish cognitive environments that can effectively negotiate the possibilities of the new, while restricting their development to the logic of the old (that is, profit accumulation). In other words, in the graveyard of concepts that is the intellectual history of capitalist ideology, capitalism is nonetheless an engine of conceptual differences that must constantly invent new ways of obscuring the economic relations while providing the skills necessary for people to enter the new division of labor. If it is to remain relevant, mainstream cultural theory constantly has to adapt its reading of culture to the new possibilities for the logic of the market in order to prepare the next generation of workers for the new global marketplace. In the case of the digital condition, what this means is that the development of the forces of production are turned at the level of culture into a promise of a new heterogeneous democracy that honors difference, hybridity, and plurality. Digital capitalism, as representative of the most expansive development of the forces of production in human history as well as the most extensive development of capitalism globally, is defined instead as an economy that suspends class divisions by allowing people to escape the limits of their material bodies and enter into the fictional world of cyberspace, where all identities are said to be in play. Insofar as it is argued that life itself has become digital, this suspension of identity in cyberspace is read back onto reality to argue that all identities in the digital age exist somewhere in-between the virtual and the material. That is to say, it is argued that it exposes identity itself as a fiction that has no basis in reality, especially the reality of a world divided by class. In this way, the ideology of the digital promotes the illusion that the new digital economy is the other of class inequality because it allows anyone to transform his or her identity if the new digital society does not fulfill his or her desires.

It is in this sense that the ideology of the digital *me* collapses the material and the cultural, rendering matter to be an effect of culture and culture to be the space of desire. On these terms, the material is dematerialized and turned into a space upon which the desires of the individual can be inscribed. Desire, in turn, is described as the space of agency because it is that which provides the individual with the possibility of thinking the world differently. Desire, in other words, is defined as a productive act because it is the process by which the individual turns dissatisfaction into a new virtual reality. Central to the digital is thus a rewriting of the material world of property as the materiality of desire in which unequal property relations are turned into equal access to the realm of the digital. Within the framework of the desiring theory of materiality, interactivity and "active consumers, and even critical and creative users" replaces a world of "passive audiences or spectators."[1] It is from within this framework of "me-teriality" that the digital condition is theorized as a mode of heterogeneity without precedent: a forever virtual reality in which individuals have "a significantly greater role in authoring their own lives."[2] Moreover, that which limits the desire of the individual is seen as the violent imposition of the homogeneous. This is the logic of Antonio Negri's reading of Derrida in "The Specter's Smile." In fact, Negri argues that Derrida's theory of deconstruction, which attempted to suspend class binaries by declaring that all language was the sight of play and therefore that what any concept referred to was ultimately undecidable and could not be used to understand the world with any certainty, has been surpassed by capitalism itself. Today, Negri writes, capitalism has become a system of change to the point that "there is no longer any outside" but instead "nothing more than a real illusion before us and behind us."[3] The concept of a "real illusion" is intended to playfully mark the collapse of the virtual and the material worlds into an undecidable binary that undoes all binaries. According to Negri, capitalism is no longer a system based on the ownership of property, but instead maintains control over labor by restricting the play of individual desire. Negri argues that capitalism can only control labor by creating the illusion of property. In contrast, throughout the essay Negri celebrates Spinoza's concept of the "*pathema* of the soul" which he describes as a "dual state of mind" that exists "between passivity and activity," that "lives in the present though it is prefabricated in memory," and which endures "the past while turned towards action."[4] For Negri, "*pathema*" is the spiritual solution to class that breaks capitalism's illusory hold over the multitude by exposing "the perpetually uncertain but nevertheless open moment of an ontological passage which leads the mind to grasp the very nature of Desire, beyond the (past) determinations of existence or the (present) external dialectic of sadness and joy."[5] Negri argues that to break the illusion of property is only possible by continually creating one's own illusions that, by changing so rapidly, operate outside of capital's attempts to control desire. He writes that the only means to fight "exploitation" (by which he means the poverty of desire) is by "constituting a new reality, a new hybrid being, different each and every time, constructed and therefore snatched away from humanities arch-ghosts with each instance."[6]

What Negri proposes here is ultimately no different than what capitalism promotes every day in every film, television show, pop song, and mass-market novel—that consumption (or wage) is a fair exchange for labor because it provides one with access to the marketplace of identity. It is, in fact, another way of promoting the appearance that the free market actually does cater to *you* the *consumer* whose desires are real and therefore able to direct the markets to meet your demands. In other words, the proof that desire is real is the existence of so many commodities such that there always seems to be exactly what *you* were looking for. And if it is not there, it is argued, then just ask the company for it or keep searching as the market will eventually find *you*. However, this claim, as Adorno and Horkheimer write, that the free market responds to "satisfy the spontaneous wishes of the public" is nothing but "hot air."[7] That is to say, in the era of digital capitalism, ideology promises that through consumption "all are free to dance and enjoy themselves, just as they have been free, since the historical neutralization of religion, to join any of the innumerable sects. But freedom to choose an ideology—since ideology always reflects economic coercion—everywhere proves to be freedom to choose what is always the same."[8] In promoting a vision of markets as the realization of desires, Negri is simply providing the ideological alibi necessary for capitalism to maintain what is its real illusion—that wage labor is not the site of exploitation and that the wage-for-labor exchange is always fair and freely chosen.

Despite representing the most advanced level of scientific and technological development in human history, the digital is not in and of itself transformative; it is an extension of existing class relations. It homogenizes because capitalism cannot continue without homogenizing; for example, in turning concrete labor into abstract labor and use value into exchange value. The cultural politics of the digital are based on concealing the homogenization of humanity and representing it as heterogeneity. It appears to attend to the lifestyle of the customer and thus gives the impression of heterogeneity and cultural plurality to the homogeny of wage labor.

The Desiring Nonscience of Digital Humanities

The digital humanities are an extension of the culture industry in the sense that they are the means by which theories of culture are determined to be realistic or unrealistic, new or old. These designations have nothing to do with the substance of the arguments. Any arguments that challenge the dominance of capital will always be declared old and unrealistic and therefore not worthy to participate in the exchange of ideas. In contrast, those cultural theories that separate culture and the economic will always be read as new and therefore acceptable for public consumption. That is to say, all new bourgeois theories of culture are simply new lines within the accepted commonsense of the profession as the defenders of culture.

A prime example of the digital humanities and the way in which they update cultural theory to adapt to the new conceptual skills required by capital of the next generation of workers is Bruno Latour's *We Have Never Been Modern*. Latour, in order to position himself as the theorist of the new who is able to move beyond the clearly outdated theories of the old, has to both establish the terms of the new as well as the logic by which the division between the old and the new can be determined. In both cases, what has led to the reading of his arguments as successful among academics in the North is that he abstracts history from class struggle by disconnecting epistemology from its material conditions.

The first move is to declare that the present is in a crisis in which "[a]ll of culture and all of nature get churned up again every day"[9] and that as a result our "intellectual life is out of kilter."[10] The next move is to provide the means of reading this crisis as not the result of a growing contradiction between the forces and relations of production, but a crisis of epistemology with no connection to class conflict. Instead, he argues that the failure of theory has been in presuming that modern history—what he describes as an "emancipatory" history—came to an end with postmodernity when, in fact, history is only now coming to an end. He writes, "we have to rethink the definition of modernity, interpret the symptom of Postmodernity, and understand why we are no longer committed heart and soul to the double task of domination and emancipation."[11]

Postmodernism has become a failed concept for capital because, insofar as it promised the end of class when in reality class lines have been drawn increasingly sharper, it can no longer provide ideological cover for the interests of capital. In other words, the division of history into modern and postmodern has never been anything more than a cultural reading of history, in which different regimes of capital accumulation were read as fundamentally different modes of production. By turning economic continuity into cultural difference, cultural theory was able to sell, for a period of time, the idea that capitalism had changed, that social inequality was a thing of the past, and that the present had no need for historical materialism or ideology critique. History, on the contrary, is the making and remaking of the mode of production through class struggle and it is this history that capitalism has to deny regularly at the level of ideology. It is for this reason that *theory*, in which all theory was equated with postmodernism, is said to have come to an end. The numerous "end of theory" narratives that have emerged in recent years are less about getting theory right, than using the ideological exhaustion of postmodernism as a means of attempting once again to remove class theory from the academy. This is accomplished by declaring that all theories (even the ones that critiqued postmodernism) were equally poor readers of culture, while at the same time clearing the conceptual brush in order to install new ideological concepts so as to make variations in the same old economic logic appear as new and thus able to enter the publishing market as replacements for the ideology of postmodernism. For example, in "Medium Theory: Preface to the 2003 *Critical Inquiry Symposium,*" W. J. T. Mitchell writes that now is the time for "medium theory" that is "sober" about the "expectations that critical theory can realistically envision today" and "does not hold out much prospect of revolutionary change."[12] In other words, at the end of theory is a politics that doesn't take sides, hopelessly and despairingly trapped in-between reality and the virtual.

It is on similar terms that Latour collapses and eliminates modernism and postmodernism, as a means not of actually moving beyond either modernism or postmodernism, but in an attempt to sell a new theory for explaining the contradictions of the digital condition as having nothing to do with private property. He proposes that the failure of modernity is a central fallacy that there is a clear and defined boundary between the "laws of external nature" and the "conventions of society."[13] Modernism, on these terms, is based upon maintaining a strict division at the level of ideas between the barbarism of the past, in which the social is dominated by the "natural," and the civilization of the future, marked by the domination of the natural by the "social." According to this reading, to be modern requires an epistemological constitution of strict and recognizable difference. He writes, "The process of partitioning" between past and future, the domain of objects and the domain of society, "was accompanied by a coherent and continuous front of radical revolutions in science, technology, administration, economy and religion, a veritable bulldozer operation behind which the past disappeared forever, but in front of which, at least, the future opened up."[14] As such, the modernist belief in science and rationality, which for Latour means both industrial capitalism and socialism, is described as regularly and routinely operating as an exclusionary logic against the other. He states,

> The various manifestations of socialism destroyed both their peoples and their ecosystems, whereas the powers of the North and the West have been able to save their peoples and some of their countrysides by destroying the rest of the world and reducing its peoples to abject poverty.[15]

On the contrary, "the double failure that was my starting point, that of socialism (at stage left) and that of naturalism (at stage right) has made the work of purification less plausible and the contradictions more visible. There are no more revolutions in store to impel a continued flight forward."[16] It is in the same terms that Latour argues that postmodernism is no better insofar as it means giving up entirely on the project of science. He writes, "Postmodernism is a symptom, not a fresh solution" because it "senses that something has gone awry in the modern critique, but is not able to do anything but prolong that critique, though without believing in its foundations."[17] Reading postmodernists as "disappointed rationalists," Latour states, "instead of moving on to empirical studies of the networks that give meaning to the work of purification it denounces, postmodernism rejects all empirical work as illusory and deceptively scientific."[18] In other words, he declares that the failure of postmodernism is that rather than reject the modernist binary between the natural and social, and thus open a space for rethinking both, they reject the natural entirely and limit the possibilities for analysis to "disconnected instants and groundless denunciations."[19] In short, for Latour postmodernism is as absolute in its thinking as modernism, it merely takes the other side.

The purpose of collapsing socialism and naturalism, or modernism and postmodernism as mirror images of the same epistemological drives is to establish himself as a fair dealer, who can read without the so-called biases of the history of the past so as to be recognized as apparently nonideological and therefore beyond the failures of past cultural theory. What he proposes is that rather than simply abandon the boundaries between the natural and the unnatural, which are used to justify the effects of progress—poverty, war, racism, ecological destruction, and so on—we need to replace the concepts of social and natural with a more fluid and less determined set of criteria for reading the world without theories of progress and scientific rationality. He states that "modernity is often described in terms of humanism, either as a way of saluting the birth of 'man' or as a way of announcing his death . . . it overlooks the simultaneous birth of 'nonhumanity'—things, objects, or beasts."[20] It is from within the space of the nonmodern and the nonhuman that he proposes that "we can combine association freely without ever confronting the choice between archaism and modernization, the local and the global, the cultural and the universal, the natural and the social."[21] For Latour, to be nonmodern, as opposed to modern or postmodern, means giving up concepts such as truth, objectivity, and extraterritoriality in favor of uncertainty, daring, warmth, and the "crazy ability to reconstitute the social bond."[22] It is a desiring nonscience without conclusions or consequences.

Latour's nonhuman proposal is a reading of identity as shaped by the genealogy of social meanings, which, by separating the history of ideas from the history of the social relations of production, denies that his reading of history has anything to do with economic relations. That this is the case is evident in his arguments concerning what he calls the "reductionism" of all modernist theories. He writes, "we cannot retain the illusion (whether they deem it positive or negative) that moderns have about themselves and want to generalize to everyone: atheist, materialist, spiritualist, theist, rational, effective, objective, universal, critical . . . prisoners of an absolute dichotomy between things and signs, facts and values."[23] Instead, the nonmodernist digital consciousness is defined by the multiplication of "new definitions of humans" which do not "displace the former ones, reduce them to any homogeneous one, or unify them."[24] The reduction of capitalism and socialism, atheists and spiritualists, into the singular category of modernism shows that Latour is not opposed to collapsing binary opposites into broad generalizations. As such, it must be the case that Latour is not opposed to reduction, but is only opposed to certain kinds of reduction. That is to say, by reducing history to the conflict between the human and the nonhuman, he ultimately reads all of social history as a conflict of epistemology, while denying that this epistemology has its own social history. To be clear, the problem is not that Latour is reductive. Rather, the problem is that he locates the determination of all social conflict at the level of ideas, thereby erasing the material differences between modes of production. There is no difference, in his arguments, between the progressive and regressive societies of the modern period—socialism is described as equally reductive as capitalism—and thus there is no reason to change the economic relations of the contemporary. Instead, it is about finding differences at the level of culture while denying that science should reach any global conclusions about these differences. In defining the possibilities for social change as a matter of locating difference while limiting this inquiry to a search for only those differences that emerge within the fissures of epistemology, it becomes clear that what Latour is opposed to is the possibility of radical economic change. For Latour, there is no outside to capitalism.

What Latour establishes is the perfect ideology for digital capital. In praising the development of the nonhuman as creating an open space without determination, he is simply repeating in a new idiom the argument that the digital economy operates beyond the restrictions of class by providing a virtual space for the realization of desires. If desire was restricted conceptually—that is to say, if one had to fit into a certain identity (atheist or spiritualist) before—then in the digital age there is no reason to make any such decision. One can be both an atheist and a spiritualist in cyberspace because identities are nothing but conceptual models that have no material basis. What this is really saying is that property no longer matters in an age when anyone can escape into the virtual world, where the owner and worker compete on equal footing. The ideology of desire as productive in the digital age is thus a spiritual solution to class conflict. It creates the appearance of the kingdom of heaven (cyberspace) in which all will be judged equally, regardless of what exists in the kingdoms of earth (capitalism) and, furthermore, argues that in the coming of digital society, heaven will be realized on earth.

Cyborg as Postclass Fantasy

The erasure of class in the ideology of the digital increasingly takes place through the substitution of desire (spirit) for need (matter) as the force of historical change. From the possibilities of cloning, stem cell research and nanotechnologies to the development of social networking sites such as Facebook, it is argued that the ability of science to turn reality into a narrative that can be re-edited endlessly to fulfill the desires of the digital me forever undoes the concept of reality. For example, N. Katherine Hayles argues that our knowledge of the emerging nanorealities requires knowledge that is "in some sense already virtual," an in-between space that is both "on display" and "invisible" as it is "mediated through precision scanning probe microscopes, data streams, and computer-generated visualizations."[25] Similarly, Colin Milburn argues that to "think nanotechnologically"[26] requires "a new epistemological orientation toward the world, a new thinking of being that is no longer the perspective of the human, but instead that of the posthuman, the postbiological, the machinic, the cyborg, the networked, the uploaded, the synthetic, the schizophrenic, the alien, the monstrous, the wired, and the weird."[27] At the core of these arguments is the idea that as technology grows in its ability to transform reality it is increasingly the autonomous desire of the individual that drives reality and therefore it is desire that is the remaining space for agency. In turn, because it is argued that desire always exceeds the conceptual, it suspends the possibility of locating the individual in any regime of truth. Instead, because the digital is read as a dual consciousness of a simultaneously real and virtual existence, the individual is understood as operating in-between social binaries— between truth and illusion, reality and fiction, and, ultimately, between producer (labor) and consumer (capital). Mark Poster, for example, argues that the "electronic mediation" of digital desires "subverts the autonomous, rational subject" in favor of "an abyss of indeterminate exchanges between subject and object in which the real and the fictional, the outside and the inside, the true and false oscillate."[28] Likewise, in *The Inhuman*, Lyotard posits the inevitability of "oscillation" between "native indetermination" (the natural) and "self-instituting reason" (the social) as the resultant of what is the basis of what he has termed the "inhuman," namely the "deregulation" of meaning.[29] The problem, to be clear, is not that the new scientific developments don't hold tremendous potential for transforming our lives. Rather, what I am arguing is that the limit is the way in which they become the basis within contemporary cultural theory for providing a spiritual resolution to the economic contradictions of society.

Privileging the discourses of exchange, oscillation, and fluidity, the new digital subject seeks refuge in the indeterminacy of a spiritual dynamism represented most explicitly by the theory of the *cyborg*—the subject who is described as neither human nor machine, neither subject nor object, neither rational nor irrational, but a contingent construction operating within the network of localized desiring flows. As Ollivier Dyens writes, the cyborg is based upon the idea that:

> When a human is digitalized (when his image is digitalized), the resulting image is no longer the "mirror" of a living being. A digitalized human becomes other . . . an impure being (phantom, simulacrum) with no stable definitions of who or what he (she? it?) is, several things, several sexes, several organs, and several machines all at once . . . Once digitalized, the image of a human being is released from its origin and can transform itself into a multitude of landscapes; it becomes a system unimpeded by any conceptual limits.[30]

It is on these terms that Dyens goes on to argue that to deal with the new digital reality historical and social analysis must become a form of *ghost hunting*; a "simulacrum," he writes, "is a ghost, an illusion. It is at the same time here and there, true and false. It falsifies time, it questions the ordering of memories, it forces the multiplication of realities, and it compels phenomena and their representations to collide and contaminate each other."[31] In other words, reading the reality of the cyborg is about the surface play and the resistance of digital culture against any shaping by any social forces. In the most basic terms, then, the cyborg is based upon the assumption that in the configuring of the digital me all fixed social divisions of class, race, and gender are replaced with fluid spaces of self-creation.

Perhaps the most influential version of this argument is put forward in the work of cyborg-theorist Donna Haraway. In her often reprinted essay, "A Manifesto for Cyborgs: Science, Technology, and Socialist-Feminism in the 1980s," Haraway argues that digital culture results in the ironic production of the cyborg: a hybrid subjectivity that is neither natural nor social and, on these terms, opens a playful space of resistance *within* the very logic of science and reason. Haraway bases her reading on the presupposition that the forms capital takes are more important than its underlying logic of exploitation. She declares, for example, that digital capitalism represents "an emerging system of world order analogous in its novelty and scope to that created by industrial capital . . . from an organic, industrial society to a polymorphous, information system"[32] such that the concept of a more "'Advanced capitalism' . . . is inadequate to convey the structure of the historical moment."[33] It is the polymorphous logic of the digital economy which, according to Haraway, pressures the possibility of any grand narrative that ignores the specificity of individualized relations. Positioning cyborg theory as against "the tradition of progress" and the "tradition of the appropriation of nature,"[34] which she describes as an outdated modernist logic of objectivity versus the new logic of hybridity, Haraway declares that the new relations between human and machine blur the binary capitalist relations of owners and workers, enabling the production of the economic, cultural, and political heterogeneity which defines cyborg consciousness. It is the cyborg, as "a condensed image of both imagination and material reality," realized in the collapse of "science fiction and social reality,"[35] which is said to resist the conceptualization and totality that marks the homogenous culture of past capitalisms. "Exchange in this world," she writes, "transcends the universal translation effected by capitalist markets."[36] On these terms, the logic of the cyborg shifts from the struggle against exploitation to finding "pleasure in the confusion of boundaries"[37] and "contradictory standpoints."[38] It is, she writes, no longer "'clear-sighted critique grounding a solid political epistemology' versus 'manipulated false consciousness'" but rather a position of "ambivalence" and "subtle understanding of emerging pleasures, experiences and powers, with serious potential for changing the rules of the game."[39]

Similar, then, to Latour's argument that history is now no longer characterized by "revolution," but by the "small modifications of old beliefs,"[40]

Haraway's theory of the cyborg is said to correspond to the end of "salvation history" and the West's "escalating dominations of abstract individuation."[41] According to Haraway, the primary failure of radical social movements has been that in reducing individuals to abstract categories of class, gender, and race they have been unable to escape the homogenizing logic of capitalism they claim to be opposed to. The emergence of the digital me means that instead of essentialized groupings of "class, race, and gender"[42] cultural politics in the digital age becomes a process of exploring the surface contradictions of capitalism in order to locate "new kinds of unity"[43] based upon affinity, not class consciousness.[44] Within this narrative Haraway posits that there is no difference between socialism and capitalism and both are read as movements of modernity which attempt to reduce the play of subjectivity.[45] On the contrary, the possibility of cultural heterogeneity is said to exist today *within* capitalism, rather than *outside* of it. In other words, by denying that there is any difference between the economic relations of socialism and capitalism, Haraway's theory of revolutionary social change no longer depends upon a transformation of the mode of production. Instead, insofar as it is understood as the difference between two different but equally homogenizing cultural logics, Haraway creates the appearance that liberation is something that can occur *in spite of* capitalism. Cyborg politics are thus described as, "the struggle for language and the struggle against perfect communication, against the one code that translates all meaning perfectly."[46] That is to say, it is a struggle for plurality from within rather than collectivity from without. What are the terms for heterogeneity from within capitalism except those of the free market. If we assume that radical change is possible from within capitalism, then we must accept the terms of capitalism—the exploitation of labor. This reduces the possibilities of the political to a project of working *within* the existing to negotiate better terms. As such, the global project of human emancipation from exploitation is turned into a local process of cultural liberation and the pluralizing of identities within the structure of class relations.

It's All Up to Me: The Digital Future in Contemporary Film

The narrative of finding liberation and pleasure through consumption rather than outside of it has become a popular representation within digital culture and one finds such ideas in mainstream cyber-films such as *Dark City* and *The Matrix*. The effect of these films is to take the discursively complex theories of writers such as Negri, Latour, and Haraway and make them available for a wider audience. In other words, they are the means by which new ideologies are popularized. In turn, because they provide a surface narrative in which the alienation of work under capitalism is resolved in the dimensions of a coming digital society, they help to foster the notion that it is not the wage labor/capital relation that is the problem. Instead, class inequality is read as a purely technological issue and that digital technologies and the new avenues of consumption they engender are the solution. What is particularly interesting is the way in which both films make use of multiple techniques in order to speak to different segments of the work force, in this way continuing to foster the idea that the digital economy is driven by desire because there is always a commodity that responds to the interests of *you*.

Dark City combines the imagery of the 1927 German science-fiction classic *Metropolis* with the tone of the Noir films of the 1930s and 1940s such as the *Maltese Falcon* and *The Big Sleep* in order to appeal to both the more educated sectors of the work force who are trained to read such intertextual references as the mark of sophistication and subtly, thereby reinforcing their self-identification as smart readers, as well as those who might be interested in the more popular cultural forms of the detective novel and science-fiction narratives in the mold of *The Twilight Zone* and *The Outer Limits*. The film opens with the protagonist, John Murdoch, awakening in a strange hotel room to find that he has no memory and no history beyond vague recollections of a traditional middle-class life cut short by the tragic loss of guidance (signified by the death of his parents in a house fire). In a panic over his inability to remember how he got there, he looks in the mirror and finds that he no longer has a clear image of who he is: the mirror is broken, his image is seen by both him and the viewer as fractured, and, thus, that the correspondence between what he knows and what he sees is no longer reliable. It is the way in which the film is able to raise as a possibility that the middle-class life that he once believed in might not exist as he remembered and, as a result, might not be what he really desired. In other words, it opens up the possibility that our desires might be false, or at least, directed at a false object.

The plot then follows Murdoch as he both dodges the police—he has been falsely accused of several murders—and attempts to find his way back to Shell Beach, his childhood home. As the plot progresses, it becomes clear, however, that the film is not going to be a traditional "noir-ish" story as something besides Murdoch is out of place. The city, it seems, never emerges from darkness and, as he soon finds out, physically changes every evening at midnight. In addition, everyone he meets has heard of Shell Beach, but no one remembers how to get there. It is as if Shell Beach has become a mass delusion, a symbol of lost pleasures which the system once provided but which seem no longer attainable. In this sense, the film addresses the anxieties of the working class in the United States who are constantly fed the images of the American Dream, but whose wages have not risen since the 1960s, thereby rendering the idea of Shell Beach, much less the reality, virtually impossible to even dream of, much less realize.

It is at the end of the film that we learn the truth about the Dark City and John Murdoch. The city is actually an island floating in space, constructed by a group of alien parasites known as the Strangers, who are trying to find out what makes humanity *human* in order to escape their fate as a dying race. Each night they place all of the inhabitants in a trance and rearrange their surroundings so as to monitor how and why they respond to difference. Murdoch, of course, represents a threat to their plans because he is no longer subject to the mechanisms of the trance. Through the process by which the Strangers attempt to regain control over Murdoch to find out why he is able to escape the evening rituals and thus see their project—they attempt to harness his memories directly and share them among the group—he is implanted with their powers. He gains the same telekinetic powers they have, with the ability to overcome all of the boundaries of the material world, and engages in a battle that takes both he and the leader of the Strangers (because they can fly) to the skies above the city. At the film's conclusion Murdoch defeats the aliens to become the new leader of the city. Unlike the leaders who wanted to keep the city in the dark, he begins to metaphorically tear down the walls surrounding the city and opens the skies so that sunlight shines for the first time. He then surrounds the city with an ocean in order to recreate and return to Shell Beach. We are, of course, aware that what appears real is false—the Shell Beach to which he returns never existed—but more importantly we learn that the logic of reality is not the same. Whereas the memories of the past were directed by the owners of the city, under Murdoch's control reality has become malleable and shaped by the heterogeneity of individual desire. He is not *required* to return to structures of the past; he *wants* to. Reality has become a matter of personal choice and it is desire that makes reality happen. The film is thus a narrative that reinscribes the idea of the American Dream and locates its possibilities not in the material world, but at the level of ideas. The failure of the past was the attempt to impose the desires from above, while in the new reality desires are achieved because they come from the individual. This is the narrative of the digital economy, which promises that it is knowledge, not labor, that creates value and that it is through knowledge that everyone will be able to escape the rigid structures of the past and find their way to Shell Beach.

The Matrix makes use of almost the same imagery, the same cultural references, and in fact actually shared some of the same sets with *Dark City* which, even if for unintended economic reasons, makes their shared imagery important to consider for thinking about how the future is being represented. *The Matrix* is, perhaps, an even more culturally complex film even though it was marketed for a more popular audience. On the one hand, it directly references the high theory of Jean Baudrillard, while, on the other hand, it is a catalog of pop culture references, from the Hong Kong action movies of John Woo, to comics such as *Superman* and the *X-Men*, to classic fairy tales such as *Cinderella* and *Sleeping Beauty*. In this sense, the film is an attempt to be all things to all consumers, to be the plural commodity that gives everyone what they want and, therefore, be the ultimate digital space: the commodity that actually does respond to what the audience has been asking for, regardless of what the request was.

The film centers on Thomas Anderson, a typical dot-com worker who, at least on the surface, is living an alienated and mundane life. The initial imagery of this world is dreary: Anderson works in a cubicle with dozens of other identical-looking workers, and is clearly bored with the terms of his life. The visual effects of the film mimic this tone. The opening sequences are colored with a greenish hue that resembles the stale florescent lighting of the modern office. In this sense, the film reproduces a world that is not very different from what has come before. Despite entering the information age, Anderson's job as a symbolic analyst does not seem to fulfill its initial promise of a new economy. Far from the imagery of a plural world beyond work, the digital world appears in the beginning of the film to be an extension of the social relations of the past. However, following a scene in which Anderson is confronted by his boss and told that if he continues to believe that he is "special" and that "the rules do not apply to him" he will be fired, the viewer begins to learn that there is in fact another side to Thomas Anderson—in his private life he is known on the web by the hacker alias Neo and spends his time selling cracked software and searching for the world's most famous computer hacker, Morpheus.

What is particularly interesting is that even this exciting alter-ego is not enough to satisfy Anderson's unfulfilled desires. Despite his life as a hacker, he remains alone. For example, when he is apprehended by what appear to be members of the FBI or Secret Service and is interrogated about his knowledge of Morpheus, the lead interrogator, Agent Smith, makes it clear that despite his cool hacker alias, he is still the same person who helps his "land-lady take out the garbage." In other words, the viewer is meant to identify with the possibility that the promises of the digital economy are false, and have not produced anything but a stunted adolescence. Like *Dark City*, the viewer is meant to question whether their desires are just unfulfilled or whether what they desired has been an illusion that will never be realized.

Ultimately he learns that Morpheus is, in fact, actually looking *for him* because he believes Anderson is "the one." Following his encounter with the agents, Anderson sets up a meeting with Morpheus to learn what the *matrix* is, but, in an endless doubling that is the hallmark of the film, is told that one cannot be told what the matrix is. In this scene the matrix is established as both in experience and not in experience, as both the truth of the world and its illusion, thereby picking up the narrative that in the digital age, all conceptual boundaries are in crisis. Of course, that the film wants Anderson to both question all of his experiences and yet rely on his experiences to tell him the truth of reality—he is given the choice to either go back to his boring life as a computer programmer or to find out "how deep the rabbit hole goes"—is an indication of how disruptive of ideology the film will ultimately be.

It is at this point that Neo, like Murdoch, learns that the world he thought he knew does not exist. Instead, reality has been replaced by an ideological simulacra, described by Morpheus as "a prison for your mind," that was established sometime in the past to ensure that humans do not question their enslavement to the instrumental reason of machines in the present. What is interesting is how both films, at the moment the main character learns about the nature of reality, incorporate what have become the aesthetic of dark lighting found in many science fiction films into part of the narrative. The truth of reality is that humans have been overthrown by artificial intelligence and instead of humans using machines to produce the means of subsistence machines now "farm" humans, using their neural-electrical energy to support a tenuous existence in a world that, in an echo of *Dark City*, is absent of sunlight. Humans, in turn, have become cyborgs: half human, half machine, batteries whose bio power serves as the powers supply for the AI's power plant. The paradox, at least in the first film of the trilogy, is that humans are only able to participate in acts of resistance against the machines from inside the matrix. Their resistance is further limited, Neo is told, by a lingering attachment to the past: if they die in virtual reality of the matrix, then they die in the real world.

The turning point of the film comes when humanity is forced to confront the limits of existence as he once believed it to be—rational and scientific. When Morpheus is captured by the computer program guardians of the matrix—the Secret Service agents seen earlier in the film—he is told that what has occurred is the natural and inevitable outcome of the post-Fordist transition from labor to knowledge. Agent Smith, one of the human forms assumed by the guardians of the matrix, argues that having been freed from the burden of labor, there is no longer any use for humanity. Instead, he states, "Human beings are a disease, a cancer of this planet. You are a plague. And we are the cure." Agent Smith here is thus intended to represent in the extreme the instrumental logic of progress, rationality, and homogenization—the "singular consciousness" that brought about the downfall of humanity. Humanity, in its commitment to rationality and instrumental reason, has effected its own enslavement. It is during Morpheus's capture, however, that Neo also begins to realize that he might, in fact, be *the one*. What makes him the one is that he ultimately accepts the terms of the matrix. Unlike the other freed humans—and in particular the character of Cypher, a freed human who makes a deal with the Agents to betray Morpheus in return for being re-entered into the false consciousness of the matrix—he gives up entirely the idea of returning to the materiality of the past and, instead, accepts the fluidity and virtuality of the future. He realizes instead that the very logic of death in the matrix that others were so afraid of—in which the mind (that is, knowledge) determines the materiality of real life (that is, labor)—actually represents a new cultural realm of freedom based upon individual desire. What makes him a truly digital hero for the contemporary age, in other words, is the realization that culture has become excessive, operating independently from the historical and social relations of the past, and thus that he no longer has to try to fit into a modernist framework. Accepting that resistance to the matrix requires that one gives up any notion of an outside to the existing, he gains the ability to see that the world he inhabits is nothing but lines of code that can be rewritten to fit the desires of the individual. This triumph over materiality is complete when, in a decidedly symbolic act of resistance, he takes over the image of Agent Smith and explodes it from the inside. The film then ends not with Neo's escape from the matrix, but rather with a declaration that he is going to create a new matrix, one without "rules and controls . . . borders and boundaries . . . a world where anything is possible," at which point, like John Murdoch, he demonstrates his rejection of the limits of materiality by flying away from the city into the sky. That is to say, while the fact that the film represents a world in which knowledge is in flux and thus that anything might be unreliable, what the film actually represents as most important is the truth of desire. What will ultimately turn Anderson into Neo is that after resisting it for most of the film, he finally realizes that all of the time he really did want to be *the one*, and that it was by putting his desires into action that he is able to change his reality so that it matches his desire.

What has made both films such popular representations of the digital economy is the way in which they acknowledge the social contradictions of wage labor while also providing a way of understanding these contradictions not in terms of the division of labor, but in terms of the limits of mass production to meet the expanding individual desires of the new me. In this context, the digital economy is defined as the opening of new spaces of cultural democracy and not the extension of exploitation. In this sense, they are the popular forms of digital theory in which class divisions are reduced to a state of mind. That both films accept the idea that resistance today occurs at the level of consumption, rather than the relations of production, can be seen by the way in which both films hinge on the narrative of choice. John Murdoch might desire returning to his false memories of a middle-class life, but it is precisely that it is a matter of choice that makes his reality different despite its appearance as the same. Similarly, Neo does not have to be Thomas Anderson, a lonely computer programmer. Instead, by consuming the wonders of digital technology, he becomes part of a hip and fashionable clique at the cutting edge of culture. In fact, the narrative of choice in *The Matrix* becomes so overwhelming as to almost be parodic. At every stage of the film—regardless of whether it is saving Morpheus from torture or opening an apartment door—Neo cannot advance without being reminded that he is faced with a choice of whether to continue on his path of becoming *the one*. Furthermore, by the third film, *The Matrix: Revolutions*, this ideology of choice reaches its pinnacle when we learn that Neo's entire purpose as *the one* is essentially nothing more than to reboot the matrix program, only this time giving people the free choice of whether they want to live in the real world or spend their lives in the virtual world of the matrix. On these terms, just as John Murdoch and Thomas Anderson can only escape their fates by learning how to remake the images that surround them without making any significant changes to their actual conditions of life—neither fundamentally transforms their society, rather they learn that *revolution* means to work within the existing—so too does the viewer learn that in the digital age they can remake their lives with a simple change of mind. By declaring that society is shaped by matters of personal choice, what is obscured in both films is that choice is always historical. The choices we can make, however, are determined not by what we consume, but rather are dependent upon developments at the mode of production. In promoting acts of consumption as resistance, *Dark City* and *The Matrix* thus offer readings of the contemporary that extend, rather than challenge, capitalist relations.

Human Labor and the Schizophrenic Machine

Reading digitally, as I have argued, is an attempt to address the growing contradiction between technological advances in the forces of production and the limits of the relations of production, which restrict the development of technology to the production of profit. Instead of locating the contradiction at the site of production, the main reading put forward by theorists such as Bruno Latour and Donna Haraway and in the films *Dark City* and

The Matrix is that the development of digital capitalism severs the connection between culture and the economy, thereby fostering the idea of social change within the framework of capitalism without the necessity of addressing the logic of exploitation. This theory of a digital culture beyond the exploitation of labor, far from representing the cutting edge theory of a postexploitative stage of capitalism, extends capitalist relations by positing that material differences can be located in the terms of the market. That is to say, politics essentially becomes a matter of negotiating of better terms rather than challenging the market itself.

According to the theory of a postexploitative and pluralized digital economy driven by individual desire, what enables the emergence of a heterogeneous culture is the substitution of *accumulated* or *dead* labor (technology) for *living labor* (human labor power). In this reading, contemporary capitalism can no longer be considered capitalism because of the increasing importance that knowledge and innovation plays in the economy. In other words, what critics such as Latour, Haraway and others are suggesting is that the labor theory of value no longer applies in a knowledge economy and, as such, it is no longer necessary to confront the primary contradiction of capitalism between owners and workers because the primary commodity (information) cannot be exhausted. This, however, mistakes developments in the forms that production takes with the logic of production itself. As Chris Harman writes in *Economics of the Madhouse*, "some forms of capital—machines, factory buildings and so on—do make labor much more productive than it would be otherwise."[47] However, even though "the most elementary tool adds enormously to human productivity," technology cannot replace labor. "Machines and factory buildings are not things that exist in their own right," he explains, "they are the product of previous human labor."[48] That is to say, while a "human being can make things without the machine," the machine "cannot make anything without the human being setting it to work."[49] Although technology can enhance production, it always does so within the terms established by the relations of production. For example, while the productivity of labor in the United States has continued to increase over the past fifty years, wages over the same period of time have remained virtually stagnant. In fact, as Robert Brenner remarks, one of the main reasons that the U.S. economy has remained attractive to foreign investment in the latter half of the twentieth century is that it has maintained a relatively regular growth in the productivity of labor—

growing at an average of 2.9 percent in the period 1979–90 and increasing to 3.5 percent in the years 1990–96—while simultaneously restricting the growth of wages to near zero levels in terms of real wage growth.[50] In other words, while labor productivity has created numerous advances in both manufacturing as well as consumer technologies, what is amazing about this period is not the creation of the iPod or the World Wide Web. It is that despite the increasing productivity of labor, the gap between the richest and poorest Americans has continued to grow at an increasing rate. According to the "State of Working America 2008/2009," published by the Economic Policy Institute, "in 1962, the wealthiest 1% of households averaged 125 times the wealth of the median household" while "in 2004, the wealthiest 1% of households averaged 190 times the wealth of the median household, with particularly large increases in the 1980s and from 2001 to 2004."[51]

What is occluded, then, in the assumption that a digital economy shifts the logic of capitalism through the introduction of new technologies is that while the revolutionizing of the means of production is central to capitalist development, the substitution of machinery for labor power cannot, in itself, supplant capitalism. Capitalism depends upon extracting surplus labor from living labor, and not the accumulated labor of machinery, as the basis of surplus value. Instead, because of the irrationality of the system, overinvestment in technology leads to a falling rate of profit and a crisis of overproduction. Harman writes, "The pressure on each capitalist to keep ahead of every other leads to continual upgrading of plant and machinery, and continual pressure on workers to provide the profits which make the upgrading possible."[52] However, insofar as it is "labour, not machinery, that creates value," the effect is that as "dead" labor increases over living labor, the costs of investment "rises much faster than profit."[53] In other words, technological development is a double-edged sword for the capitalist. It enables the capitalist to increase the productivity of labor, and thus gain a competitive advantage in the marketplace, while simultaneously diminishing the rate of surplus value. In turn, for working people while increased productivity results in the availability of commodities and resources, it results in a lowering of wages and the inability to buy said commodities, as productivity increases while wages remain stagnant or grow slower than the cost of living.

For example, the complex computer skills that were said to have replaced the regimented industrial jobs of Fordism, and which once required years of study but were said to be rewarded with a high-paying job, a nice home, and other aspects that are said to make up the heterogeneity of middle-class life, have been made simple by more recent technological developments and no longer command the kinds of high wages they once did. New electronic devices are manufactured at accelerated rates and at lower cost; as an article in *Fortune* magazine explains:

> Increasingly, supereducated and highly paid workers are finding themselves traveling the same road their blue-collar peers took in the late '80s. Then, hardhats in places like Flint, Mich., and Pittsburgh were suffering from the triple threat of computerization, tech-led productivity gains, and the relocation of their jobs to offshore sites. Machines—or low-wage foreigners—could just as easily do their work. The white-collar crowd was concerned, but they knew that those three forces would also help get the American economy humming. And they did. Now that trust has come back to haunt them. Technology has allowed companies to handle rising sales without adding manpower. Gains in productivity mean one white-collar worker can do the work that would have taken two or three of his peers to do ten years ago.[54]

This is the cruel reality of life under capitalism. Skills that today make workers employable in jobs in which they can earn enough to provide for their families are no guarantee that tomorrow they will not be facing the possibility of being out of work or of no longer being able to earn enough to survive, much less maintain middle-class status. The fact that under capitalism workers have nothing to sell but their labor power means that any skills they have spent tremendous time to acquire to make their labor power more valuable could just as easily tomorrow command lower wages, or become entirely unnecessary. It is this fact that condemns working people to a life of constant uncertainty as long as capitalism remains. As Marx and Engels explain in *The Manifesto of the Communist Party*, "The various interests and conditions of life within the ranks of the proletariat are more and more equalized, in proportion as the machinery obliterates all distinctions of labor and nearly everywhere reduces wages to the same low level."[55] In other words, the cultural heterogeneity that appears at one moment is quickly shown to be an illusion as the fundamental homogeneity of capitalism is once again exposed.

In suggesting that any remaining contradiction between capital and labor is one of a residue of living labor that will be eliminated by the automation of production, digital culture theories substitute conflict between *living* and *dead* labor that capitalism produces for the cause of exploitation itself, thus proposing that freeing living labor through the automation of production will eliminate the binary class division without having to change the terms of capitalism. Capitalism can go on, it is argued, without labor. The substitution of the secondary antagonism between living and dead labor for that of the fundamental antagonism between capital and labor assumes that the automation of production negates exploitation when, in fact, as long as technological advancement is harnessed to the interests of capitalism, it only further heightens the contradictions between capital and labor. While advancements in technology make possible the meeting of the needs of all, the subjection of such advancements to the production of profit means that what disappears is not *work* (in the abstract), but rather the means by which millions of workers can meet their basic needs. The contradiction of the systematic exploitation of the working class through technological advancement is thus ideologically transformed in dominant discussions of technology into a liberatory potentiality from within. It is such that the theories of reading culture digitally reflect the real material conditions of life, but from the position of the capitalist. While technological advances in the means of production have created the potential to meet the needs of the world's population, the concentration of capital in the hands of the capitalist means that rather than having their needs met, workers today are subjected to the most brutal, and intensified, division of labor in which they become, as Marx and Engels argue, "an appendage of the machine."[56]

The substitution of the fundamental antagonism between capital and labor with that of a conflict between the reductionist logic of a "failed" epistemology of the past and a pluralized digital future which exceeds the capitalist mode of production is evident in what has become one of the most canonical texts in contemporary digital theory, Gilles Deleuze and Felix Guattari's *Anti-Oedipus: Capitalism and Schizophrenia*. This text characterizes the digital economy as an *automated* capitalism premised not on the production of commodities as much as the circulation of "spectral values" which transverse the antagonism between capital and labor such that "there is no such thing as either man or nature now, only a process that produces the one within the other and couples the machines together. Producing-machines, desiring-machines, everywhere schizophrenic machines."[57] This theory of class as a hybrid entity assumes the possibility of technological development in itself to transcend social antagonisms by representing the

wage labor/capital relation as having been replaced by a spontaneous cou-
pling fueled by the mutual desires of all market participants. Deleuze and
Guattari's articulation of capitalist production, in which the social division
of labor is rearticulated as a machine of production and consumption, thus
collapses the class division between owners and workers into a circular theory of class-as-lifestyle—without the economic compulsion of necessity that
results from the private ownership of the means of production—and thus
substitutes for the exploitation of production the liberation of consumption.

To achieve this, Deleuze and Guattari must rewrite history as the drive
towards posthuman labor, and thus posit that the primary conflict of the
modern period was between the philosophic division of the *human* and *nature* that has now been effaced by the development of the machine. According to this reading, technological development fractures the modernist
attempt at theorizing culture as part of a social totality and replaces it with
the figure of the "schizophrenic." In the new cultural climate of digital
capitalism, they write, "we no longer believe in the myth of the existence of
fragments that, like pieces of an antique statue, are merely waiting for the
last one to be turned up, so that they may all be glued back together to
create a unity that is precisely the same as the original unity."[58] "Schizo"
analysis, on the contrary, is represented as the alternative to what they define as the metaphysics of *presence*—regardless of whether this presence is
understood as either the materiality of class or the process of signification.
The "schizophrenic" operates in their text as that which disrupts boundaries through the introduction of *desire* into all modes of investigation. The
"schizophrenic," they write, is:

> at the very limit of the social codes, where a despotic Signifier destroys all chains,
> linearizes them, biunivocalizes them, and uses the bricks as so many immobile
> units for the construction of an imperial Great Wall of China. But the schizo
> continually detaches them, continually works them loose and carries them off in
> every direction in order to create a new polyvocity that is the code of desire.[59]

That is to say, the schizophrenic becomes the figure for a postanalytic,
postscientific, posthistorical subject who cannot be reduced to any one reading. On these terms, Deleuze and Guattari argue that the singular desires
of the individual and not labor are the real motor of history. They state,
"Desire is not bolstered by needs, but rather the contrary; needs are derived
from desire: they are counterproducts within the real that desire

produces . . . Desire always remains in close touch with the conditions of objective existence; it embraces them and follows them, shifts when they shift, and does not outlive them."[60] By casting *desire* as that which produces the *real*—as that which "is at work everywhere, functioning smoothly at times, at other times in fits and starts. It breathes, it heats, it eats, it shits and fucks"[61]—Deleuze and Guattari claim that we can move beyond any need to understand culture in relation to the economic. Instead, what is necessary is releasing the heterogeneous desires of the individual as a means of overcoming the homogenous logic of past forms of capitalism. They write,

> Desire is the set of *passive syntheses* that engineer partial objects, flows, and bodies, and that function as units of production. The real is the end product, the result of the passive syntheses of desire as autoproduction of the unconscious . . . The truth of the matter is that *social production is purely and simply desiring-production itself under determinate conditions.*[62]

There is, according to this argument, no logic that can account for the heterogeneous workings of desire as it represents that which always exceeds attempts at explanation and resists conceptualization. "Universal history," they argue, "is the history of contingencies, and not the history of necessity"; it is an unending play between the "ruptures" and "limits" of desire against the forms of oppression which inevitably emerge to control it.[63] On these terms, what Deleuze and Guattari situate as the alternative to the labor theory of value is the valorization of desire as a means of resisting all cultural determinations.

Once again, we are back to the argument that shifts in the mode of accumulation exceed the logic of exploitation, such that there is no necessity for addressing one in relation to the other. On their terms, technological development is always a contradictory process because it creates the possibilities of desire while simultaneously engendering the means by which desire is controlled. In other words, within the logic of their argument, history is reduced to the play of desire and control regardless of any specifics. In all corners of history, in other words, and regardless of the organization of production, there is always a structure of desire and control. As such, while their theory of the schizophrenic is all about difference, it cannot ever lead to any real material difference since all future historical formations are reduced to the same, eternal logic of the past.

On the contrary, in their work Marx and Engels provide a critical theory of difference, in which the differences between oppressor and oppressed,

exploiter and exploited, are not read as *eternal,* but rather as historical relations dependent upon material conditions. That is to say, in contrast to the
readings of Deleuze and Guattari, by reading difference as it is defined by
material conditions, Marx and Engels open a space for analyzing the representations of society against its actual conditions. In turn, it becomes possible to consider the ways in which the actual conditions can be transformed
so that the way differences exist in society can also be changed. They write,
"In the present epoch, the domination of material relations over individuals,
and the suppression of individuality by fortuitous circumstances, has assumed its sharpest and most universal forms."[64] However,

> It was only possible to discover the connection between the kinds of enjoyment
> open to individuals at any particular time and the class relations in which they
> live, and the conditions of production and intercourse which give rise to these
> relations, the narrowness of the hitherto existing forms of enjoyment, which were
> outside the actual content of the life of the people and in contradiction to it, the
> connection between everyday philosophy of enjoyment and the enjoyment actu-
> ally present and the hypocrisy of such a philosophy which treated all individuals
> without distinction—it was, of course, only possible to discover all of this when
> it became possible to criticize the conditions of production and intercourse in
> the hitherto existing world, i.e., when the contradiction between the bourgeoisie
> and the proletariat had given rise to communist and socialist views.[65]

While Deleuze and Guattari assume the inevitability of inequality in the
very structure of desire, as Marx and Engels make clear in this passage, the
current forms of inequality are only one form of difference and that other
forms of difference, not exploitative relations based upon the meeting of the
needs of all, are possible. Technological developments cannot, therefore, be
read ahistorically as the effect of desire. Instead, technology is an index both
of the level of development of production as well as the social relations
under which that labor is carried out. On these terms, the developments in
production which enable the meeting of the needs of all, but which through
private ownership are used only to meet the needs of the few, serve as the
objective basis for the possibility of eliminating inequality through social
transformation.

Theories of digital culture as escaping the boundaries of the economic
are, therefore, the ideological reflection of the fact that as capitalism develops it invests increasing amounts of capital in revolutionizing the means
of production over and against the relations of living labor as a means of

maximizing profit. While it can thus be objectively recognized that recent technological developments increasingly point to the material possibility of the end of wage labor, under capitalism this is impossible as the development of the forces of production is tied to the interests of profit. Instead of being judged based on the priority of social necessity, technological advancements are judged on their ability to valorize capital. It is in the interests of profit that the possibility of emancipation from wage labor, which increases as capitalism develops, becomes the image of liberation through consumption, which extends rather than challenges the logic of exploitation. As Engels argues, technological advancements will not allow us to escape from the contradictions of capitalism; there can be no emancipation from wage labor without ending the logic of exploitation, because the fundamental antagonism between capital and labor is intensified, not transcended, by automation:

> During the first period of machinery, when it possess a *monopoly* character, profits are enormous, and hence the thirst for more, for boundless lengthening of the working day. With the general introduction of machinery this monopoly profit vanishes, and the law asserts itself that surplus-value arises, not from the labor *supplanted* by the machine, but from the labor employed by it.[66]

The dominance of the imagery of the *digital* in contemporary cultural theory is an index of this contradiction and the attempt to solve it at the level of ideas. The dominant readings of the digital condition in both popular media as well as most cultural theory represent the process of increasing productivity through the intensification of the production process—in which capitalists accumulate tremendous profits while workers are subjected either to increased domination by machinery or to the poverty of the industrial reserve army—as the transformation from a system based upon the exploitation of labor to a network of social relations in which the individual has been liberated through the introduction of technology: a postcapitalist, postproduction era of endless free time. However, as Marx argues in *The Poverty of Philosophy*, "nothing is more absurd than to see in machinery the *antithesis* of the division of labor."[67] In other words, far from a new stage of capitalist relations in which technology liberates workers from the exploitative constraints of the past, in actuality digital capitalism becomes a *hindrance* to progress, with numerous examples of innovations and advancements that were not introduced because of a possible negative effect on the rate of profit. Capitalism, in short, will not end because its relations of production have been "desired" away through consumption or by increasing developments in productivity alone. It homogenizes all social relations and reduces them to the terms of exchange value. In response, the primary role played by cultural theory has been to legitimate exploitation through the production of knowledge that promotes the appearance of increasing heterogeneity at the level of culture by severing its connection to the economic.

We live at a time of tremendous contradictions between what is and what could be. Given the material conditions that exist for actual radical transformation and not just cultural refiguration, I argue that what is most urgently needed today for true heterogeneity and difference to be realized is for cultural theory to return to the concepts of class, labor, and production so as to be able to understand how the forms of everyday life are shaped by the economic relations and thus how and why the development of technology means they can be transformed in the interests of all.

INTRODUCTION

1. Ernest Mandel, *Marxist Economic Theory* (New York/London: Monthly Review Press, 1968), 672.

2. Karl Marx and Frederick Engels, *Manifesto of the Communist Party*, in *Marx–Engels Collected Works*, vol. 6 (New York: International Publishers, 1976), 485.

3. Ibid., 519.

4. Jean-François Lyotard, *The Postmodern Condition: A Report on Knowledge*, trans. Geoff Bennington and Brian Massumi (Minneapolis: University of Minnesota Press, 1993), 5.

5. Ibid., xvi.

6. Ibid., 60.

7. Lawrence Grossberg, *Bringing It All Back Home: Essays on Cultural Studies* (Durham, N.C.: Duke University Press, 1997), 1.

8. Ibid., 10.

9. Ibid., 12.

10. Ibid., 4.

11. David Trend, *Reading Digital Culture* (Malden, Mass./Oxford, UK: Blackwell Publishers, 2001), 2.

12. Chris Hables Gray, *Cyborg Citizen: Politics in the Posthuman Age* (New York/London: Routledge, 2001), 13.

13. Stanley Aronowitz and Michael Menser, "On Cultural Studies, Science, and Technology," in *Technoscience and Cyberculture*, ed. Stanley Aronowitz, Barbara Martinsons, and Michael Menser (New York: Routledge, 1996), 8.

14. Geert Lovink, *Zero Comments: Blogging and Critical Internet Culture* (New York/London: Routledge, 2008), 232.

15. Ibid., 229.

16. Ibid., xii.

17. Ibid., xvii–xviii.

18. Ibid., 231.

19. Ibid., xviii.

20. Stuart Hall, "The Meaning of New Times," in *Stuart Hall: Critical Dialogues in Cultural Studies*, ed. David Morley and Kuan-Hsing Chen (London/New York: Routledge, 1996), 235.

21. Lovink, *Zero Comments*, 242.

22. Slavoj Žižek, *Living in the End Times* (London/New York: Verso, 2010), x.

23. Karl Marx, *Capital Volume I*, in *Marx-Engels Collected Works*, vol. 35 (New York: International Publishers, 1996), 19.

24. Karl Marx, preface to *A Contribution to a Critique of Political Economy*, ed. Maurice Dobb (New York: International Publishers, 1970), 21.

25. Terry Eagleton, "Lenin in the Postmodern Age," in *Lenin Reloaded: Toward a Politics of Truth*, ed. Sebastian Budgen, Stathis Kouvelakis, and Slavoj Žižek (Durham, N.C.: Duke University Press, 2007), 43.

1. THE SPIRIT TECHNOLOGICAL

1. Karl Marx, *Contribution to the Critique of Hegel's Philosophy of Law: Introduction*, in *Marx-Engels Collected Works*, vol. 3 (New York: International Publishers, 1975), 175.

2. Robert Hassan, *Information Society* (Cambridge, UK/Malden, Mass.: Polity Press, 2008), 23.

3. Helmut Willke, *Smart Governance: Governing the Global Knowledge Society*, (Frankfurt, Germany/New York: Campus Verlag, 2007), 195.

4. Frederick Engels, "Letter to Heinz Starkenburg," in *Marx & Engels on the Means of Communication*, ed. Yves de la Hayae (New York: International General, 1979), 70.

5. Timothy Druckery, introduction to *Culture on the Brink: Ideologies of Technology*, ed. Gretchen Bender and Timothy Druckery (Seattle, Wash.: Bay Press, 1994), 3.

6. Steven Best and Douglas Kellner, *The Postmodern Adventure: Science, Technology, and Cultural Studies at the Third Millennium* (New York: Guilford Press, 2001), 13.

7. Karl Marx and Frederick Engels, *Manifesto of the Communist Party*, in *Marx–Engels Collected Works*, vol. 6 (New York: International Publishers, 1976), 484–485.

8. Bill Gates, Nathan Myhrvold, and Peter Rinearson, *The Road Ahead* (New York: Viking, 1995).

9. Thomas L. Friedman, *The World Is Flat: A Brief History of the Twenty-First Century* (New York: Farrar, Straus and Giroux, 2005).

10. Nicholas Negroponte, *Being Digital* (New York: Knopf, 1995), 6.

11. Frederic Jameson, *Postmodernism, or the Cultural Logic of Late Capitalism* (Durham: Duke University Press, 1991), 5.

12. Ibid., 48.

13. Ibid., 17.

14. Ibid., 5.

15. Robert Hassan, *Information Society* (Digital Media and Society Series), 5.

16. Jeremy Rifkin, *The Age of Access: The New Culture of Hypercapitalism, Where All of Life Is a Paid–for Experience* (New York: J.P. Tarcher/Putnam, 2000), 41.

17. Ibid., 114.

18. Ibid., 5.

19. Ibid., 47.

20. Ibid., 45.

21. Ibid., 50.

22. Ibid., 13.

23. Roger Sullivan, introduction to *The Metaphysics of Morals*, by Immanuel Kant. (Cambridge, UK/New York: Cambridge University Press, 1996), xiii.

24. Immanuel Kant, *The Metaphysics of Morals*, (Cambridge, UK/New York: Cambridge University Press, 1996), 41.

25. Ibid., 45.

26. Ibid., 51.

27. Karl Marx, *Capital Volume I*, in *Marx-Engels Collected Works*, vol. 35 (New York: International Publishers, 1996), 583.

28. Ibid., 705.

29. Ibid., 706.

30. Ibid., 705.

31. Stuart Hall, "The Meaning of New Times," in *Stuart Hall: Critical Dialogues in Cultural Studies*, edited by David Morley and Kuan-Hsing Chen (London and New York: Routledge, 1996), 226.

32. Peter Hitchcock, *Oscillate Wildly: Space, Body, and Spirit of Millennial Materialism* (Minneapolis: University of Minnesota Press, 1999), xiii.

33. Ernesto Laclau and Chantal Mouffe, *Hegemony and Socialist Strategy: Towards a Radical Democratic Politics, 2nd ed.* (London and New York: Verso, 2001), 111.

34. Jean Burgess and Joshua Green, *YouTube* (Cambridge, UK/Malden, Mass.: Polity Press, 2009), 75.

35. Zillah Eisenstein, *Global Obscenities: Patriarchy, Capitalism and the Lure of Cyberfantasy* (New York: New York University Press, 1998), 1.

36. Ibid., 1.

37. Ibid., 46.

38. Ibid., 71.

39. Ibid., 93.

40. Jan van Dijk, *The Deepening Divide: Inequality in the Information Society* (Thousand Oaks, Calif.: Sage Publications, 2005).

41. Manuel Castells, *The Rise of the Network Society* (Cambridge, Mass.: Blackwell Publishers, 1996).

42. Michel Hardt and Antonio Negri, *Empire* (Cambridge, Mass.: Harvard University Press, 2000).

43. Mark Poster, *What's the Matter with the Internet?* (Minneapolis: University of Minnesota Press, 2001), 2.

44. Ibid., 184.

45. Ibid., 49.

46. Jean Baudrillard, *Simulacra and Simulation* (Ann Arbor: University of Michigan Press, 1994).

47. Poster, *What's the Matter with the Internet*, 2.

48. Ibid., 11.

49. Ibid., 48.

50. Peter Drucker, *Post-Capitalist Society* (New York: Harper Business, 1993), 8.

51. Ibid., 8.

52. Richard L. Florida, *The Rise of the Creative Class: And How It's Transforming Work, Leisure, Community and Everyday Life* (New York: Basic Books, 2004).

53. Poster, *What's the Matter with the Internet*, 40.

54. Ibid., 49.

55. Ibid., 43.

56. Ibid., 47.

57. Ibid., 58.

58. Ibid., 46.

59. Max Weber, "Class, Status, Party," in *From Max Weber: Essays in Sociology*, trans. by H.H. Gerht and C. Wright Mills. (London: Routledge, 1961), 183.

60. Ibid., 187.

61. Hall, "The Meaning of New Times," 235.

62. Hall, "On Postmodernism and articulation: An Interview with Stuart Hall," in *Stuart Hall: Critical Dialogues in Cultural Studies*, 143.

63. Lindsey German, *A Question of Class* (London: Bookmarks, 1996), 14.

64. Ibid., 16.

65. Ibid., 12.

66. Ibid., 18.

67. John Frow, *Cultural Studies and Cultural Value* (Oxford: Oxford University Press, 1995), 1.

68. Ibid., 5.

69. Yochai Benkler, *The Wealth of Networks: How Social Production Transforms Markets and Freedom* (New Haven, Conn./London: Yale University Press, 2006), 2.

70. Ibid., 6.

71. Ibid., 2.

72. John Allen, "Fordism and Modern Industry," *Modernity: An Introduction to Modern Societies*, ed. Stuart Hall, David Held, Don Hubert, and Kenneth Thompson (Oxford: Blackwell, 1996), 281.

73. Ibid., 282.

74. Ibid., 286.

75. John Allen, "Post-Industrialism/Post-Fordism," in *Modernity: An Introduction to Modern Societies*, 534.

76. Ibid., 535.

77. Alvin Toffler, *The Third Wave* (New York: Morrow, 1980), 11, 37–45, 265–288.

78. Ibid., 274.

79. Negroponte, *Being Digital*, 164.

80. Jacques Ellul, *The Technological Society* (New York: Knopf, 1965), 5.

81. Constance Penley and Andrew Ross, *Technoculture* (Minneapolis: University of Minnesota Press, 1991), xi.

82. Daniel Bell, *The Coming of Post-Industrial Society: A Venture in Social Forecasting* (New York: Basic Books, 1973), x.

83. Ibid., x.

84. Ibid., x.

85. Ibid., xii.

86. Ibid., xi.

87. Ibid., xi.

88. Ibid., xii.

89. Ibid., xi.

90. Ibid., x.

91. Ibid., xii.

92. Ibid., xiii, xv.

93. Ibid., xiii.

94. Ibid., xix.

95. Ibid., x.

96. Ibid., xvi.

97. Ibid., xiv.

98. Ibid., xvi-xvii.

99. Jean Baudrillard, *Symbolic Exchange and Death* (London/Thousand Oaks, Calif.: Sage Publications, 1993), 125.

100. Ibid., 127.

101. Ibid., 140.

102. Daniel Bell, *The Coming of Post-Industrial Society: A Venture in Social Forecasting*, xiv.

103. Henry Giroux, *Impure Acts: The Practical Politics of Cultural Studies* (New York and London: Routledge, 2000), 2.

104. Karl Marx, *Poverty of Philosophy*, in *Marx-Engels Collected Works*, vol. 6 (New York: International Publishers, 1976), 166.

105. Ibid., 165–166.

106. Ibid., 166.

107. Martin Heidegger, "The Question Concerning Technology," in *Basic Writings*, trans. David Farrell Krell (San Francisco, Calf.: Harper San Francisco, 1993), 311.

108. Ibid., 312.

109. Ibid., 313.

110. Ibid., 320.

111. Ibid., 322.

112. Ibid., 321.

113. Ibid., 323.

114. Ibid., 332.

115. Ibid., 333.

116. Ibid., 313.

117. Ibid., 315.

118. Ibid., 315.

119. Ibid., 318.

120. Ibid., 318.

121. Bernard Stiegler, *Technics and Time, 1: The Fault of Epimetheus* (Stanford: Stanford University Press, 1998), 7.

122. R. L. Rutsky, *High Technē: Art and Technology from the Machine Aesthetic to the Posthuman* (Minneapolis: University of Minnesota Press, 1999), 1.

123. Ibid., 6.

124. Ibid., 2.

125. Ibid., 4.

126. Ibid., 4.

127. Samuel Weber, *Mass Mediauras: Form, Technics, Media*, edited By Alan Cholodenko (Stanford: Stanford University Press, 1996), 73.

128. Ibid., 69.

129. Ibid., 64.

130. Ibid., 74.

131. Ibid., 8.

132. David Golumbia, *The Cultural Logic of Computation* (Cambridge, Mass./London: Harvard University Press, 2009), 9.

133. Ibid., 130.

134. Ibid., 173.

135. Ibid., 151.

136. Ibid., 185.

137. Ibid., 110.

138. Ibid., 13.

139. Karl Marx, *Economic and Philosophic Manuscripts of 1844*, in *Marx–Engels Collected Works*, vol. 3 (New York: International Publishers, 1975), 272.

140. Ibid., 278.

141. V. I. Lenin, "Dialectics and Formal Logic," in *Reader in Marxist Philosophy*, edited by Howard Selsam and Harry Martel, (New York: International Publishers, 1987), 116.

142. Ibid., 116.

143. Ibid., 116–117.

144. Leander Kahney, *The Cult of iPod* (San Francisco: No Starch Press, 2005).

145. Steven Levy, *The Perfect Thing: How the iPod Shuffles Commerce, Culture, and Coolness* (New York: Simon & Schuster, 2007), 5.

146. Ibid., 4.

147. Friedman, *The World Is Flat*, 155.

148. Robert McChesney, *The Problem of the Media: U.S. Communication Politics in the Twenty-First Century* (New York: Monthly Review Press, 2004), 178.

149. Karl Marx, *Capital Volume I*, in *Marx–Engels Collected Works*, vol. 35 (New York: International Publishers, 1996), 83.

150. "Where Would Jesus Queue? Marketing the iPhone," *The Economist*, July 7 (2007): 65.

151. Marx, *Marx–Engels Collected Works*, 35:82.

152. "Reader Comments," *Engadget*, http://tinyurl.com/engadget2004.

153. Kahney, *The Cult of iPod*, 139.

154. Ibid., 139.

155. Michael Bull, *Sound Moves: iPod Culture and Urban Experience* (New York: Routledge, 2008), 147.

156. Ibid., 110.

157. Ernest Mandel, *Marxist Economic Theory* (New York and London: Monthly Review Press, 1968), 172.

158. Ibid., 172.

159. Ibid., 172.

160. Ibid., 172.

161. Ibid., 172.

162. Ibid., 173.

163. Ibid., 673.

164. Ibid., 672.

165. Ibid., 672.

166. Marx, *Marx–Engels Collected Works*, 35:177.

167. Ibid., 219.

168. Ibid., 397.

169. Ibid., 489.

170. Ibid., 409.

171. Marx, *Marx–Engels Collected Works*, 6:188.

2. GLOBAL NETWORKS AND THE MATERIALITY OF IMMATERIAL LABOR

1. Jean-François Lyotard, *The Postmodern Condition: A Report on Knowledge*, trans. Geoff Bennington and Brian Massumi (Minneapolis: University of Minnesota, 1993), 63.

2. Karl Marx, preface to *A Contribution to a Critique of Political Economy*, ed. Maurice Dobb (New York: International Publishers, 1970), 21.

3. Robert Brenner, "The Economics of Global Turbulence," *New Left Review* 229 (1998), 265.

4. Yochai Benkler, *The Wealth of Networks: How Social Production Transforms Markets and Freedom* (New Haven, Conn./London: Yale University Press, 2006), 6.

5. Ibid., 19.

6. Clay Shirky, *Here Comes Everybody: The Power of Organizing Without Organizations* (New York: The Penguin Press, 2008), 47.

7. Ibid., 47.

8. Chris Harman, "Globalisation: A Critique of A New Global Orthodoxy," *International Socialism* 73 (1996): 3.

9. Anthony Giddens and Will Hutton, "Anthony Giddens and Will Hutton in Conversation," in *Global Capitalism*, ed. Anthony Giddens and Will Hutton (New York: The New Press, 2000), 11.

10. John Tomlinson, *Globalization and Culture* (Chicago: University of Chicago Press, 1999), 88.

11. Helmut Willke, *Smart Governance: Governing the Global Knowledge Society*, (Frankfurt, Germany/New York: Campus Verlag, 2007), 199.

12. Mark Poster, *Information Please: Culture and Politics in the Age of Digital Machines*, (Durham and London: Duke University Press, 2006), 195–196.

13. Jan Nederveen Pieterse, *Globalization and Culture: Global Mélange* (New York: Rowan and Littlefield, 2003), 83.

14. Ulrich Beck, *The Cosmopolitan Vision* (Cambridge, UK/Malden, Mass.: Polity, 2006), 91.

15. Malcolm Waters, *Globalization* (London; New York: Routledge, 2001), 24.

16. Klaus Götz and Nadine Bleher, "Towards the Transnationalisation of Corporate Culture," in *Borderless Business: Managing the Far-Flung Enterprise*, ed. Clarence J. Mann and Klaus Götz (Westport, Conn./London: Praeger Publishers, 2006), 297.

17. See, for example, Thomas L. Friedman, *The World Is Flat: A Brief History of the Twenty-First Century* (New York: Farrar, Straus and Giroux, 2005) and Kenichi Omahe, *The Borderless World: Power and Strategy in the Interlinked Economy* (New York: HarperBusiness, 1990).

18. Rafael X. Reuveny and William R. Thompson, introduction to "The North-South Divide and International Studies: A Symposium," in International *Studies Review* 9, no. 4 (2007): 556–564.

19. International Monetary Fund, *World Economic Outlook: October 2007* (Washington D.C.: International Monetary Fund, 2007), 137.

20. Francis Fukuyama, *The End of History and the Last Man* (New York: Avon Books, 1992), xv.

21. Martin Wolf, *Why Globalization Works* (New Haven, Conn./London: Yale University Press, 2004), 147.

22. World Bank, *2007 World Development Indicators*. (Washington D.C.: The World Bank, 2007), 4.

23. International Monetary Fund, *World Economic Outlook*, 158–159.

24. Karl Marx, *Wage-Labour and Capital/Value, Price and Profit* (New York: International Publishers, 1997), 39.

25. Nederveen Pieterse, *Globalization and Culture*, 117.

26. Roland Robertson, *Globalization: Social Theory and Global Culture* (London: Sage, 1992), 184.

27. Tiziana Terranova, *Network Culture: Politics for the Information Age* (London and Ann Arbor, Mich.: Pluto Press, 2004), 82.

28. Beck, *The Cosmopolitan Vision*, 100.

29. Bruce Robbins, *Feeling Global: Internationalism in Distress* (New York: New York University Press, 1999), 108.

30. Waters, *Globalization*, 56.

31. David Held, "Democracy and the Global System," in *Political Theory Today*, ed. David Held (Stanford, Calif.: Stanford University Press, 1991), 211.

32. Arjun Appadurai, "Disjunction and Difference in the Global Cultural Economy," in *The Cultural Studies Reader* (London/New York: Routledge, 1999), 221.

33. Tomlinson, *Globalization and Culture*, 7.

34. George Ritzer, *The Globalization of Nothing* (Thousand Oaks, Calif.: Pine Forge Press, 2004), 81.

35. Ibid., 82.

36. Ibid., xi.

37. Ibid., 75.

38. Ibid., 7.

39. Ibid., 75.

40. Ibid., 90.

41. Ibid., xii.

42. Ibid., xiii.

43. George Ritzer, *The Globalization of Nothing 2* (Thousand Oaks, Calif.: Pine Forge Press, 2007), 207.

44. David Pryce-Jones, "Why They Hate Us", *National Review* (October 1, 2001): 8.

45. Samuel P. Huntington, *The Clash of Civilizations and the Remaking of World Order* (New York: Simon & Schuster, 1996), 21.

46. Ibid., 28.

47. Ibid., 184.

48. Niall Ferguson, *Colossus: The Price of America's Empire* (New York: Penguin Press, 2004), 25.

49. Nederveen Pieterse, *Globalization and Culture*, 77.

50. Michael Hardt and Antonio Negri, *Empire* (Cambridge, Mass.: Harvard University Press, 2000), xiv.

51. Manfred B. Steger, *Globalization: A Very Short Introduction* (Oxford, UK/ New York: Oxford University Press, 2003), 14.

52. Waters, *Globalization*, 186.

53. Appadurai, "Disjunction and Difference in the Global Cultural Economy," 221.

54. See, for example, Robert Brenner, "The Economics of Global Turbulence," *New Left Review* 229 (1998), 11; Immanuel Wallerstein, *World-Systems Analysis: An Introduction*. (Durham, N.C./London: Duke University Press, 2004), 20; Michael Hardt and Antonio Negri, *Empire* (Cambridge, Mass.: Harvard University Press, 2000), 150.

55. Slavoj Žižek, *Living in the End Times* (London/New York: Verso, 2010) 241.

56. Waters, *Globalization*, 1.

57. John Quelch and Rohit Deshpande, *The Global Market: Developing a Strategy to Manage Across Borders* (San Fransisco, Calif.: Jossey-Bass, 2004), 25.

58. Mike Featherstone, *Global Culture: Nationalism, Globalization, and Modernity*, (London: Newbury Park: Sage Publications, 1990), 1.

59. Kenichi Omhae, "The End of the Nation State." *The Globalization Reader*, ed. Frank J. Lechner and John Boli (Oxford, UK/Malden, Mass.: Blackwell Publishers 2000), 211.

60. Ibid., 205.

61. Kenichi Omhae, *The Borderless World: Power and Strategy in the Interlinked Economy* (New York: HarperBusiness, 1990), xii.

62. Ibid., xii.

63. Karl Marx and Frederick Engels, *Manifesto of the Communist Party*, in *Marx–Engels Collected Works, vol. 6* (New York: International Publishers, 1976), 487.

64. Chris Harman, "Globalisation: A Critique of A New Global Orthodoxy," 9.

65. Paul Q. Hirst, and Grahame Thompson, *Globalization in Question: The International Economy and the Possibilities of Governance* (Oxford, UK/Malden, Mass.: Blackwell Publishers, 1996), 20.

66. Brenner, "The Economics of Global Turbulence," 55.

67. Ibid., 39.

68. Ibid., 56.

69. Gérard Duménil and Dominique Lévy, *Capital Resurgent: Roots of the Neoliberal Revolution* (Cambridge: Harvard University Press, 2004), 21–28.

70. Brenner, "The Economics of Global Turbulence," 201.

71. Guillermo de la Dehesa, *Winners and Losers in Globalization* (Oxford, UK/ Malden, Mass.: Blackwell Publishing, 2006), 3.

72. Jan van Dijk, *The Network Society: Social Aspects of New Media* (Thousand Oaks, Calif.: Sage Publications, 2006), 24.

73. Ibid., 24.

74. Terranova, *Network Culture: Politics for the Information Age*, 1–2.

75. Chwo-Ming Joseph Yu, "Restructuring of Production Networks in Foreign Countries: The Case of Taiwanese Firms," in *Foreign Direct Investment*, ed. John-Ren Chen (New York: St. Martin's Press, 2000), 96–97.

76. Gilles Deleuze and Felix Guattari, *Anti-Oedipus: Capitalism and Schizophrenia*, trans. Robert Hurley, Mark Seem, and Helen R. Lane (Minneapolis: University of Minnesota Press, 1983).

77. Manuel Castells, *The Rise of the Network Society* (Cambridge, Mass.: Blackwell Publishers, 1996), 1.

78. Ibid., 66.

79. Ibid., 417.

80. Ibid., 18.

81. Ibid., 477.

82. Ibid., 474.

83. Ibid., 17.

84. Ibid., 243.

85. Ibid., 472.

86. Ibid., 371.

87. Ibid., 374.

88. Ibid., 195.

89. Ibid., 475.

90. Ibid., 475.

91. Ibid., 473.

92. Ibid., 6–7.

93. Ibid., 199.

94. Manuel Castells, *The Internet Galaxy: Reflections on the Internet, Business, and Society* (Oxford and New York: Oxford University Press, 2001), 1.

95. Steve Lohr, "A Cyberfueled Growth Spurt: The Web Upends Old Ideas About the Little Guy's Role," *The New York Times* (21 Feb. 2006): G1.

96. Daniel H. Pink, "Why the World Is Flat," *Wired* (May 2005). http://www.wired.com/wired/archive/13.05/.

97. Thomas L. Friedman's *The World Is Flat: A Brief History of the Twenty-First Century*, (New York: Farrar, Straus and Giroux, 2005), 8.

98. Ibid., 16.

99. Ibid., 45.

100. Ibid., 129.

101. Ibid., 131.

102. Ibid., 135.

103. Ibid., 129.

104. Ibid., 137.

105. Ibid., 129.

106. Ibid., 139.

107. Ibid., 139.

108. Brenner, "The Economics of Global Turbulence," 80–82.

109. Friedman *The World Is Flat,* 139.

110. Ibid., 421.

111. Karl Marx, *Capital Volume I,* in *Marx–Engels Collected Works,* vol. 35 (New York: International Publishers, 1996), 177.

112. Ibid., 219.

113. Manuel Castells, *The Rise of the Network Society,* 475.

114. V. I. Lenin, *Imperialism, The Highest Stage of Capitalism. Lenin Collected Works,* vol. 22, (Moscow: Progress Publishers, 1977), 246.

115. Ibid., 260.

116. Ibid., 241.

117. Ibid., 241.

118. Ibid., 241.

119. Karl Marx, *Capital Volume III,* in *Marx–Engels Collected Works,* vol. 37 (New York: International Publishers, 1998), 209–265.

120. Lenin, *Imperialism, The Highest Stage of Capitalism,* 242.

121. Ernest Mandel, *Marxist Economic Theory* (New York/London: Monthly Review Press, 1968), 454.

122. Lenin, *Imperialism, The Highest Stage of Capitalism,* 246.

123. Ibid., 266–267.

124. Brenner, "The Economics of Global Turbulence," 11.

125. Ibid., 48.

126. Ibid., 48.

127. Ibid., 56.

128. Duménil and Lévy, *Capital Resurgent,* 28.

129. Ibid., 153.

130. Ibid., 154.

131. Aaron Cobet and Gregory Wilson, "Comparing 50 years of labor productivity in U.S. and foreign manufacturing," *Monthly Labor Review* (June 2002): 55.

132. Lawrence Mishel, Jared Bernstein, and Heidi Shierholz, *The State of Working America 2008–2009* (Ithaca, N.Y./London: ILR Press, 2009), 209.

133. Brenner, "The Economics of Global Turbulence," 196.

134. Ibid., 211.

135. John-Ren Chen, "Foreign Direct Investment, International Financial Flows, and Geography," *Foreign Direct Investment,* ed. John-Ren Chen (New York: St. Martin's Press, 2000), 6.

136. Robert J. Flanagan, *Globalization and Labor Conditions: Working Conditions and Worker Rights in a Global Economy* (Oxford: Oxford University Press, 2006), 120.

137. Clarence J. Mann, "Overview: Forces Shaping the Global Business Environment," in *Borderless Business: Managing the Far-Flung Enterprise*, ed. by Clarence J. Mann and Klaus Götz (Westport, Conn./London: Praeger Publishers, 2006), 7.

138. Christian Smekal and Rupert Sausgruber, "Determinants of FDI in Europe," in *Foreign Direct Investment*, ed. John-Ren Chen (New York: St. Martin's Press, 2000), 38.

139. Karl Kautsky, "Ultra-Imperialism," *New Left Review* 59 (1970): 44–45.

140. Ibid., 46.

141. Lenin, *Imperialism, The Highest Stage of Capitalism*, 216.

142. "The Future of Europe: Staring into an Abyss," *The Economist*, http://www.economist.com/node/16536898.

143. Ernest Mandel, *Late Capitalism*, trans. Joris De Bres (London: Verso, 1987), 474.

144. Sidney Lens, *The Forging of the American Empire* (New York: Thomas Y. Cromwell Company, 1971), 195.

145. Guillermo de la Dehesa, *Winners and Losers in Globalization* (Oxford, UK/ Malden, Mass.: Blackwell Publishing, 2006), 13.

146. Hardt and Negri, *Empire*, xi.

147. Ibid., xi.

148. Ibid., xii.

149. Ibid., 302.

150. Ibid., xii.

151. Ibid., 335.

152. Ibid., 295.

153. Ibid., 258.

154. Ibid., 294.

155. Ibid., 290.

156. Karl Marx, *Grundrisse*, trans. Martin Nicolaus (New York: Vintage Books, 1973), 700.

157. Antonio Negri, *Marx Beyond Marx: Lessons on the Grundrisse*, trans. Harry Cleaver, Michael Ryan, and Maurizio Vianom, ed. Jim Fleming, (New York: Autonomedia, 1991), 145.

158. Ibid., 147.

159. Ibid., 23.

160. Ibid., 179.

161. Ibid., 183.

162. Michael Hardt and Antonio Negri, *Multitude: War and Democracy in the Age of Empire* (New York: Penguin Press, 2004), 135.

163. Ibid., 109.

164. Ibid., 113.

165. Ibid., 108.

166. Ibid., 146.

167. Hardt and Negri, *Empire*, 405.

168. Ibid., 48.

169. Hardt and Negri, *Multitude*, 102.

170. Hardt and Negri, *Empire*, 46.

171. Ibid., 294.

172. Alain Touraine, "New Classes, New Conflicts," in *The Worker in "Post-Industrial" Capitalism*, ed. Bertram Silverman and Murray Yanowitch (New York: Free Press, 1974), 182.

173. Stanley Aronowitz and William DiFazio, *The Jobless Future* (Minneapolis: University of Minnesota Press, 1994), 17.

174. Maurizio Lazzarato, "Immaterial Labor," in *Radical Thought in Italy: A Potential Politics*, ed. Paolo Virno and Michael Hardt (Minneapolis: University of Minneapolis Press, 1996), 132.

175. Ibid., 140.

176. Ibid., 138.

177. Ibid., 140.

178. Hardt and Negri, *Empire*, 299.

179. Ibid., 299.

180. Ibid., 303.

181. Castells, *The Rise of the Network Society*, 195.

182. Ibid., 374.

183. Ibid., 341.

184. Thomas L. Friedman, *The Lexus and the Olive Tree: Understanding Globalization*, (New York: Knopf Publishing Group, 2000), 9.

185. Karl Marx, *Capital Volume II*, in *Marx–Engels Collected Works*, vol. 35 (New York: International Publishers, 1997) 133.

186. Ibid., 133–134.

187. Ibid., 136.

188. Ibid., 135.

189. Ibid., 135.

190. Ibid., 319.

191. Duménil and Lévy, *Capital Resurgent: Roots of the Neoliberal Revolution*, 155.

192. Justin Lahart. "U.S. Firms Build Up Record Cash Piles," *The Wall Street Journal*, (June 10, 2010), http://tinyurl.com/wsjlahart.

193. Mandel, *Late Capitalism*, 387–388.

194. Guillermo de la Dehesa, *Winners and Losers in Globalization*, 31.

195. Christopher Caldwell, "Old School Economics," *The New York Times Magazine* (January 27, 2008), 11.

196. Chris Harman, "The rate of profit and the world today," *International Socialism* 115 (2007), http://tinyurl.com/intsoc115.

197. Ernest Mandel, introduction to *Capital Volume II*, trans. David Fernbach (New York: Penguin Classics, 1992), 41.

198. Ibid., 42.
199. Ibid., 41.
200. Catherine McKercher and Vincent Mosco, "Introduction: Theorizing Knowledge Labor and the Information Society," in *Knowledge Workers in the Information Society*, ed. Cathering McKercher and Vincent Mosco (Lanham, Md.: Lexington Books, 2007), xii.
201. Ibid, x.
202. David Harvie, "Value Production and struggle in the classroom: Teachers within, against, and beyond capital," *Capital & Class* 88 (2006): 1.
203. Ibid., 18.
204. Ibid., 5.
205. Ibid., 6.
206. Ibid., 4.
207. Ibid., 12.
208. Ibid., 12.
209. Ibid., 8.
210. Ibid., 4.
211. Ibid., 10.
212. Ibid., 10.
213. Ibid., 20.
214. Ibid., 20–23.
215. Ibid., 23–24.
216. Karl Marx, *Marx–Engels Collected Works*, 35:726.
217. Mark C. Taylor, "End the University as We Know It," *New York Times* (27 Apr. 2009), 23.
218. Karl Marx, *Grundrisse*, 700.
219. Ibid., 701.
220. Ibid., 701.
221. Ibid., 706.
222. Ibid., 706.
223. Ibid., 701.
224. Bruce Sterling, introduction to *Mirrorshades: The Cyberpunk Anthology* (New York: Arbor House, 1986), xii.
225. Frederic Jameson, *Postmodernism, or the Cultural Logic of Late Capitalism* (Durham: Duke University Press, 1991), 419.
226. Bruce Sterling, introduction to *Mirrorshades*, xiii.
227. James Patrick Kelly and John Kessel, eds., *Rewired: The Post-Cyberpunk Anthology* (San Francisco, Calif.: Trachyon Publications, 2007), ix.
228. Person, Lawrence. "Notes Toward a Postcyberpunk Manifesto," http://slashdot.org/features/99/10/08/2123255.shtml.
229. Ibid.
230. S. N. Nadel, *Contemporary Capitalism and the Middle Classes* (New York: International Publishers, 1982), 11.

231. "Home Entertainment," *The Economist* (6 Dec. 2003), 78.

232. William Gibson, *Pattern Recognition* (New York: G. P. Putnam's Sons, 2003), 137.

233. Ibid., 10.

234. Ibid., 1.

235. Ibid., 1.

236. Ibid., 1.

237. Ibid., 137.

238. Ibid., 134.

239. Ibid., 1.

240. Ibid., 86.

241. Ibid., 2.

242. Ibid., 8.

243. Ibid., 17–18.

244. Ibid., 97.

245. Ibid., 127.

246. Ibid., 11.

247. Ibid., 270.

248. Ibid., 23.

249. Ibid., 23.

250. Ibid., 4.

251. Ibid., 194.

252. Ibid., 104.

253. Ibid., 305.

254. Ibid., 356.

255. Frederic Jameson, "Fear and Loathing in Globalization," *New Left Review* 23 (2003): 110.

256. Ibid., 111–112.

257. Ibid., 114.

258. Ibid., 114.

259. Lawrence Mishel, Jared Bernstein and Heidi Shierholz, *The State of Working America 2008–2009*, (Ithaca and London: ILR Press, 2009), 227.

260. Jeanne Sahadi, "White House: Unemployment at 9% Until 2012," CNNMoney.com, http://tinyurl.com/jswhitehouse.

261. Karl Marx, *Marx–Engels Collected Works*, 35:490.

262. Karl Marx and Frederick Engels, *Manifesto of the Communist Party*, in *Marx–Engels Collected Works*, vol. 6 (New York: International Publishers, 1976), 498.

263. Lenin, *Imperialism, The Highest Stage of Capitalism*, 243.

264. Ibid., 237.

265. Ibid., 187.

266. John Holloway, *Change the World without Taking Power* (London/Ann Arbor, Mich.: Pluto Press, 2005), 173.

267. Ibid., 146.

268. Poster, *Information Please.* 56.

269. Ibid., 65.

270. Paul Thompson, "Foundation and Empire: A Critique of Hardt and Negri," *Capital and Class* 86 (Summer 2005): 78.

271. Ibid., 78.

272. Michael Hardt and Antonio Negri, "Response," *Artforum* (November 2009): 212.

273. Michael Hardt and Antonio Negri, *Commonwealth* (Cambridge, Mass.: The Belknap Press of Harvard University Press, 2009), 125.

274. David Harvey, "Analysis," *Artforum* (November 2009): 210.

275. Ibid., 258.

276. Hardt and Negri, "Response," 211.

277. Harvey, "Analysis," 212.

278. Ibid., 256.

279. Hardt and Negri, *Commonwealth*, 319.

280. Harvey, "Analysis," 260.

281. David Harvey, *The Limits to Capital: New and Fully Updated Edition* (London/New York: Verso, 2006), xxiii.

282. Ibid., 191.

283. Ibid., 325.

284. Ibid., 424.

285. Ibid., 191.

286. Ibid., xvi.

287. Ibid., 440.

288. Rosa Luxemburg, *The Accumulation of Capital*, trans. Agnes Schwarzchild (London/New York: Routledge, 2003), 398.

289. Ibid., 426.

290. Hannah Arendt, *The Origins of Totalitarianism*, (New York: Harcourt, Brace and Company, 1951), 148.

291. David Harvey, *The New Imperialism* (Oxford: Oxford University Press, 2003), 138–140.

292. Ibid., 144.

293. Ibid., 145.

294. Karl Marx, *Capital Volume III*, in *Marx–Engels Collected Works*, vol. 37 (New York: International Publishers, 1998), 212.

295. Ibid., 212.

296. Harvey, *The Limits to Capital*, xvii.

297. Ibid., 450.

298. Harvey, *The New Imperialism*, 176.

299. Lenin, *Imperialism, The Highest Stage of Capitalism*, 212.

3. READING AND WRITING IN THE DIGITAL AGE

1. Karl Marx, *Capital Volume I*, in *Marx–Engels Collected Works*, vol. 35 (New York: International Publishers, 1996), 84–94.

2. Jacques Derrida, Guy Scarpetta, and J. L Houdebine, "Interview: Jacques Derrida," *Diacritics* 2, no. 4 (1972): 36.

3. Richard J. Finneran, ed., *The Literary Text in the Digital Age* (Ann Arbor: University of Michigan Press, 1996), ix.

4. Alan Kirby, *Digimodernism: How New Technologies Dismantle, the Postmodern and Reconfigure our Culture* (New York/London: The Continuum International Publishing Group Inc, 2009), 1.

5. Ibid., 149.

6. Jacques Derrida, "'Genesis and Structure' and Phenomenology," in *Writing and Difference*, trans. Alan Bass (Chicago, Ill.: University of Chicago Press, 1978), 167.

7. Jacques Derrida, "The Right to Philosophy from the Cosmopolitical Point of View (The Example of an International Institution)," in *Ethics, Institutions, and the Right to Philosophy*, translated by Peter Pericles Trifonas (Lanham, Boulder, New York, and Oxford: Rowman and Littlefield Publishers, Inc., 2002), 10.

8. Jacques Derrida, "'Genesis and Structure' and Phenomenology," 162.

9. Ibid., 160.

10. Karl Marx, preface to *A Contribution to a Critique of Political Economy*, ed. Maurice Dobb (New York: International Publishers, 1970), 21.

11. George P. Landow, *Hypertext 3.0: Critical Theory and New Media in the Age of Globalization* (Baltimore, Md.: The Johns Hopkins University Press, 2006), 1.

12. Ibid., 56.

13. Jacques Derrida, "'Genesis and Structure' and Phenomenology," 163.

14. Roland Barthes, *The Rustle of Language*, trans. Richard Howard (Berkeley, Calif.: University of California Press, 1989), 138.

15. Jacques Derrida, *Paper Machine*, trans. Rachel Bowlby (Stanford, Calif.: Stanford University Press, 2005), 5.

16. Jean Baudrillard, *Selected Writings*, ed. Mark Poster, (Stanford, Calif.: Stanford University Press, 2001), 146.

17. Peter Lunenfeld, *The Digital Dialectic: New Essays on New Media* (Cambridge, Mass.: MIT Press, 1999), xiv.

18. Samuel Weber, *Benjamin's –abilities*, (Cambridge, Mass./London: Harvard University Press, 2008), 47.

19. Gunnar Liestol, Andrew Morrison, and Terje Rasmussen, eds., *Digital Media Revisited: Theoretical and Conceptual Innovation in Digital Domains* (Cambridge, Mass.: MIT Press, 2003), 2.

20. Ibid., 2.

21. Robert Markley, "History, Theory, and Virtual Reality," in *Reading Digital Culture*, ed. David Trend (Malden, Mass./Oxford: Blackwell Publishers, Inc., 2001), 299.

22. Robert Brenner, "The Economics of Global Turbulence," *New Left Review* 229 (1998): 93.

23. Ibid., 62.

24. Karl Popper, *The Open Society and Its Enemies*, vol. 1 (Princeton, N.J.: Princeton University Press, 1966), 190.

25. Henry Jenkins, *Convergence Culture: Where Old and New Media Collide* (New York/London: New York University Press, 2006), 3–4.

26. Mark Poster, *Information Please: Culture and Politics in the Age of Digital Machines* (Durham and London: Duke University Press, 2006), 127.

27. Silvio Gaggi, *From Text to Hypertext: Decentering the Subject in Fiction, Film, the Visual Arts, and Electronic Media* (Philadelphia, Penn.: University of Pennsylvania Press, 1997), 103.

28. Ibid., 130.

29. Chrisian Vandendorpe, *From Papyrus to Hypertext: Toward the Universal Digital Library*, trans. Phyllis Aronoff and Howard Scott, (Urbana, Ill./Chicago, Ill.: University of Chicago Press, 2009), 2.

30. Richard A. Lanham, *The Electronic Word: Democracy, Technology, and the Arts* (Chicago: University of Chicago Press, 1993), 5.

31. Henry James, "The Art of Fiction," in *Critical Theory Since Plato*, ed. Hazard Adams (New York: Harcourt Brace Jovanovich, Inc., 1971), 662.

32. Ibid., 664.

33. Lanham, *The Electronic Word*, 31.

34. Ibid., 7.

35. Ibid., 5.

36. Ibid., 31.

37. Ibid., 73.

38. Ibid., 11.

39. Karl Marx, *Contribution to the Critique of Hegel's Philosophy of Law: Introduction*, in *Marx–Engels Collected Works*, vol. 3 (New York: International Publishers, 1975), 175.

40. Tiziana Terranova, *Network Culture: Politics for the Information Age* (London and Ann Arbor, Mich.: Pluto Press, 2004), 27.

41. Walter Benjamin, "Brecht's *Threepenny Novel*," in *Reflections: Essays Aphorisms, Autobiographical Writings*, ed. Peter Demetz, trans. Edmund Jephcott (New York: Schocken Books, 1986), 199.

42. Roland Barthes, *The Pleasure of the Text*, trans. Richard Miller (New York: Wang and Hill, 1975), 4, 13.

43. Jacques Derrida, "The End of the Book and the Beginning of Writing," in *Of Grammatology*, trans. Gayatri Chakravority Spivak (Baltimore, Md.: The Johns Hopkins University Press, 1976), 24.

44. Jacques Derrida, "The Double Session," in *Dissemination*, trans. Barbara Johnson, (Chicago, Ill.: University of Chicago Press, 1981), 285.

45. Ibid., 268.

46. Ibid., 183.
47. Ibid., 184.
48. Ibid., 191.
49. Ibid., 206.
50. Ibid., 262.
51. Ibid., 175.
52. Ibid., 175.
53. Ibid., 175.
54. Ibid., 184.
55. Ibid., 184.
56. Ibid., 184–185.
57. Ibid., 185.
58. Ibid., 185.
59. Ibid., 191.
60. Ibid., 188.
61. Ibid., 185.
62. Plato, *The Republic*, trans. Desmond Lee (New York/London: Penguin Books, 1974), 431.
63. Jacques Derrida, "The Double Session," 187.
64. Ibid., 189.
65. Ibid., 190.
66. Ibid., 189.
67. Ibid., 191.
68. Ibid., 193.
69. Ibid., 191.
70. Ibid., 206.
71. Ibid., 201.
72. Ibid., 201.
73. Ibid., 201.
74. Ibid., 202.
75. Ibid., 198.
76. Ibid., 199.
77. Ibid., 198.
78. Ibid., 205.
79. Ibid., 210.
80. Ibid., 210.
81. Ibid., 208.
82. Ibid., 206.
83. Ibid., 195.
84. Ibid., 175.
85. Ibid., 197.
86. Ibid., 212.
87. Ibid., 231.

88. Ibid., 252.

89. Ibid., 253.

90. Ibid., 253.

91. Ibid., 258.

92. Ibid., 257.

93. Ibid., 251.

94. Ellen Meiksins Wood, *Peasant-Citizen and Slave: The Foundations of Athenian Democracy* (London/New York: Verso, 1989), 148.

95. Jacques Derrida, "The Double Session," 201.

96. Karl Marx and Frederick Engels, *Manifesto of the Communist Party*, in *Marx–Engels Collected Works*, vol. 6 (New York: International Publishers, 1976), 505.

97. Ibid., 504.

98. Georg Lukács, "Art and Objective Reality," in *Writer & Critic and Other Essays*, ed. and trans. Arthur D. Kahn (New York: Grosset & Dunlap, 1970), 43.

99. Ibid., 43.

100. Ibid., 43.

101. Jacques Derrida, "The Double Session," 206.

102. Ibid., 195.

103. Ibid., 207.

104. Ibid., 205.

105. Frederick Engels, *The Origin of the Family, Private Property, and the State*, in *Marx–Engels Collected Works*, vol. 26 (New York: International Publishers, 1990), 173.

106. Ibid., 187.

107. Ibid., 170.

108. Ibid., 183.

109. Jacques Derrida, "The Double Session," 203.

110. Ibid., 285.

111. David Jay Bolter, *Writing Space: The Computer, Hypertext, and the History of Writing* (Hillsdale, N.J.: L. Erlbaum Associates, 1991), 2.

112. Ibid., 55.

113. Ibid., 31.

114. Ibid., 9.

115. Ibid., 97.

116. Ibid., 11.

117. Ibid., 155.

118. Ibid., 238.

119. Jacques Derrida, "That Dangerous Supplement," in *Of Grammatology*, trans. Gayatri Chakravority Spivak (Baltimore, Md.: The Johns Hopkins University Press, 1976), 158.

120. David Jay Bolter, *Writing Space*, 9.

121. Ibid., 5.

122. Ibid., 6.

123. I. A. Richards, *Principles of Literary Criticism* (New York: Harcourt Brace & World, 1961), 25.

124. Ibid., 229.

125. David Jay Bolter, *Writing Space*, 198.

126. Ibid., 166.

127. Ibid., 166.

128. Ibid., 232.

129. Ibid., 232.

130. Ibid., 232.

131. Ibid., 233.

132. Karl Marx, preface to *A Contribution to a Critique of Political Economy*, 21.

133. Peter Hitchcock, *Oscillate Wildly: Space, Body, and Spirit of Millennial Materialism* (Minneapolis: University of Minnesota Press, 1999), xii.

134. Antonio Callari, David F. Ruccio, and Louis Althusser, *Postmodern Materialism and the Future of Marxist Theory: Essays in the Althusserian Tradition* (Hanover, N.H.: University Press of New England for Wesleyan University Press, 1996), 7.

135. Michael Hardt and Antonio Negri, *Multitude: War and Democracy in the Age of Empire* (New York: Penguin Press, 2004), 102.

136. Angela McRobbie, "Post-Marxism and Cultural Studies: A Postscript," in *Cultural Studies*, ed. by Lawrence, Grossberg, Lawrence, Cary Nelson, and Paula Treichler (New York: Routledge, 1992), 724.

137. Lawrence Grossberg, *Bringing It All Back Home: Essays on Cultural Studies* (Durham, N.C.: Duke University Press, 1997), 12.

138. Karl Marx and Frederick Engels, *The German Ideology*, in *Marx–Engels Collected Works*, vol. 5 (New York: International Publishers, 1976), 35.

139. Ibid., 35–36.

140. John Frow, *Cultural Studies and Cultural Value* (Oxford: Oxford University Press, 1995), 1.

141. Marx and Engels, *The German Ideology*, 42.

142. Stuart Hall, "The Meaning of New Times," in *Stuart Hall: Critical Dialogues in Cultural Studies*, ed. David Morley and Kuan-Hsing Chen (London/New York: Routledge, 1996), 235.

143. Louis Althusser, "Ideology and Ideological State Apparatuses (Notes towards an Investigation)," in *Lenin and Philosophy and Other Essays* (New York: Monthly Review Press, 1971), 172.

144. Marx and Engels, *The German Ideology*, 43.

145. Karl Marx, *Wage-Labour and Capital/Value, Price and Profit* (New York: International Publishers, 1997), 28–29.

146. Karl Marx, preface to *A Contribution to a Critique of Political Economy*, 21.

147. Karl Marx, *Capital Volume I*, in *Marx–Engels Collected Works*, vol. 35 (New York: International Publishers, 1996), 85.

148. F. R. Leavis, *Education and the University; A Sketch for an English School* (London: Chatto & Windus, 1965), 38.

149. Ibid., 16.

150. Louis Althusser, "A Letter on Art in Reply to André Daspre," in *Lenin and Philosophy and Other Essays* (New York: Monthly Review Press, 1971), 223.

151. Karl Marx, "Thesis on Feuerbach." *Marx–Engels Collected Works*, vol. 5 (New York: International Publishers, 1976), 3.

152. Roland Barthes, *The Pleasure of the Text* (New York: Hill and Wang, 1975), 54.

153. Bertolt Brecht, *Brecht on Theatre*, ed. John Willet (New York: Hill and Wang, 1992), 29.

154. Marx and Engels, *The German Ideology*, 39.

155. Ibid., 40.

156. Frederick Engels, "Role of Production in the Development of the Sciences," in *Reader in Marxist Philosophy*, ed. Howard Selsam and Harry Martel (New York: International Publishers, 1987), 169–170.

157. Ernest Mandel, *Late Capitalism*, trans. Joris De Bres, (London: Verso, 1987), 508.

158. Karl Marx, *Economic and Philosophic Manuscripts of 1844*, *Marx–Engels Collected Works*, vol. 3 (New York: International Publishers, 1975), 296.

159. Marx and Engels, *The German Ideology*, 59.

4. THE IDEOLOGY OF THE DIGITAL ME

1. Sidney Eve Matrix, *Cyberpop: Digital Lifestyles and Commodity Culture* (New York/London: Routledge, 2006), 22.

2. Yochai Benkler, *The Wealth of Networks: How Social Production Transforms Markets and Freedom* (New Haven, Conn./London: Yale University Press, 2006), 9.

3. Antonio Negri, "The Specter's Smile," in *Ghostly Demarcations: A Symposium on Jacques Derrida's Specters of Marx*, ed. Michael Sprinker (London: Verso: 1999), 9.

4. Ibid., 11.

5. Ibid., 11.

6. Ibid., 14–15.

7. Theodor Adorno and Max Horkheimer, "The Culture Industry: Enlightenment as Mass Deception," in *Dialectic of Enlightenment*, trans. John Cumming (New York: Continuum, 1990), 122.

8. Ibid., 166–167.

9. Bruno Latour, *We Have Never Been Modern* (Cambridge, Mass.: Harvard University Press, 1993), 2.

10. Ibid., 5.

11. Ibid., 1.

12. W.J.T. Mitchell, "Medium Theory: Preface to the 2003 'Critical Inquiry' Symposium," *Critical Inquiry* 30, no. 2 (Winter 2004): 334.

13. Latour, *We Have Never Been Modern*, 130.

14. Ibid., 130.

15. Ibid., 9.

16. Ibid., 131.

17. Ibid., 46.

18. Ibid., 46.

19. Ibid., 46.

20. Ibid., 13.

21. Ibid., 141.

22. Ibid., 142.

23. Ibid., 133.

24. Ibid., 136–137.

25. N. Katherine Hayles, "Connecting the Quantum Dots: Nanotechscience and Culture," in *Nanoculture: Implications of the New Technologies*, ed. N. Katherine Hayles (Bristol, UK: Intellect Books, 2004), 16–17.

26. Colin Milburn, *Nanovision: Engineering the Future* (Durham, N.C./London: Duke University Press, 2008), 13.

27. Ibid., 5.

28. Mark Poster, *Mode of Information: Poststructuralism and Social Context* (Chicago: University of Chicago Press, 1990), 11.

29. Jean-François Lyotard, *The Inhuman*, trans. Geoffrey Bennington and Rachel Bowlby, (Stanford, Calif.: Stanford University Press, 1991), 4–5.

30. Ollivier Dyens, *Metal and Flesh: The Evolution of Man: Technology Takes Over*, trans. Evan J. Bibbee and Ollivier Dyens (Cambridge, Mass./London: The MIT Press, 2001), 85.

31. Ibid., 82.

32. Donna Haraway, "A Manifesto for Cyborgs: Science, Technology, and Socialist Feminism in the 1980s," *Feminism/Postmodernism*, ed. Linda J. Nicholson (New York: Routledge, 1990), 203.

33. Ibid., 202.

34. Ibid., 191.

35. Ibid., 191.

36. Ibid., 205.

37. Ibid. 191.

38. Ibid., 196.

39. Ibid., 215.

40. Latour, *We Have Never Been Modern*, 48.

41. Haraway, *Feminism/Postmodernism*, 192.

42. Ibid., 203.

43. Ibid., 215.

44. Ibid., 197.

45. Ibid., 193, 219.

46. Ibid., 218.

47. Chris Harman, *Economics of the Madhouse: Capitalism and the Market Today* (London, Chicago, and Melbourne: Bookmarks, 1995), 21.

48. Ibid., 21.

49. Ibid., 21.

50. Brenner, "The Economics of Global Turbulence," 196–199.

51. Lawrence Mishel, Jared Bernstein, and Heidi Shierholz, *The State of Working America 2008–2009* (Ithica, N.Y./London: ILR Press, 2009), 269.

52. Harman, *Economics of the Madhouse*, 31.

53. Ibid., 47.

54. Nelson D. Schwartz and Ann Harrington, "Down and Out in White-Collar America," *Fortune* 147 (2003): 78–79.

55. Karl Marx and Frederick Engels, *Manifesto of the Communist Party*, in *Marx–Engels Collected Works*, vol. 6 (New York: International Publishers, 1976), 492.

56. Ibid., 491.

57. Gilles Deleuze and Felix Guattari, *Anti-Oedipus: Capitalism and Schizophrenia*, trans. Robert Hurley, Mark Seem, and Helen R. Lane (Minneapolis: University of Minnesota Press, 1983), 2.

58. Ibid., 42.

59. Ibid., 40.

60. Ibid., 27.

61. Ibid., 1.

62. Ibid., 26–29.

63. Ibid., 140.

64. Karl Marx and Frederick Engels, *The German Ideology*, in *Marx–Engels Collected Works*, vol. 5 (New York: International Publishers, 1976), 438.

65. Ibid., 418.

66. Frederick Engels, *Frederick Engels on Capital*, trans. Leonard E. Mins (New York: International Publishers, 1974), 90.

67. Karl Marx, *Poverty of Philosophy*, in *Marx–Engels Collected Works*, vol. 6 (New York: International Publishers, 1976), 186.

WORKS CITED

Adorno, Theodor, and Max Horkheimer. "The Culture Industry: Enlightenment as Mass Deception." In *Dialectic of Enlightenment*, translated by John Cumming, 120–67. New York: Continuum, 1990.

Allen, John. "Fordism and Modern Industry." In *Modernity: An Introduction to Modern Societies*, edited by Stuart Hall, David Held, Don Hubert, and Kenneth Thompson, 280–306. Oxford: Blackwell, 1996.

———. "Post-Industrialism/Post-Fordism." In *Modernity: An Introduction to Modern Societies*, edited by Stuart Hall, David Held, Don Hubert, and Kenneth Thompson, 533–64. Oxford: Blackwell, 1996.

Althusser, Louis. "Ideology and Ideological State Apparatuses (Notes towards an Investigation)." In *Lenin and Philosophy and Other Essays*, 127–86. New York: Monthly Review Press, 1971.

———. "A Letter on Art in Reply to André Daspre." In *Lenin and Philosophy and Other Essays*. 221–27. New York: Monthly Review Press, 1971.

Appadurai, Arjun. "Disjunction and Difference in the Global Cultural Economy." In *The Cultural Studies Reader*, 220–30. London and New York: Routledge, 1999.

Arendt, Hannah. *The Origins of Totalitarianism*. New York: Harcourt, Brace and Company, 1951.

Aronowitz, Stanley. *The Knowledge Factory: Dismantling the Corporate University and Creating True Higher Learning*. Boston: Beacon Press, 2000.

Aronowitz, Stanley, and William DiFazio. *The Jobless Future*. Minneapolis: University of Minnesota Press, 1994.

Aronowitz, Stanley, and Michael Menser. "On Cultural Studies, Science, and Technology." In *Technoscience and Cyberculture*, edited by Stanley Aronowitz, Barbara Martinsons, and Michael Menser, 7–28. New York: Routledge, 1996.

Barabási, Albert-Lászláo. *Linked: How Everything Is Connected to Everything Else and What It Means for Business, Science, and Everyday Life*. New York: Plume, 2003.

Barthes, Roland. *The Pleasure of the Text*. New York: Hill and Wang, 1975.

223

———. *The Rustle of Language*. Translated by Richard Howard. Berkeley: University of California Press, 1989.

Baudrillard, Jean. *Selected Writings*. Edited by Mark Poster. Stanford, Calif.: Stanford University Press, 1998.

———. *Simulacra and Simulation*. Ann Arbor: University of Michigan Press, 1994.

———. *Symbolic Exchange and Death*. London/Thousand Oaks, Calif.: Sage Publications, 1993.

Beck, Ulrich. *The Cosmopolitan Vision*. Cambridge, UK/Malden, Mass.: Polity Press, 2006.

Bell, Daniel. *The Coming of Post-Industrial Society: A Venture in Social Forecasting.* New York: Basic Books, 1973.

Benjamin, Walter. "Brecht's *Threepenny Novel*," in *Reflections: Essays, Aphorisms, Autobiographical Writings*, edited by Peter Demetz, translated by Edmund Jephcott, 193–202. New York: Schocken Books, 1986.

Benkler, Yochai. *The Wealth of Networks: How Social Production Transforms Markets and Freedom*. New Haven, Conn./London: Yale University Press, 2006.

Best, Steven, and Douglas Kellner. *The Postmodern Adventure: Science, Technology, and Cultural Studies at the Third Millennium*. New York: Guilford Press, 2001.

Bolter, J. David. *Writing Space: The Computer, Hypertext, and the History of Writing*. Hillsdale, N.J.: L. Erlbaum Associates, 1991.

Bousquet, Marc. *How the University Works: Higher Education and the Low-Wage Nation*. New York: New York University Press, 2008.

Brecht, Bertolt. *Brecht on Theatre*. Edited by John Willet. New York: Hill and Wang, 1998.

Brenner, Robert. "The Economics of Global Turbulence." *New Left Review* 229 (1998): i–265.

Bull, Michael. *Sound Moves: iPod Culture and Urban Experience*. New York: Routledge, 2008.

Burbach, Roger, Orlando Nunez, and Boris Kagarlitsky. *Globalization and Its Discontents: The Rise of Postmodern Socialisms*. London/Chicago: Pluto Press, 1997.

Burgess, Jean, and Joshua Green. *YouTube (Digital Media and Society Series)*. Cambridge, UK/Malden, Mass.: Polity Press, 2009.

Caldwell, Christopher. "Old School Economics." *The New York Times Magazine*. January 27, 2008: 11.

Callari, Antonio, David F. Ruccio, and Louis Althusser. *Postmodern Materialism and the Future of Marxist Theory: Essays in the Althusserian Tradition*. Hanover, N.H.: University Press of New England, 1996.

Castells, Manuel. *The Rise of the Network Society*. Cambridge, Mass.: Blackwell Publishers, 1996.

————. *The Internet Galaxy: Reflections on the Internet, Business, and Society.* Oxford/New York: Oxford University Press, 2001.

Chen, John-Ren. "Foreign Direct Investment, International Financial Flows, and Geography." In *Foreign Direct Investment,* 6–32. New York: St. Martin's Press, 2000.

Cobet, Aaron, and Gregory Wilson. "Comparing 50 years of labor productivity in U.S. and foreign manufacturing." *Monthly Labor Review* (June 2002): 51–65.

Coupland, Douglas. *Microserfs.* New York: Regan Books, 1995.

Dalla Costa, Mariarosa, and Selma James. *The Power of Women and the Subversion of the Community.* Bristol, UK: Falling Wall Press, 1972.

Dark City. DVD. Directed by Alex Proyas. Los Angeles, Calif.: New Line Home Video, 1998.

de la Dehesa, Guillermo. *Winners and Losers in Globalization.* Oxford, UK/Malden, Mass.: Blackwell Publishing, 2006.

Deleuze, Gilles, and Felix Guattari. *Anti-Oedipus: Capitalism and Schizophrenia.* Translated by Robert Hurley, Mark Seem, and Helen R. Lane. Minneapolis: University of Minnesota Press, 1983.

Derrida, Jacques. "Différance." In *Margins of Philosophy,* translated by Alan Bass, 1–28. Chicago: University of Chicago Press, 1982.

————. "The Double Session." In *Dissemination,* translated by Barbara Johnson, 173–226. Chicago: University of Chicago Press, 1981.

————. "The End of the Book and the Beginning of Writing." In *Of Grammatology,* 6–26.

————. "'Genesis and Structure' and Phenomenology." In *Writing and Difference,* 154–231.

————. *Of Grammatology.* Translated by Gayatri Chakravorty Spivak. Baltimore: The Johns Hopkins University Press, 1976.

————. *Paper Machine.* Translated by Rachel Bowlby. Stanford, Calif.: Stanford University Press, 2005.

————. "The Right to Philosophy from the Cosmopolitical Point of View (The Example of an International Institution)." In *Ethics, Institutions, and the Right to Philosophy,* translated by Peter Pericles Trifonas, 1–18. Lanham, Boulder, New York, and Oxford: Rowman and Littlefield Publishers, Inc., 2002.

————. "Structure, Sign, and Play in the Discourse of the Human Sciences." In *Writing and Difference,* 278–94.

————. "That Dangerous Supplement." In *Of Grammatology,* 141–64.

————. *Writing and Difference.* Translated by Alan Bass. Chicago, Ill.: University of Chicago Press, 1978.

Derrida, Jacques, Guy Scarpetta, and Jean-Louis Houdebine. "Interview: Jacques Derrida." *Diacritics* 2, no. 4 (1972): 35–43.

Donoghue, Frank. *The Last Professors: The Corporate University and the Fate of the Humanities*. New York: Fordham University Press, 2008.

Drucker, Peter. *Post-Capitalist Society*. New York: Harper Business, 1993.

Druckery, Timothy. Introduction to *Culture on the Brink: Ideologies of Technology*. Edited by Gretchen Bender and Timothy Druckery, 1–14. Seattle: Bay Press, 1994.

Duménil, Gáerard, and Dominique Lévy. *Capital Resurgent: Roots of the Neoliberal Revolution*. Cambridge, Mass.: Harvard University Press, 2004.

Dyens, Ollivier. *Metal and Flesh: The Evolution of Man: Technology Takes Over*. Translated by Evan J. Bibbee and Ollivier Dyens. Cambridge, Mass./London: MIT Press, 2001.

Eagleton, Terry. "Lenin in the Postmodern Age." In *Lenin Reloaded: Toward a Politics of Truth*, edited by Sebastian Budgen, Stathis Kouvelakis, and Slavoj Žižek, 42–58. Durham: Duke University Press, 2007.

Economist. "Home Entertainment." December 6, 2003: 78.

Economist. "Where Would Jesus Queue? Marketing the iPhone." July 7, 2007: 65.

Economist. "The Future of Europe: Staring into an Abyss." July 8, 2010. http://tinyurl.com/economist07082010.

Eisenstein, Zillah. *Global Obscenities: Patriarchy, Capitalism and the Lure of Cyberfantasy*. New York: New York University Press, 1998.

Ellul, Jacques. *The Technological Society*. New York: Knopf, 1965.

Engadget. "Reader Comments." http://tinyurl.com/engadget2004.

Engels, Frederick. *Frederick Engels on Capital*. Translated by Leonard E. Mins. New York: International Publishers, 1974.

———. "Letter to Heinz Starkenburg." In *Marx & Engels on the Means of Communication*, edited by Yves de la Hayae, 70. New York: International General, 1979.

———. *The Origin of the Family, Private Property, and the State*. Marx–Engels Collected Works, vol. 26. New York: International Publishers, 1990.

———. "Role of Production in the Development of the Sciences." In *Reader in Marxist Philosophy*, edited by Howard Selsam and Harry Martel. 1963. New York: International Publishers, 1987.

Featherstone, Mike. *Global Culture: Nationalism, Globalization, and Modernity*. London/Newbury Park, Calif.: Sage Publications, 1990.

Ferguson, Niall. *Colossus: The Price of America's Empire*. New York: Penguin Press, 2004.

Finneran, Richard J., ed. *The Literary Text in the Digital Age*. Ann Arbor: University of Michigan Press, 1996.

Flanagan, Robert J. *Globalization and Labor Conditions: Working Conditions and Worker Rights in a Global Economy*. Oxford: Oxford University Press, 2006.

Florida, Richard L. *The Rise of the Creative Class: And How It's Transforming Work, Leisure, Community and Everyday Life*. New York: Basic Books, 2004.

Fortunati, Leopoldina. *The Arcane of Reproduction: Housework, Prostitution, Labor and Capital*. New York: Autonomedia, 1995.

Friedman, Thomas L. *The Lexus and the Olive Tree: Understanding Globalization*. New York: Knopf, 2000.

———. *The World Is Flat: A Brief History of the Twenty-First Century*. New York: Farrar, Straus and Giroux, 2005.

Frow, John. *Cultural Studies and Cultural Value*. Oxford: Oxford University Press, 1995.

Fukuyama, Francis. *The End of History and the Last Man*. New York: Avon Books, 1992.

Gaggi, Silvio. *From Text to Hypertext: Decentering the Subject in Fiction, Film, the Visual Arts, and Electronic Media*. Philadelphia: University of Pennsylvania Press, 1997.

Gates, Bill, Nathan Myhrvold, and Peter Rinearson. *The Road Ahead*. New York: Viking, 1995.

German, Lindsey. *A Question of Class*. London: Bookmarks, 1996.

Gibson, William. *Pattern Recognition*. New York: G. P. Putnam's Sons, 2003.

Giddens, Anthony, and Will Hutton. "Anthony Giddens and Will Hutton in Conversation." In *Global Capitalism*, edited by Anthony Giddens and Will Hutton, 1–52. New York: The New Press, 2000.

Giroux, Henry. *Impure Acts: The Practical Politics of Cultural Studies*. New York/London: Routledge, 2000.

Golumbia, David. *The Cultural Logic of Computation*. Cambridge, Mass./London: Harvard University Press, 2009.

Götz, Klaus, and Nadine Bleher. "Towards the Transnationalisation of Corporate Culture." In *Borderless Business: Managing the Far-Flung Enterprise*, edited by Clarence J. Mann and Klaus Götz. Westport, Conn./London: Praeger Publishers, 2006.

Gray, Chris Hables. *Cyborg Citizen: Politics in the Posthuman Age*. New York/London: Routledge, 2001.

Grossberg, Lawrence. *Bringing It All Back Home: Essays on Cultural Studies*. Durham, N.C.: Duke University Press, 1997.

Hall, Stuart. "Cultural Studies: Two Paradigms." *Media, Culture and Society* 2 (1980): 57–72. Reprinted in *Culture/Power/History: A Reader in Contemporary Social Theory*, edited by Nicholas B. Dirks, Geoff Eley, and Sherry B. Ortner, 520–38. Princeton, N.J.: Princeton University Press, 1994.

———. "The Meaning of New Times." In Morley and Chen, *Stuart Hall: Critical Dialogues in Cultural Studies*, 223–37.

———. "On Postmodernism and articulation: An Interview with Stuart Hall." In Morley and Chen, *Stuart Hall: Critical Dialogues in Cultural Studies*, 131–50.

Haraway, Donna J. "A Manifesto for Cyborgs: Science, Technology, and Socialist Feminism in the 1980s." In *Feminism/Postmodernism*, edited by Linda J. Nicholson, 190–233. New York: Routledge: 1990.

Hardt, Michael, and Antonio Negri. *Commonwealth*. Cambridge, Mass.: The Belknap Press of Harvard University Press, 2009.

———. *Empire*. Cambridge, Mass.: Harvard University Press, 2000.

———. *Multitude: War and Democracy in the Age of Empire*. New York: Penguin Press, 2004.

———. "Response." *Artforum*. November 2009: 211.

Harman, Chris. *Economics of the Madhouse: Capitalism and the Market Today*. London/Chicago/Melbourne: Bookmarks, 1995.

———. "Globalisation: A Critique of A New Global Orthodoxy." *International Socialism* 73 (1996): 3–33.

———. "The rate of profit and the world today." *International Socialism* 115 (2007). http://tinyurl.com/intsoc115.

Harvie, David. "Value Production and struggle in the classroom: Teachers within, against, and beyond capital." *Capital & Class* 88 (2006): 1–32.

Harvey, David. "Analysis." *Artforum*. November 2009: 210.

———. *The Condition of Postmodernity*. Cambridge, Mass./Oxford: Blackwell Publishers, 1989.

———. *The Limits to Capital: New and Fully Updated Edition*. London/New York: Verso, 2006.

———. *The New Imperialism*. Oxford: Oxford University Press, 2003.

Hassan, Ihab. *The Postmodern Turn: Essays in Postmodern Theory and Culture*. Columbus: Ohio State University Press, 1987.

Hassan, Robert. *Information Society (Digital Media and Society Series)*. Cambridge, UK/Malden, Mass.: Polity Press, 2008.

Hayles, Katherine N. "Connecting the Quantum Dots: Nanotechscience and Culture." In *Nanoculture: Implications of the New Technologies*, edited by N. Katherine Hayles, 11–23. Bristol, UK: Intellect Books, 2004.

———. *Writing Machines*. Cambridge and London: MIT Press, 2002.

Heidegger, Martin. "The Question Concerning Technology." In *Basic Writings*, translated by David Farrell Krell, 307–342. 1977. Reprint, San Francisco: Harper San Francisco, 1993.

Held, David. "Democracy and the Global System." In *Political Theory Today*, edited by David Held, 197–236. Stanford, Calif.: Stanford University Press, 1991.

Hirst, Paul Q., and Grahame Thompson. *Globalization in Question: The International Economy and the Possibilities of Governance*. Oxford, UK/Malden, Mass.: Blackwell Publishers, 1996.

Hitchcock, Peter. *Oscillate Wildly: Space, Body, and Spirit of Millennial Materialism.* Minneapolis: University of Minnesota Press, 1999.

Holloway, John. *Change the World Without Taking Power.* 2nd ed. London/Ann Arbor, Mich.: Pluto Press, 2005.

Huntington, Samuel P. *The Clash of Civilizations and the Remaking of World Order.* New York: Simon & Schuster, 1996.

International Monetary Fund. *World Economic Outlook: October 2007.* Washington, D.C.: International Monetary Fund, 2007.

James, Henry. "The Art of Fiction." *Critical Theory Since Plato.* Edited by Hazard Adams, 660–670. New York: Harcourt Brace Jovanovich, Inc., 1971.

Jameson, Frederic. "Fear and Loathing in Globalization." *New Left Review* 23 (2003): 105–114.

———. *Postmodernism, or the Cultural Logic of Late Capitalism.* Durham, N.C.: Duke University Press, 1991.

Jenkins, Henry. *Convergence Culture: Where Old and New Media Collide.* New York/London: New York University Press, 2006.

Johnson, Steven. *Emergence: The Connected Lives of Ants, Brains, Cities, and Software.* New York: Scribner, 2001.

Kant, Immanuel. *The Metaphysics of Morals.* Cambridge, UK/New York: Cambridge University Press, 1996.

Kahney, Leander. *The Cult of iPod.* San Francisco: No Starch Press, 2005.

Kautsky, Karl. "Ultra-Imperialism." *New Left Review* 59 (1970): 41–46.

Kelly, James Patrick, and John Kessel, eds. *Rewired: The Post-Cyberpunk Anthology.* San Francisco: Trachyon Publications, 2007.

Kirby, Alan. *Digimodernism: How New Technologies Dismantle, the Postmodern and Reconfigure Our Culture.* New York/London: The Continuum International Publishing Group Inc, 2009.

Laclau, Ernesto, and Chantal Mouffe. *Hegemony and Socialist Strategy: Towards a Radical Democratic Politics.* 2nd ed. London and New York: Verso, 2001.

Landow, George. *Hypertext 3.0: Critical Theory and New Media in the Age of Globalization.* Baltimore: The Johns Hopkins University Press, 2006.

Lanham, Richard A. *The Electronic Word: Democracy, Technology, and the Arts.* Chicago: University of Chicago Press, 1993.

Lanhart, Justin. "U.S. Firms Build Up Record Cash Piles." *The Wall Street Journal.* June 10, 2010. http://tinyurl.com/wsjlahart.

Latour, Bruno. *We Have Never Been Modern.* Cambridge, Mass.: Harvard University Press, 1993.

Lazzarato, Maurizio. "Immaterial Labor." In *Radical Thought in Italy: A Potential Politics,* edited by Paolo Virno and Michael Hardt, 133–47. Minneapolis: University of Minneapolis Press, 1996.

Leavis, F. R. *Education and the University; a Sketch for an English School.* London: Chatto & Windus, 1965.

Lenin, V. I. "Dialectics and Formal Logic." In *Reader in Marxist Philosophy*, edited by Howard Selsam and Harry Martel, 114–17. 1963. Reprint, New York: International Publishers, 1987.

———. *Imperialism, The Highest Stage of Capitalism.* Lenin Collected Works, vol. 22. 1964. Moscow: Progress Publishers, 1977.

Lens, Sidney. *The Forging of the American Empire.* New York: Thomas Y. Cromwell Company, 1971.

Lessig, Lawrence. *Free Culture: The Nature and Future of Creativity.* New York: Penguin Press, 2004.

Levy, Steven. *The Perfect Thing: How the iPod Shuffles Commerce, Culture, and Coolness.* New York: Simon & Schuster Paperbacks, 2007.

Liestol, Gunnar, Andrew Morrison, and Terje Rasmussen, eds. *Digital Media Revisited: Theoretical and Conceptual Innovation in Digital Domains.* Cambridge, Mass.: MIT Press, 2003.

Liu, Alan. *The Laws of Cool: Knowledge Work and the Culture of Information.* Chicago/London: University of Chicago Press, 2004.

Lohr, Steve. "A Cyberfueled Growth Spurt: The Web Upends Old Ideas About The Little Guy's Role." *The New York Times.* February 21, 2006: G1–G10.

Lovink, Geert. *My First Recession: Critical Internet Culture in Transition.* Rotterdam: V2_NAi Publishers, 2003.

———. *Zero Comments: Blogging and Critical Internet Culture.* New York/London: Routledge, 2008.

Lukács, Georg. "Art and Objective Reality." In *Writer & Critic and Other Essays*, edited and translated by Arthur D. Kahn, 25–60. New York: Grosset & Dunlap, 1970.

Lunenfeld, Peter. *The Digital Dialectic: New Essays on New Media.* Cambridge, Mass.: MIT Press, 1999.

Luxemburg, Rosa. *The Accumulation of Capital.* Translated by Agnes Schwarzchild. London/New York: Routledge, 2003.

Lyotard, Jean-François. *The Inhuman.* Translated by Geoffrey Bennington and Rachel Bowlby. Stanford, Calif.: Stanford University Press, 1991.

———. *The Postmodern Condition: A Report on Knowledge.* Translated by Geoff Bennington and Brian Massumi. 1984. Reprint, Minneapolis: University of Minnesota, 1993.

Mandel, Ernest. Introduction to *Capital Volume II*, translated by David Fernbach, 11–79. New York: Penguin Classics, 1992.

———. *Late Capitalism.* Translated by Joris De Bres. 1978. Reprint, London: Verso, 1987.

―――. *Marxist Economic Theory*. New York and London: Monthly Review Press, 1968.

Mann, Clarence J. "Overview: Forces Shaping the Global Business Environment." In *Borderless Business: Managing the Far-Flung Enterprise*, edited by Clarence J. Mann and Klaus Götz, 1–29. Westport, Conn./London: Praeger Publishers, 2006.

Markley, Robert. "History, Theory, and Virtual Reality." In *Reading Digital Culture*, edited by David Trend, 297–304. Oxford, UK/Malden, Mass.: Blackwell Publishers, Inc., 2001.

Marx, Karl. *Capital Volume I*. Marx–Engels Collected Works, vol. 35. New York: International Publishers, 1996.

―――. *Capital Volume II*. Marx–Engels Collected Works, vol. 35. New York: International Publishers, 1997.

―――. *Capital Volume III*. Marx–Engels Collected Works, vol. 37. New York: International Publishers, 1998.

―――. *Contribution to the Critique of Hegel's Philosophy of Law: Introduction*. Marx–Engels Collected Works, vol. 3. New York: International Publishers, 1975.

―――. *Economic and Philosophic Manuscripts of 1844*. Marx–Engels Collected Works, vol. 3. New York: International Publishers, 1975.

―――. *Grundrisse*. Translated by Martin Nicolaus. New York: Vintage Books, 1973.

―――. *Poverty of Philosophy*. Marx–Engels Collected Works, vol. 6. New York: International Publishers, 1976.

―――. Preface to *A Contribution to a Critique of Political Economy*. Edited by Maurice Dobb. New York: International Publishers, 1970.

―――. "Thesis on Feuerbach." Marx–Engels Collected Works, vol. 5. New York: International Publishers, 1976.

―――. Wage-Labour and Capital/Value, Price and Profit. 1976. Reprint, New York: International Publishers, 1997.

Marx, Karl, and Frederick Engels. *The German Ideology*. Marx–Engels Collected Works, vol. 5. New York: International Publishers, 1976.

―――. *Manifesto of the Communist Party*. Marx–Engels Collected Works, vol. 6. New York: International Publishers, 1976.

Matrix, Sidney Eve. *Cyberpop: Digital Lifestyles and Commodity Culture*. New York/London: Routledge, 2006.

The Matrix. DVD. Directed by Andy Wachowski and Larry Wachowski. Burbank, Calif.: Warner Home Video, 1999.

Mattelart, Armand. *Networking the World, 1794–2000*. Minneapolis: University of Minnesota Press, 2000.

McBride, Stephen, and John Richard Wiseman. *Globalization and Its Discontents.* New York: Palgrave Macmillan Press, 2000.

McChesney, Robert Waterman. *The Problem of the Media: U.S. Communication Politics in the Twenty-First Century.* New York: Monthly Review Press, 2004.

McGann, Jerome. *Radiant Textuality: Literature After the World Wide Web.* New York: Palgrave Macmillan, 2001.

McLuhan, Marshall, and Quentin Fiore. *The Medium Is the Massage: An Inventory of Effects.* Corte Madera, Calif.: Ginko Press, 2005.

McRobbie, Angela. "Post-Marxism and Cultural Studies: A Postscript." In *Cultural Studies,* edited by Lawrence Grossberg, Cary Nelson, and Paula Treichler, 719–730. New York: Routledge, 1992.

Milburn, Colin. *Nanovision: Engineering the Future.* Durham, N.C./London: Duke University Press, 2008.

Mishel, Lawrence, Jared Bernstein, and Heidi Shierholz. *The State of Working America 2008–2009.* Ithica, N.Y./London: ILR Press, 2009.

Mitchell, W. J. T. "Medium Theory: Preface to the 2003 'Critical Inquiry' Symposium." *Critical Inquiry* 30, no. 2 (Winter 2004): 324–335.

Morley, David, and Kuan-Hsing Chen, eds. *Stuart Hall: Critical Dialogues in Cultural Studies.* London/New York: Routledge, 1996.

Mosco, Vincent, and Catherine McKercher. Introduction to *Knowledge Workers in the Information Society,* edited by Cathering McKercher and Vincent Mosco, vii–xxiv. Lanham, M.D.: Lexington Books, 2007.

Nadel, S. N. *Contemporary Capitalism and the Middle Classes.* New York: International Publishers, 1982.

Negri, Antonio. *Marx Beyond Marx: Lessons on the Grundrisse.* Translated by Harry Cleaver, Michael Ryan, and Maurizio Viano. Edited by Jim Fleming. New York: Autonomedia, 1991.

———. "The Specter's Smile." In *Ghostly Demarcations: A Symposium on Jacques Derrida's* Specters of Marx, edited by Michael Sprinker, 5–16. London: Verso: 1999.

Negroponte, Nicholas. *Being Digital.* New York: Knopf, 1995.

Ohmae, Kenichi. *The Borderless World: Power and Strategy in the Interlinked Economy.* New York: HarperBusiness, 1990.

———. "The End of the Nation State." In *The Globalization Reader,* edited by Frank J. Lechner and John Boli, 207–211. Oxford, UK/Malden, Mass.: Blackwell Publishers, 2000.

Penley, Constance, and Andrew Ross. *Technoculture.* Minneapolis: University of Minnesota Press, 1991.

Person, Lawrence. "Notes Toward a Postcyberpunk Manifesto." http://tinyurl.com/postcyberpunkmanifesto.

Pieterse, Jan Nederveen. *Globalization and Culture: Global Mélange*. New York: Rowan and Littlefield, 2003.

Pink, Daniel H. "Why the World Is Flat." *Wired* (May 2005). http://tinyurl.com/friedmanwired.

Pirandello, Luigi. *Il Turno*. Milan, Italy: A. Mondadori, 1953.

———. *Suo Marito*. Florence, Italy: Giunti, 1994.

Plato. *The Republic*. Translated by Desmond Lee. 1955. Reprint, New York/London: Penguin Books, 1974.

Popper, Karl. *The Open Society and its Enemies*. Vol. 1. Princeton, N.J.: Princeton University Press, 1966.

Poster, Mark. *Information Please: Culture and Politics in the Age of Digital Machines*. Durham, N.C./London: Duke University Press, 2006.

———. *Mode of Information: Poststructuralism and Social Context*. Chicago: University of Chicago Press, 1990.

———. *What's the Matter with the Internet?* Minneapolis: University of Minneapolis Press, 2001.

Pryce-Jones, David. "Why They Hate Us." *National Review*. September 11, 2001. http://tinyurl.com/nroprcejns.

Quelch, John, and Rohit Deshpande. *The Global Market: Developing a Strategy to Manage Across Borders*. San Fransisco: Jossey-Bass, 2004.

Reuveny, Rafael X. and William R. Thompson. Introduction to "The North-South Divide and International Studies: A Symposium." *International Studies Review* 9, no. 4 (2007): 556–564.

Richards, I. A. *Principles of Literary Criticism*. 1925. Reprint, New York: Harcourt Brace & World, 1961.

Rifkin, Jeremy. *The Age of Access: The New Culture of Hypercapitalism, Where All of Life Is a Paid-for Experience*. New York: J.P. Tarcher/Putnam, 2000.

Ritzer, George. *The Globalization of Nothing*. Thousand Oaks, Calif.: Pine Forge Press, 2004.

———. *The Globalization of Nothing 2*. Thousand Oaks, Calif.: Pine Forge Press, 2007.

Robbins, Bruce. *Feeling Global: Internationalism in Distress*. New York: New York University Press, 1999.

Robertson, Roland. *Globalization: Social Theory and Global Culture*. London: Sage, 1992.

Robins, Kevin, and Frank Webster. *Times of the Technoculture: From Information Society to the Virtual Life*. New York/London: Routledge, 1999.

Ronell, Avital. *The Telephone Book: Technology, Schizophrenia, Electric Speech*. Lincoln/London: University of Nebraska Press, 1989.

Rutsky, R. L. *High Technē: Art and Technology from the Machine Aesthetic to the Posthuman.* Minneapolis: University of Minnesota Press, 1999.

Sahadi, Jeanne. "White House: Unemployment at 9% Until 2012." CNNMoney .com. http://tinyurl.com/cnn07232010.

Sassen, Saskia. *Globalization and Its Discontents: Essays on the New Mobility of People and Money.* New York: New Press, 1998.

Schwartz, Nelson D., and Ann Harrington. "Down and Out in White-Collar America." *Fortune* 147 (2003): 78–86.

Shirky, Clay. *Here Comes Everybody: The Power of Organizing Without Organizations.* New York: The Penguin Press, 2008.

Smekal, Christian, and Rupert Sausgruber. "Determinants of FDI in Europe." In *Foreign Direct Investment,* edited by John-Ren Chen, 33–42. New York: St. Martin's Press, 2000.

Steger, Manfred B. *Globalization: A Very Short Introduction.* Oxford/New York: Oxford University Press, 2003.

Sterling, Bruce. Introduction to *Mirrorshades: The Cyberpunk Anthology.* New York: Arbor House, 1986.

Stiegler, Bernard. *Technics and Time, 1: The Fault of Epimetheus.* Stanford: Stanford University Press, 1998.

———. *Technics and Time, 2: Disorientation.* Stanford: Stanford University Press, 2008.

———. *Technics and Time, 3: Cinematic Time and the Question of Malaise.* Stanford: Stanford University Press, 2010.

Stiglitz, Joseph E. *Globalization and Its Discontents.* New York: W. W. Norton, 2002.

Sullivan, Roger J. Introduction to *The Metaphysics of Morals,* by Immanuel Kant. Cambridge/New York: Cambridge University Press, 1996.

Taylor, Mark C. "End the University as We Know It." *New York Times* April 27, 2009: 23. http://www.ebscohost.com/.

Terranova, Tiziana. *Network Culture: Politics for the Information Age.* London/Ann Arbor, Mich.: Pluto Press, 2004.

Thompson, Paul. "Foundation and Empire: A Critique of Hardt and Negri." *Capital and Class* 86 (Summer 2005): 99–134.

Toffler, Alvin. *The Third Wave.* New York: Morrow, 1980.

Tomlinson, John. *Globalization and Culture.* Chicago: University of Chicago Press, 1999.

Touraine, Alaine. "New Classes, New Conflicts." In *The Worker in "Post-Industrial" Capitalism,* edited by Bertram Silverman and Murray Yanowitch, 180–187. New York: Free Press, 1974.

Trend, David. *Reading Digital Culture.* Malden, Mass./Oxford: Blackwell Publishers, 2001.

Vandendorpe, Christian. *From Papyrus to Hypertext: Toward the Universal Digital Library*. Translated by Phyllis Aronoff and Howard Scott. Urbana, Ill./Chicago: University of Chicago Press, 2009.

van Dijk, Jan. *The Deepening Divide: Inequality in the Information Society*. Thousand Oaks, Calif.: Sage Publications, 2005.

———. *The Network Society: Social Aspects of New Media*. Thousand Oaks, Calif.: Sage Publications, 2006.

Wallerstein, Immanuel. *World-Systems Analysis: An Introduction*. 2004. Reprint, Durham, N.C./London: Duke University Press, 2005.

Waters, Malcolm. *Globalization*. 2nd ed. London; New York: Routledge, 2001.

Weber, Max. "Class, Status, Party." In *Max Weber: Essays in Sociology*, translated by H. H. Gerht and C. Wright Mills, 180–195. London: Routledge, 1961.

Weber, Samuel. *Benjamin's -abilities*. Cambridge, Mass./London: Harvard University Press, 2008.

———. *Mass Mediauras: Form, Technics, Media*. Edited by Alan Cholodenko. Stanford, Calif.: Stanford University Press, 1996.

Willke, Helmut. *Smart Governance: Governing the Global Knowledge Society*. Frankfurt/New York: Campus Verlag, 2007.

Wolf, Martin. *Why Globalization Works*. New Haven, Conn./London: Yale University Press, 2004.

World Bank. *2007 World Development Indicators*. Washington, D.C.: The World Bank, 2007.

Wood, Ellen Meiksins. *Peasant-Citizen and Slave: The Foundations of Athenian Democracy*. London/New York: Verso, 1989.

Yu, Chwo-Ming Joseph. "Restructuring of Production Networks in Foreign Countries: The Case of Taiwanese Firms." In *Foreign Direct Investment*, edited by John-Ren Chen, 96–114. New York: St. Martin's Press, 2000.

Žižek, Slavoj. *Living in the End Times*. London/New York: Verso, 2010.